ISLAM'S RESPONSE TO CONTEMPORARY ISSUES

HADHRAT MIRZA TAHIR AHMAD,
KHALIFATUL MASIH IV
Head of the world wide Ahmadiyya Muslim Jamaat (Community)

ISLAM INTERNATIONAL PUBLICATIONS LTD

ISLAM'S RESPONSE TO CONTEMPORARY ISSUES

First published in English July 1992
Reprinted in 1993
Present edition 1997

© Islam International Publications Ltd.

Published by:
    Islam International Publications Ltd.
    Islamabad, Sheephatch Lane,
    Tilford, Surrey GU10 2AQ
Printed by:
    The Bath Press,
    Bath

ISBN 1 85372 498 X

The Author

HADHRAT MIRZA TAHIR AHMAD is the supreme head of a
dynamic worldwide missionary sect, the Ahmadiyya Muslim
Jamaat. He has delivered numerous lectures on religious topics
and answered thousands of questions on key issues of the
contemporary age. His book, *Murder in the Name of Allah* has
been reprinted in several languages.

CONTENTS

PREFACE

Jamaat Ahmadiyya was founded in 1889 by Hadhrat Mirza Ghulam Ahmad of Qadian who claimed on divine authority that he was the Promised Messiah and World Reformer of the latter centuries whose advent was prophesied in the ancient sacred scriptures of all great religions.

In 1989, this community of Muslims celebrated its first centenary. The last major event in the celebrations was a lecture, delivered on 24th February 1990, at the Queen Elizabeth II Conference Centre in London by the Head of Jamaat Ahmadiyya, Hadhrat Mirza Tahir Ahmad, Khalifatul Masih the Fourth (Successor to the Promised Messiah).

This keynote lecture was attended by eight hundred distinguished guests including politicians, Arabists, journalists, professors, teachers, men and women from other professions and vocations and eminent religious scholars. Mr. Aftab A. Khan, National Amir of the Ahmadiyya Muslim Association (UK) welcomed the guests. Mr. Edward Mortimer presided and Mr. Hugo Summerson MP proposed the vote of thanks. After the lecture there was a brief session of questions and answers.

As it was not possible to do full justice to such a vast subject in the space of time traditionally provided for such public addresses, only partial treatment was possible. However, in view of numerous demands by many who attended or those who missed this lecture, the book based on the original manuscript is being published separately.

Since the original text of this address was dictated by the Speaker, every effort was made to faithfully record the dictation. During the first revision, some minor mistakes were discovered here and there which were duly corrected by the Speaker himself. Later on, it was considered advisable to have parts of the text reviewed by an Englishman so that he could point out any areas where the text needed further elaboration or if some expressions were unfamiliar to the English ear. We are grateful to Mr. Barry Jeffries of Queensbury, Yorkshire and Mr. Muzaffar Clarke of Stirchley, Birmingham, who volunteered their services and carried out this task admirably. Their advice was most valuable in regard to some passages which may have conveyed a different impression to the reader than was intended mainly because of the gradual change in the connotation of some expressions and idiom in current use. Also their advice with regard to the hypersensitivity of the western mind concerning some cultural differences between the east and west was of considerable help. Of course everyone has a right to disagree with anyone else, but disagreement merely because of a misunderstanding of points of view should be avoided as far as possible. It is here that both these gentlemen helped immensely.

As we go to print, albeit very belatedly, we are deeply conscious of the fact that a number of issues addressed herein have assumed centre stage. A number of possibilities seen by the far-sightedness of the Speaker have miraculously begun to prove true. For instance, there has been considerable debate on inter-religious harmony in view of the renewed fatwa on blasphemy. Enormous changes have taken place after the collapse of communism in East European countries. The UN's Security Council has acquired a new role. In Great Britain, the interest rate policy has precipitated economic recession. All these issues and events, and indeed many more, were fully and squarely discussed beforehand in this address. Alas! Had we gone to print earlier?

All that remains to be said is a humble reminder to the reader that the text of this address was dictated by the Speaker in early

1990 when the omens for these changes were yet in their formative stage. Seldom is a warning given in such clear terms. The message is timeless and relates to the future prospects for peace for the entire world. If the Speaker is proved right in most of his 'predictions,' as he has already been proved right in some of them, it would only be appropriate for the leaders of the world to take the message of this address seriously and make a genuine attempt to draw the maximum benefit out of it in the shaping of the new world order.

May God enable them to do so. Amen.

Mansoor A. Shah

London: July 1992.

PUBLISHER'S NOTES

According to our system of counting, the verse *Bismillah irrahman irrahim* (In the name of Allah, the Most Gracious, Ever Merciful) is counted as the first verse of the chapter which it precedes. Some publishers of the Holy Quran however, begin following *Bismillah irrahman irrahim*. Should the reader not find the relevant verse under the number mentioned in this book, he or she is advised to deduct 1 from the number e.g. p.16 of this book quotes Ch. 2: Al-Baqarah: 286 which in some copies of the Holy Quran will be found under Ch. 2: Al-Baqarah: 285.

Where necessary, translation of the Arabic text has been elaborated by additional words to explain the meaning. Such words are not in italics. The word *And* at the commencement of a translated verse has been omitted.

In view of numerous editions of the Books of *Hadith* (traditions), only the Compiler's name has been indicated, and, for brevity, volume and chapter references omitted.

The name Muhammad, the Holy Prophet, or Founder of Islam, have generally been followed by the symbol[sa] for the salutation *salallaho alaihi wassalam or may peace and blessings of Allah be upon him*. The names of other Prophets and Messengers of God are followed by the symbol[as] for *alaihi salato wassalam* meaning *on whom be peace*. The actual salutations have not been set out in full, except in a few instances, in order to accommodate the text to the non-Muslim readers. Muslims readers should treat the full salutation as being implicit in the text.

The form *ibn* has been used in both initial and medial position in the names of persons, in order to conform with current usage, although *bin* also occurs medially in some original texts (abbreviated usually as b.)

Local geographic transliterations for Makkah and Madinah have been used in lieu of Mecca and Medina.

Quotations from the Holy Bible are from the New World Translation.

INTRODUCTION

After the traditional recitation and reciting the Surah Fatiha (the opening chapter of the Holy Quran), the Head of Jamaat Ahmadiyya commenced as follows:

Mr Edward Mortimer (the Chairman), all our distinguished guests, ladies and gentlemen!

Let me express my deep sense of gratitude for your scholarly presence here this afternoon. Permit me to confess that the address I am going to make poses a great challenge to me. It is a wide subject, and as such I am over-awed.

May I begin, however, by raising two fundamental questions. What are the modern challenges? What modern situation can any religion address? These are the fundamental questions.

ABSENCE OF PEACE

The single most important malady of the world today is the absence of peace.

In the contemporary world, man, as a whole, has reached a high standard of achievement in material progress, made possible by the advancement of science and technology in every sphere of human requirement at a mind-boggling pace.

No doubt, the more fortunate sections of human society, known as the First and Second World, have a much larger share of the fruits of scientific progress in the contemporary age, but the Third World has also benefitted to a degree. Rays of progress have penetrated even the innermost recesses of the darkest areas, where a section of human society still lives in a remote past.

Nevertheless, man is not happy and content. There is growing restlessness, fear, premonition, lack of trust in the future and dissatisfaction with one's heritage.

These are some of the important elements which challenge the nature of the contemporary world. It, in turn, gives birth to a deep-seated dissatisfaction of man either with his past or with his present; particularly, it runs deep in the formative thought processes of the younger generation. Man is in search of peace.

ISLAM'S CONTRIBUTION TO WORLD PEACE

The word ISLAM literally means peace. In this single word, all Islamic teachings and attitudes are most beautifully and concisely reflected. Islam is a religion of peace. Its teachings guarantee peace in every sphere of human interest and aspiration.

For today's address, I have catergorised some areas in which the contemporary world stands in need of guidance:

1. Inter-religious peace and harmony;
2. Social peace, in general;
3. Socio-economic peace;
4. Economic peace;
5. Peace in national and international politics;
6. Individual peace.

1

INTER-RELIGIOUS PEACE AND HARMONY

1. Religious values have become redundant
2. Universality of prophethood
3. All prophets are equal
4. Can rank be different if authenticity is equal?
5. Salvation cannot be monopolised by any single religion
6. Promotion of harmony and mutual respect amongst religions
7. The universality concept
8. Islam is a universal religion
9. Instruments of struggle - no compulsion
10. Survival of the fittest
11. Freedom of speech
12. Liberty and emancipation in the context of the contemporary world
13. Blasphemy
14. Inter-religious cooperation
15. Conclusion

Verily, We have sent thee with the truth, as a Bearer of glad tidings and as a Warner; and there is no people on earth in any age who did not receive a Warner from God. (Ch. 35: Al-Fatir:25)

Surely those who have believed in Muhammad as a Messenger of God, and the Jews, and the Sabians, and the Christians - whoso believes in Allah and the Last Day and does good deeds, on them shall come no fear, nor shall they grieve. (Ch. 5: Al-Ma'idah: 70)

RELIGIOUS VALUES HAVE BECOME REDUNDANT

Examining the overall religious scenario, one cannot fail to notice that in religion there seems to prevail a paradoxical situation today. In general, religion is losing its grip yet simultaneously tightening it in different areas. In some sections of society, in almost all religions, there seems to be a powerful swing back in the direction of dogmas with medieval rigidity and intolerence of opposition.

On the moral side, religion is on the retreat; crime is rampant; truth is disappearing fast; equity and the deliverance of justice are on the verge of extinction; social responsibilities to the society are being ignored; and a selfish individualism is gaining strength in its stead even in such countries of the world as would otherwise claim to be religious. These and many other social evils which are positive signs of a morally decadent society have become the order of the day. If moral values in any religion form the life and soul of religion itself, then a progressive strangulation of these values can lead us to the inevitable conclusion that while the body of religion is being resurrected, the soul is fast ebbing out of the body. So, what we observe in religion today, the so-called revival of religion, becomes tantamount to resurrecting dead corpses so that they walk about like zombies.

In other areas long stagnation and a lack of exciting developments generates boredom among religiously inclined people. Miraculous things which they expect to happen do not take place. The bizarre phenomenon of supernatural intervention in world events to change the world to their liking does not materialise. They want to see strange prophecies fulfilled to give credence to their faith. Yet nothing materialises. Such are the people who provide fodder for new cults which thrive on the humus of their frustrations. The urge to escape from the past generates a desire to fill the void with something new.

Apart from these destructive trends, another extremely disturbing phenomenon, which, perhaps, is related to the revival of dogmas in religion, is threatening the peace of the world. With the rise of such dogmas a toxic atmosphere is generated which proves fatal to the healthy spirit of dialogue and free flow of ideas. As if this were not enough, wilful attempts by unscrupulous politicians, ever ready to exploit volatile situations to their own advantage, are being made to tarnish the image of religion itself. Again, historic inter-religious rivalries and feuds have their part to play. In addition, the so-called `free' media is generally controlled by unseen hands rather than being at liberty to play a completely neutral role in the affairs of the world. Therefore, when the media of a country with a predominant population belonging to one religion joins the battle in maligning the image of a rival religion, the scenario becomes very complex. The first victim of this melee is, undoubtedly, religion itself.

I really feel deeply concerned and disturbed at what is happening in the world of religion today. There is a deep urgency for religions to make a genuine and serious effort to remove misunderstanding between themselves.

I believe that Islam can deliver the goods with distinction in a manner that can fully satisfy our demands and requirements.

To facilitate a better understanding, I have further categorised the subject into different sections.

For instance, I believe that for a religion to be helpful in establishing peace in the world, it is essential that a religion which is universally capable of uniting man ultimately, must itself accept the universality of religion in the sense that human beings, whatever their colour, race or geographic denomination, are all creatures of the same Creator. As such, they are equally entitled to receive divine instruction - if ever divine instructions were given to any section of human society. This view obviates the concept of monopolisation of truth by any religion.

All religions, whatever their name or doctrines, wherever they be found and to whichever age they belong, have the right to claim the possession of some divine truth. Also, one has to admit that, despite the differences in their doctrines and teachings, religions are most likely to have a common origin. The same divine Authority which gave birth to any religion in one area of the world must also have looked after the religous and spiritual needs of other human beings in other parts of the world and belonging to different ages.

This exactly is the Message of the Holy Quran, the Sacred Scripture of Islam.

UNIVERSALITY OF PROPHETHOOD

The Holy Quran has the following to say in this regard:

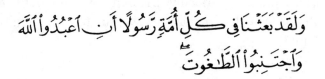

We did raise among every people a Messenger with the teaching 'Worship Allah and shun the evil one'. (Ch. 16: Al-Nahl:37)

Secondly, the Holy Quran declares that: O Prophet of God, you are not the only Prophet in the world.

وَلَقَدۡ أَرۡسَلۡنَا رُسُلًا مِّن قَبۡلِكَ مِنۡهُم مَّن قَصَصۡنَا عَلَيۡكَ وَمِنۡهُم مَّن لَّمۡ نَقۡصُصۡ عَلَيۡكَ

We indeed, sent Messengers before thee; of them are some whom We have mentioned to thee, and of them are some We have not mentioned to thee. (Ch. 40: Al-Mu'min: 79)

The Holy Quran reminds the Holy Prophet of Islam:

إِنۡ أَنتَ إِلَّا نَذِيرٌ ۞ إِنَّا أَرۡسَلۡنَٰكَ بِٱلۡحَقِّ بَشِيرًا وَنَذِيرًا وَإِن مِّنۡ أُمَّةٍ إِلَّا خَلَا فِيهَا نَذِيرٌ ۞

Thou art but a Warner. Verily, We have sent thee with the Truth, as a bearer of glad tidings and as a Warner; and there is no people, to whom a Warner has not been sent. (Ch. 35: Al-Fatir: 24-25)

In view of the above, it is manifestly clear that Islam does not monopolise truth to the elimination of all other religions but categorically declares that in all ages and in all parts of the world, God has been looking after the spiritual and religious needs of mankind by raising Messengers who delivered the divine message to the people for whom they were raised and commissioned.

ALL PROPHETS ARE EQUAL

The question arises that if there are so many Prophets of God sent to all peoples of the world, in different parts of the world and in different ages, do they have the same divine authority? According to the Holy Quran, all Prophets belong to God, and as such, insofar as their divine authority is concerned, they exercise such authority with equal force and strength. No one has a right to discriminate between one Prophet and another. As far as the authenticity of their message is concerned, all Prophets must be equal. This attitude of Islam towards other religions and their Founders as well as minor Prophets, can work as a very important uniting and cementing factor between various religions. The principle that the authenticity of each Prophet's revelation enjoys the same status can be used as a very powerful unifying force, bringing various religions together. This transforms the attitude of hostility towards the revelation of Prophets of other religions to that of respect and reverence. This, again, is the clear and logical position taken by the Holy Quran:

$$ءَامَنَ ٱلرَّسُولُ بِمَآ أُنزِلَ إِلَيْهِ مِن رَّبِّهِۦ وَٱلْمُؤْمِنُونَ كُلٌّ ءَامَنَ بِٱللَّهِ وَمَلَـٰٓئِكَتِهِۦ وَكُتُبِهِۦ وَرُسُلِهِۦ لَا نُفَرِّقُ بَيْنَ أَحَدٍ مِّن رُّسُلِهِۦ وَقَالُوا۟ سَمِعْنَا وَأَطَعْنَا$$

This Messenger (the Holy Founder of Islam) *believes in that which was revealed to him from his Lord, and so do the believers; all of them believe in Allah; and in His angels, and in His Books, and in His Messengers saying, 'We make no distinction between any of His Messengers. And they say, We have heard and we are obedient . . .' (Ch. 2: Al-Baqarah: 286)*

This subject is repeated in other verses of the Holy Quran. For instance:

$$إِنَّ ٱلَّذِينَ يَكْفُرُونَ بِٱللَّهِ وَرُسُلِهِۦ وَيُرِيدُونَ أَن يُفَرِّقُوا۟ بَيْنَ ٱللَّهِ وَرُسُلِهِۦ$$

وَيَقُولُونَ نُؤْمِنُ بِبَعْضٍ وَنَكْفُرُ بِبَعْضٍ وَيُرِيدُونَ أَن يَتَّخِذُواْ بَيْنَ ذَلِكَ سَبِيلًا ۝ أُوْلَٰئِكَ هُمُ ٱلْكَٰفِرُونَ حَقًّا ۚ وَأَعْتَدْنَا لِلْكَٰفِرِينَ عَذَابًا مُّهِينًا ۝ وَٱلَّذِينَ ءَامَنُواْ بِٱللَّهِ وَرُسُلِهِ وَلَمْ يُفَرِّقُواْ بَيْنَ أَحَدٍ مِّنْهُمْ أُوْلَٰئِكَ سَوْفَ يُؤْتِيهِمْ أُجُورَهُمْ ۗ وَكَانَ ٱللَّهُ غَفُورًا رَّحِيمًا ۝

Surely, those who disbelieve in Allah and His Messengers and seek to make a distinction between Allah and His Messengers, and say, 'We believe in some and disbelieve in others', and seek to take a way in between, these really are the disbelievers, and We have prepared for the disbelievers a humiliating punishment. And those who believe in Allah and in all of His Messengers and make no distinction between any of them, to such He will soon give their rewards. And Allah is Most Forgiving, Merciful. (Ch. 4: Al-Nisa: 151—153)

CAN RANK BE DIFFERENT IF AUTHENTICITY IS EQUAL?

If all Prophets are equal in authenticity must they also need be equal in rank? The answer to this question is that in many respects, Prophets can vary in their personal qualities and the way they discharge their responsibilities. As far as their nearness to God and the relative status they hold in the sight of God is concerned, Messengers and Prophets can differ from each other. A study of the history of Prophets from the account of the Holy Bible, the Holy Quran and other Scriptures also affirms this conclusion.

The Holy Quran admits that there are differences of status in a manner that should not disturb the peace of man. The same Holy

Quran that declares that there is no difference as far as the authenticity of Messages from God are concerned between one Prophet of God and another, declares:

$$تِلْكَ ٱلرُّسُلُ فَضَّلْنَا بَعْضَهُمْ عَلَىٰ بَعْضٍ مِّنْهُم مَّن كَلَّمَ ٱللَّهُ وَرَفَعَ بَعْضَهُمْ دَرَجَٰتٍ$$

These Messengers have We exalted, some of them above others; among them there are those to whom Allah spoke frequently; and some of them He exalted by degrees of rank . . . (Ch. 2: Al-Baqarah: 254)

Having accepted this proposition, one may wonder as to who should be considered as the highest in rank among the Prophets. This is a sensitive issue; yet one cannot close one's eyes to the importance of this question.

Adherents of almost all religions claim that the Founder of their religion stands supreme and no one else can be a match to him in excellence, dignity, piety, honour and in short all the qualities that go into the making of a Prophet. Then, does Islam also claim that Muhammad, the Holy Prophet of Islam, may peace and blessings of Allah be upon him, is the most exalted of all Prophets? Yes, Islam does make an unambiguous claim about the par excellence and supremacy of the qualities of the Holy Prophet[sa] over all the rest of the Prophets of the world. Yet, there is a very clear difference between Islam and other religions in their attitude to this claim.

First of all, it should be kept in mind that no religion other than Islam recognises the universality of prophethood. When the Jews claim, if they do, that Moses was the greatest Prophet, they are not comparing Moses[as] with Buddha[as], Krishna[as], Jesus[as], or Muhammad, may peace and blessings of Allah be upon them all,

23

because they deny the claims of all other great Founders of the religions mentioned above to be genuine and worthy of acceptance. So, in the Jewish list of Prophets, no Prophets are included other than those specifically mentioned in the Old Testament; even the possibility of there being Prophets elsewhere is ruled out. In the light of this attitude, their claim regarding the supremacy of any Judaic Prophet does not belong to the same category as that of Islam, as according to Judaism, Prophets outside the Holy Bible simply do not exist. Exactly the same is the nature of similar claims of Buddhism, Zoroastrianism, Hinduism, etc.

There is yet another difference to be kept in mind. When we talk of their Prophets, we are aware that they do not always refer to their holy religious figures as Prophets. The concept of Prophets and Messengers as understood in Judaism, Christianity and Islam is not exactly shared by most other religions. Instead, they treat the Founders of their religion and holy men as holy personages, or reincarnations of God, or God Himself, or, something approaching that. Perhaps in this respect, Jesus Christ[as] also should be understood as an exception from the vantage point of Christianity.

But according to Islam, all these so-called gods or reincarnations of God, or the so-called sons or children of God are merely Prophets and Messengers who were deified by their followers at a much later point. In fact, to be more specific, according to Islam, the deification of holy personages in various religions is a very gradual process and not that of the generation contemporary to the Prophet. But of that, we shall speak later.

When Islam, however, claims that its Holy Founder is supreme amongst the Prophets, it takes into account the holy personages of all the religions of the world in the sense understood by the Judeo-Islamic concept of Prophets. It may bear repeating that

24

Islam considers the Founders of all revealed religions to be merely human beings who were raised by God to the status of prophethood.

There is no exception in this universal phenomenon. For instance, the Holy Quran declares:

فَكَيْفَ إِذَا جِئْنَا مِن كُلِّ أُمَّةٍ بِشَهِيدٍ وَجِئْنَا بِكَ عَلَىٰ هَٰؤُلَآءِ شَهِيدًا ۝

How will it fare with them when We shall bring a
witness from every people, and shall bring thee as a witness
against these! (Ch. 4: Al-Nisa: 42)

Having made this essential clarification, we now proceed to study the status of the Holy Prophet of Islam, peace and blessings of Allah be upon him, according to the Holy Quran. The most conspicuous and incontrovertible claim regarding the Holy Prophet[sa] of Islam is made in the widely known and extensively discussed verse of the Holy Quran:

مَّا كَانَ مُحَمَّدٌ أَبَآ أَحَدٍ مِّن رِّجَالِكُمْ وَلَٰكِن رَّسُولَ اللَّهِ وَخَاتَمَ النَّبِيِّـنَ ۗ وَكَانَ اللَّهُ بِكُلِّ شَيْءٍ عَلِيمًا ۝

Muhammad is not the father of any of your men, but
he is the Messenger of Allah and (Khataman Nabiyyin) the Seal
of the Prophets and Allah has full knowledge of all things. (Ch.
33: Al-Ahzab:41)

The Arabic word *Khatam* in this verse has many connotations but the essence of the title *Khataman Nabiyyin* is, without a shadow of doubt, to be the very best; the supreme; the last word; the final authority; the one who encompasses all and testifies to the truth of others. (Lexicons of the Arabic language F.W. Lane,

Aqrab al-Muwarid, the Mufradat of Imam Raghib, Fath and Zurqani)

Another verse which speaks of the excellence of the Holy Founder[sa] of Islam declares that the teachings of the Holy Prophet[sa] are perfect and final. The verse runs as follows:

الْيَوْمَ أَكْمَلْتُ لَكُمْ دِينَكُمْ وَأَتْمَمْتُ عَلَيْكُمْ نِعْمَتِى وَرَضِيتُ لَكُمُ الْإِسْلَامَ دِينًا

. . . This day have I perfected your religion for you and completed My favour upon you and have chosen for you Islam as religion . . . (Ch. 5: Al-Ma'idah:4)

The obvious inference from this claim would be that of all law bringing Prophets of the world and in giving the world the most perfect teaching, he occupies the highest station amongst the Prophets.

Developing the theme further the Holy Founder[sa] is assured in no uncertain terms that the Book being revealed to him will be guarded and protected from interpolations. As such, not only is the teaching claimed to be perfect, but also, it is declared to be everlasting — to be kept pure and unadulterated in the very words in which they were revealed to the Holy Founder[sa] of Islam. The history of the last fourteen centuries has borne ample witness to the truth of this claim.

The following are some relevant verses:

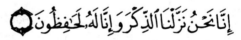

Surely, We Ourself have sent down this Exhortation and We will, most surely, be its Guardian. (Ch. 15: Al-Hijr: 10)

Surely, this is a glorious Quran in a well-guarded tablet. (Ch. 85: Al-Buruj: 22-23)

In view of the above, the Holy Founder[sa] of Islam is clearly not only declared to be supreme but also the last and final law-bearing Prophet whose authority would continue to remain good till the end of time.

Having said that, one begins to wonder if, in the eyes of some, this claim about the supremacy of the Holy Founder [sa] of Islam would be tantamount to creating ill-will or misunderstanding amongst the followers of other religions. So how can one reconcile this claim with the theme of this address, namely that Islam guarantees peace in all spheres of human interest, religion being not the least important among them?

It was with this question in mind that I had to elaborate this claim at some length. This question can be answered to the satisfaction of an unprejudiced and enquiring mind in more than one way.

As has already been mentioned before, similar claims are also made by followers of many other religions. It is only prudent for one to investigate the relative merits of the claim without being unduly excited about it. By itself such a claim should not offend the sensibilities of the followers of other religions who make similar counter-claims.

But Islam goes one step further by teaching humility and decency to its followers so that their belief in the supremacy of the Holy Founder[sa] of Islam is not expressed incautiously, thereby giving offence to others.

The following two Traditions of the Holy Founder[sa] of Islam stand aloft as beacons to illuminate the case in point.

(i) One of the Companions of the Holy Founder of Islam became involved in a rather heated discussion with a staunch follower of the Prophet Jonah[as] of the Fish (or Whale). Both parties in the debate claimed their respective Prophet to be head and shoulders above the other in excellence. It appears that the Muslim contender might have rubbed in the claim in a manner so as to hurt the sensibility of the follower of Jonah who approached Prophet Muhammad, peace and blessings of Allah be upon him, and lodged a complaint against the Muslim involved in this debate. Addressing the community in general, the Prophet issued the following words of instruction:

$$\text{لاَ تُفَضِّلُونِي عَلَى يُونُس بنِ مَتَى}$$

Do not declare me to be superior over Jonah (Yunus), son of Mattah.(Bukhari: Book on Prophets)

Some Muslim commentators of Traditions are perplexed by this Tradition as it seemingly stands counter to the Quranic claim that Muhammad, peace and blessings of Allah be upon him, is superior not only to Jonah[as] but all Prophets. But they seem to miss the point that what he said was not that he was inferior to Jonah[as], (nor superior to Jonah[as]), but simply that his followers should not declare him to be superior in a manner liable to hurt the feelings of others. In the context of what had passed, the only inference one can draw is that the Prophet[as] was teaching Muslims a lesson in decency. He was instructing them not to become involved in bragging. They should take care to avoid discussing his status in a manner that could cause offence. Such an attitude would indeed be detrimental to the cause of Islam because instead of winning hearts and minds to the Message of Islam, quite the opposite would be achieved.

(ii) This attitude of the Holy Prophet, peace and blessings of Allah be upon him, is corroborated further by another Tradition in which a Muslim was involved in a similar argument with a

Jew. Both claimed and counter-claimed the relative superiority of their spiritual leaders. Again, it was the non-Muslim contender who thought it fit to lodge a complaint against the behaviour of his Muslim adversary. The Holy Prophet, peace and blessings of Allah be upon him, responded with his habitual humility and prudence and taught the Muslim the same lesson in decency and courtesy by admonishing:

$$\text{لاَ تُفَضِّلُونِي عَلَى مُوسى}$$

Do not declare my superiority over Moses. (Bukhari: ibid)

The long and short of this is that it is for God to decide and declare the comparative ranking of the various Prophets' closeness to Him. It is quite likely that in a particular age, in the context of a particular religion, God may have expressed His pleasure with the Prophet of the time in such strong terms as to declare that he was the best. Superlatives can, after all, be also used in relative terms in the context of a limited application of time and space.

This could easily have led the followers of that holy personage to believe that he was the best and holiest for all ages and for all times to come. To genuinely believe in this should not be considered an offence against others. A civilised attitude would require that such issues should not be abused to create friction amongst religions. That exactly is the true import of the admonition of the Holy Prophet, peace and blessing of Allah be upon him, quoted above. If adherence to this principle of humility and decency is adopted by all religions, the world of religious controversy would be the better for it.

SALVATION CANNOT BE MONOPOLISED BY ANY SINGLE RELIGION

The question of salvation, howsoever innocent it may appear, is potent in its danger to peace in the religious world.

It is one thing for a religion to declare that those who seek to be redeemed from Satan and attain salvation should rush to the safe haven of that religion; it is there that they would find salvation and eternal liberation from sin. But it is quite another thing for the same religion to declare in the next breath that those who do not come hither to seek refuge will be damned eternally, one and all. Whatever they do to please God, however much they love their Creator and His creation, however much they lead a life of purity and piety, they would most certainly be condemned to an everlasting Fire.

When such a rigid, narrow-minded and non-tolerant view is expressed in a provocative language as generally is by religious zealots, it is known to have produced violent riots.

People come in all shapes and sizes. Some are educated, cultured and refined and so are their reactions to offences committed against them. Yet a large number of religiously inclined people, be they educated or illiterate, are likely to react violently when their religious sensibilities are hurt.

Unfortunately this seems to be the attitude of the clergy of almost all religions of the world against those who do not conform to their faith. Even Islam is presented by most medieval scholars as the only door to salvation, in the sense that ever since the advent of Islam, all the descendants of Adam who have lived and died outside the pale of Islam are denied salvation. Christianity does not offer a different view, nor does any religion to my knowledge.

But let me assure my audience that the attribution of this bigoted and narrow view to Islam has no justification. The Holy Quran has a completely different story to tell us in this regard.

According to the Holy Quran, salvation cannot be monopolised by any single religion of the world. Even if new truths are revealed and new eras of light have dawned, those who live a life of ignorance through no fault of their own and those who generally try to lead a life of truth even if they inherited false ideologies, will not be denied salvation by God.

The following verses from the Holy Quran elaborate this point further:

لِكُلِّ أُمَّةٍ جَعَلْنَا مَنسَكًا هُمْ نَاسِكُوهُ فَلَا يُنَازِعُنَّكَ فِى ٱلْأَمْرِ وَٱدْعُ إِلَى رَبِّكَ إِنَّكَ لَعَلَى هُدًى مُّسْتَقِيمٍ ۝

For every people We have appointed ways of worship which they observe; so let them not dispute with thee in the matter of the Islamic way of worship; and call thou the people to thy Lord, for, surely, thou art on the right guidance. (Ch. 22: Al-Hajj: 68)

In another verse, the Holy Quran declares in the same context:

إِنَّ ٱلَّذِينَ ءَامَنُوا وَٱلَّذِينَ هَادُوا وَٱلصَّٰبِئُونَ وَٱلنَّصَرَىٰ مَنْ ءَامَنَ بِٱللَّهِ وَٱلْيَوْمِ ٱلْأَخِرِ وَعَمِلَ صَلِحًا فَلَا خَوْفٌ عَلَيْهِمْ وَلَا هُمْ يَحْزَنُونَ ۝

Surely, those who have believed in Muhammad and the Jews, and the Sabians, and the Christian — whoso believes in Allah and the Last Day and does good deeds, on them shall come no fear nor shall they grieve. (Ch. 5; Al-Ma'idah: 70)

Let me remind you that although the *People of the Book* is applicable to the Jews and Christians, potentially, it has a much wider application. In the context of the Quranic assertion *'that there is no people in the world but We have sent a Warner to them'*, and similar verses (cited earlier), we are left with no room for doubt that these were not only the people of the Old Testament and the Gospel (or the Torah and the Injeel) who were given the Book, but most certainly other books were revealed for the benefit of mankind. So all religions which have a claim to be founded on divine revelation would also be included among *the People of the Book*.

Again the Holy Quran uses the term *Sabi* which further clarifies the issue and dispels doubt. *Sabi* is a term used by the Arabs to apply to the followers of all non-Arab and non-Semitic religions which have their own revealed Books. As such, followers of all religions based on divine revelation have been granted the assurance that provided they do not fail to recognise the truth of a new religion (despite their sincere efforts to understand)and stick honestly and truly to the values of their ancestral religion, they have nothing to fear from God and will not be denied salvation.

The Holy Quran, speaking of whichever party from among the Believers: Jews, Christians and Sabians, promises:

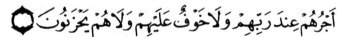

..... Shall have their reward with their Lord, and no fear shall come upon them, nor shall they grieve. (Ch. 2: Al-Baqarah: 63)

And:

وَلَوْ أَنَّهُمْ أَقَامُواْ ٱلتَّوْرَىٰةَ وَٱلْإِنجِيلَ وَمَآ أُنزِلَ إِلَيْهِم مِّن رَّبِّهِمْ لَأَكَلُواْ مِن فَوْقِهِمْ وَمِن تَحْتِ أَرْجُلِهِمْ مِّنْهُمْ أُمَّةٌ مُّقْتَصِدَةٌ وَكَثِيرٌ مِّنْهُمْ سَآءَ مَا يَعْمَلُونَ ۝

> *If they had observed the Torah and the Gospel and what has been now sent down to them from their Lord, they would surely, have eaten of good things from above them and from under their feet. Among them are people who are moderate but many of them are such that evil is what they do. (Ch. 5: Al-Ma'idah: 67)*

To prevent Muslims from censuring indiscriminately all those who do not belong to Islam, the Holy Quran categorically declares:

لَيْسُواْ سَوَآءً مِّنْ أَهْلِ ٱلْكِتَٰبِ أُمَّةٌ قَآئِمَةٌ يَتْلُونَ ءَايَٰتِ ٱللَّهِ ءَانَآءَ ٱلَّيْلِ وَهُمْ يَسْجُدُونَ ۝ يُؤْمِنُونَ بِٱللَّهِ وَٱلْيَوْمِ ٱلْأَخِرِ وَيَأْمُرُونَ بِٱلْمَعْرُوفِ وَيَنْهَوْنَ عَنِ ٱلْمُنكَرِ وَيُسَٰرِعُونَ فِى ٱلْخَيْرَٰتِ وَأُوْلَٰٓئِكَ مِنَ ٱلصَّٰلِحِينَ ۝ وَمَا يَفْعَلُواْ مِنْ خَيْرٍ فَلَن يُكْفَرُوهُ وَٱللَّهُ عَلِيمٌۢ بِٱلْمُتَّقِينَ ۝

> *They are not all alike. Among the people of the Book are those who are very pious and God-fearing, and who stand by their covenant; they recite the Word of Allah in the hours of night and prostrate themselves before Him. They believe in Allah and the Last Day, and enjoin good and forbid evil, and hasten to vie with one another in good works. These are among*

*the righteous. Whatever good they do, they shall not be denied
its due reward, and Allah well knows those who guard against
evil. (Ch. 3: Al-Imran: 114-116)*

There is a great misunderstanding today, born out of the recent
political rivalries between the Jews and the Muslims, that
according to Islam, all Jews are hellbound. This is totally false
in light of what I have recited before you from the Holy Quran,
and in light of the following verse:

وَمِن قَوْمِ مُوسَىٰٓ أُمَّةٌ يَهْدُونَ بِٱلْحَقِّ وَبِهِۦ يَعْدِلُونَ ۝

*Of the people of Moses there is a party who guides
with truth and does justice therewith. (Ch. 7: Al-A'raf: 160)*

PROMOTION OF HARMONY AND MUTUAL RESPECT AMONGST RELIGIONS

It is declared in unambiguous terms in the Holy Quran that it is
not only the Muslims who stand firmly by the truth and
admonish and dispense justice righteously amongst the
followers of other faiths. There are also other people who do the
same.

This is the attitude which the entire world of religion must adopt
today to improve the quality of relationship with other faiths.
Religious peace cannot be achieved without cultivating such
broadminded, magnanimous and humanely understanding
attitudes towards the people of other faiths.

Referring to all religions of the world, in general, the Holy
Quran declares:

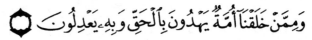

وَمِمَّنْ خَلَقْنَآ أُمَّةٌ يَهْدُونَ بِٱلْحَقِّ وَبِهِۦ يَعْدِلُونَ ۝

Of those We have created, there are a people that guide men with truth and do justice therewith. (Ch. 7: Al-A'raf: 182)

THE UNIVERSALITY CONCEPT

Since time immemorial, many philosophers have been dreaming of the moment when mankind can gather as one large human family under one flag. This concept of the unification of mankind has been entertained not only by political thinkers but also by economists and sociologists alike. But nowhere has the idea been pursued with greater fervour than in the domain of religion.

Although Islam also shares this view with other religions (some having highly ambitious programmes of world domination), within this apparent commonality, Islam stands distinctly different in its attitude to the aforementioned ambitious claim. This is no place for developing this controversial theme further and to enter into a debate as to which religion has actually been commissioned by God to gather the whole of mankind under one divine banner. But it is very important for us to understand the implications of such claims by more than one religion of the world. If two, three or four powerful religions with long-established historical tradition, simultaneously claim to be universal religions, will it not generate monstrous confusion and uncertainty in the minds of all human beings ? Will their mutual rivalry and struggle for domination not pose a real and substantial threat to world peace?

Such movements of global dimension on the part of religions are a matter of grave concern themselves. But to add to that the danger of such movements falling into the hands of an irresponsible, bigoted and intolerant leadership means that the risks will be manifold and more real than academic.

In the case of Islam, unfortunately, there is widespread propaganda to the effect that Islam promotes the use of force wherever possible for the spread of its ideology. Such words emanate not only from opponents of Islam but also from medieval-minded Muslim "clergy".

Obviously, if one religion opts for the offensive, the others will have the right to defend themselves with the same weapons.

Of course, I do not agree and strongly reject the notion that Islam advocates the use of force for the spread of ideologies - but to this aspect, I will return later.

Let us first examine the rationality of such a claim by any religion of the world. Can any religion - Islam, Christianity, or whatever you may call it - become universal in its Message, in the sense that the Message be applicable to all people of the world, whatever their colour, race or nationality? What about a host of different racial, tribal, national traditions, social habits and cultural patterns?

The concept of universality as proposed by religions, should not only transcend the geographic and national boundaries but should also transcend time. So, the question would be: can a religion be timeless, i.e. can the teachings of any religion be applicable with equal fitness to the people of this age as well as to those of a thousand years ago and a thousand years hence? Even if a religion was accepted globally by the entire mankind, how could it be competent enough to fulfil the needs of the future generation?

It is for the followers of every religion to suggest how the teachings of their religion propose to resolve the problems discussed above. However, on behalf of Islam, I should like to summarise very briefly the Islamic answer to these questions.

ISLAM IS A UNIVERSAL RELIGION

The Holy Quran repeatedly makes it clear that Islam is a religion whose teachings are related to the human psyche. Islam emphasises that any religion which is rooted in the human psyche transcends time and space. The human psyche is unchangeable. Therefore, the religion which is truly rooted in the human psyche becomes unchangeable by the same token providing that it does not get too involved with the transient situations of man, in whatever age, as he progresses forward. If the religion sticks to those principles which emanate from the human psyche, such a religion has the logical potential of becoming a universal religion.

Islam goes one step further. In its uniquely understanding attitude, it describes all religions of the world as possessing this character of universality to some degree. As such, in every divinely revealed religion, there is always found a central core of teaching which is bonded to the human psyche and eternal truth. This core of religions remains unchangeable unless, of course, the followers of that religion corrupt that teaching at a later period of time.

The following verses illustrate the case in point:

وَمَآ أُمِرُوٓاْ إِلَّا لِيَعۡبُدُواْ ٱللَّهَ مُخۡلِصِينَ لَهُ ٱلدِّينَ حُنَفَآءَ وَيُقِيمُواْ ٱلصَّلَوٰةَ وَيُؤۡتُواْ ٱلزَّكَوٰةَ‌ۚ وَذَٰلِكَ دِينُ ٱلۡقَيِّمَةِ ۝

They (the People of the Book) were not commanded but to serve Allah, being sincere to Him in obedience, and being upright, and to observe Prayer and pay the Zakat. That is the religion of the people of the right path. (Ch. 98: Al-Bayyinah: 6)

فَأَقِمْ وَجْهَكَ لِلدِّينِ حَنِيفًا فِطْرَتَ ٱللَّهِ ٱلَّتِى فَطَرَ ٱلنَّاسَ عَلَيْهَا لَا تَبْدِيلَ لِخَلْقِ ٱللَّهِ ذَٰلِكَ ٱلدِّينُ ٱلْقَيِّمُ وَلَٰكِنَّ أَكْثَرَ ٱلنَّاسِ لَا يَعْلَمُونَ ۝

So set thy face to the service of religion turning as one devoted to God. And follow the nature made by Allah - the nature in which He has created mankind. There is no altering the creation of Allah. That is the right religion. But most men know not. (Ch. 30: Al-Rum: 31)

In view of the above, the question may be raised as to the wisdom of sending one religion after another with the same teaching. Further, one may wonder why Islam claims, in relative terms, to be more universal and perfect than all the previous religions if all had the same unchangeable universal teaching applicable to human beings at all times.

1) In answer to the first question, the Holy Quran draws the attention of mankind to the indisputable historical fact that the Books and Scriptures revealed earlier than the Quran have been tampered with. Their teachings were corrupted by a process of gradual amendment or new elements were introduced through interpolation until the validity and authenticity of these Books and Scriptures became doubtful and questionable.

So, the onus of proof that no change whatsoever has been effected, of course, lies on the shoulders of the people belonging to such religions. As far as the Quran goes, it occupies a unique and distinct position amongst all religious Books and Scriptures. Even some of the staunchest enemies of Islam, who do not believe the Quran to be the Word of God, have to confess that the Holy Quran, without a shadow of doubt, remains the same unchanged and unaltered Book which was claimed by

Muhammad, peace and blessings of Allah be upon him, to be the Word of God.

For instance:

There is otherwise every security, internal and external, that we possess the text which Mohamet himself gave forth and used. (p. xxvii)

We may, upon the strongest assumption, affirm that every verse in the Quran is the genuine and unaltered composition of Mohamet himself. (p. xxviii)[Life of Mohamet by Sir William Muir (London, 1878)]

Slight clerical errors there may have been, but the Quran of Uthman contains none but genuine elements, though sometimes in very strange order. The efforts of European scholars to prove the existence of later interpolations in the Quran have failed. (Prof. Noldeke in Encyclopaedia Britannica; 9th edition, under Quran)

It is a completely different domain of controversy as to which Book was authored by whom. But the same Book whose authorship by God is challenged by the other People of the Books stands witness to the fact that, not only the Torah and the Injeel (collectively the Old Testament and the Gospels) were authored in part by God Himself, but also other Books belonging to different religions in other parts of the world were, without question, also authored by the same God - only the contradictions one finds in them today are man-made. Need it be said that the attitude of the Holy Quran is by far the most realistic and conducive to peace among religions.

2) As to the second question, the Holy Quran draws our attention to the process of evolution in every sphere of human society. New religions were needed not only for the sake of restoring the fundamental teachings of older religions which had been mutilated at the hands of man, but also, as society evolved,

more teachings had to be added to previous ones to keep up with the pace of progress.

3) That is not all. Another factor at work in this process of change was the element of time-related secondary teachings which were revealed to meet only the requirements of a certain people or period. This means that religions were not only made of central cores of unchangeable principles, but were also dressed-up with peripheral, secondary and even transient teachings.

4) Last but not least, man was not educated and trained in divine instructions in one single stride, but he was gradually carried forward step by step to a stage of mental adulthood where he was considered fit and mature to receive all the fundamental principles which were needed for his guidance. According to the Quranic claim, a secondary teaching inseparably based on everlasting fundamental principles was also revealed as a part of the final, perfect and consummate religion i.e. Islam. That which was of a purely local or temporary character was abrogated or omitted; that which was still needed henceforth was provided and retained. (see Holy Quran Ch. 5:14-16)

This in essence is the Islamic concept of religious universality which Islam claims to possess. It is for man to investigate and judge the comparative merit of different claimants.

Now, once again, we turn to the question of such religions which have set themselves the goal of global ascendancy. Clearly, Islam does entertain such ambitions. By way of prophecy, the Holy Quran declares that Islam is destined to emerge one day as the sole religion of mankind.

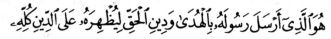

40

وَلَوْ كَرِهَ ٱلْمُشْرِكُونَ ۝

He it is Who has sent His Messenger with the guidance and the religion of the truth, that He may cause it to prevail over all religions, even if those who associate partners with God do not like it. (Ch. 61: Al-Saff: 10)

Despite its commitment to the promotion of peace and harmony between various religions, Islam does not discourage the competitive dissemination of messages and ideologies with a view to gaining ascendancy over others. In fact, it sets the ultimate ascendancy of Islam over all other faiths as a noble goal which must be pursued by the adherents of Islam.

Speaking of the Holy Founder[sa] of Islam , the Holy Quran states:

قُلْ يَا أَيُّهَا ٱلنَّاسُ إِنِّي رَسُولُ ٱللَّهِ إِلَيْكُمْ جَمِيعًا ٱلَّذِى لَهُ مُلْكُ ٱلسَّمَوَاتِ وَٱلْأَرْضِ لَا إِلَهَ إِلَّا هُوَ يُحْيِ وَيُمِيتُ فَآمِنُوا بِٱللَّهِ وَرَسُولِهِ ٱلنَّبِيِّ ٱلْأُمِّيِّ ٱلَّذِى يُؤْمِنُ بِٱللَّهِ وَكَلِمَاتِهِ وَٱتَّبِعُوهُ لَعَلَّكُمْ تَهْتَدُونَ ۝

Say, 'O mankind! truly I am a Messenger to you all from Allah to Whom belongs the kingdom of the heavens and earth. There is no God but He. He gives life, and He causes death. So believe in Allah and His Messenger, the Prophet, the Immaculate one, who believes in Allah and His words; and follow him that you may be rightly guided'. (Ch. 7: Al-A`raf: 159)

However, to pre-empt frictions and misunderstandings, Islam prescribes a set of clear cut rules of conduct which guarantee fair play, absolute justice, freedom of speech, right of expression and the right of disagreement for all alike.

INSTRUMENTS OF STRUGGLE - NO COMPULSION

How can a religion claim itself to be universal, international, or global and yet not cause frictions?

No religion with a universal message and global ambitions to unite mankind under one flag can even momentarily entertain the idea of employing force to spread its message.

Swords can win territories but not hearts.

Force can bend heads but not minds.

Islam does not permit the use of force as an instrument for the spread of its Message. It declares:

There should be no compulsion in religion. Surely, right has become distinct from wrong..........(Ch.2:Al-Baqarah: 257)

So there is no need for any coercion. Leave it to man to determine where the truth belongs. Addressing the Holy Founder[sa] of Islam, God clearly warns him of entertaining any idea of force in an attempt to reform society. His status as reformer is made very clear in the following verse:

فَذَكِّرْ إِنَّمَآ أَنتَ مُذَكِّرٌ ۝ لَّسْتَ عَلَيْهِم بِمُصَيْطِرٍ ۝

Admonish, therefore, for thou art but an admonisher; thou hast no authority to compel them. (Ch. 88: Al-Ghashiyyah: 22-23)

Further developing the same theme, Prophet Muhammad, may peace and blessings of Allah be upon him, is reminded:

فَإِنْ أَعْرَضُوا فَمَا أَرْسَلْنَاكَ عَلَيْهِمْ حَفِيظًا إِنْ عَلَيْكَ إِلَّا الْبَلَاغُ

But if they turn away, We have not sent thee as a
guardian over them. Thy duty is only to convey the Message.
Leave it to God to make the Message effective. (Ch. 42: Al-
Shura: 49)

Even if a struggle develops in the process of the propagation of
the new ideology and violent reaction ensues, then Islam
strongly exhorts its adherents to show patience and perseverance
and avoid conflict as much as possible. This is why wherever a
Muslim is admonished to deliver the Message of Islam to the
world at large, a clear-cut code of conduct is laid out for him.
Out of many verses related to this subject, we quote the
following few verses to illustrate the point:

ادْعُ إِلَى سَبِيلِ رَبِّكَ بِالْحِكْمَةِ وَالْمَوْعِظَةِ الْحَسَنَةِ
وَجَادِلْهُمْ بِالَّتِي هِيَ أَحْسَنُ إِنَّ رَبَّكَ هُوَ أَعْلَمُ بِمَنْ
ضَلَّ عَنْ سَبِيلِهِ وَهُوَ أَعْلَمُ بِالْمُهْتَدِينَ ۞

Call unto the way of thy Lord, with wisdom and
goodly exhortation, and argue with them in a way that is best.
Surely, thy Lord knows best who has strayed from His way; and
He also knows who are rightly guided. (Ch. 16: Al-Nahl: 126)

And:
ادْفَعْ بِالَّتِي هِيَ أَحْسَنُ السَّيِّئَةَ نَحْنُ أَعْلَمُ بِمَا يَصِفُونَ ۞

Repel evil with that which is best. We know very well what
they allege. (Ch. 23: Al-Mu'minun: 97)

Here, 'Ahsan' means the best, most attractive and something
beautiful.

Describing a code of conduct under which the believers deliver the Message, the Holy Quran has the following comment:

وَٱلْعَصْرِ ۞ إِنَّ ٱلْإِنسَٰنَ لَفِى خُسْرٍ ۞ إِلَّا ٱلَّذِينَ ءَامَنُواْ وَعَمِلُواْ ٱلصَّٰلِحَٰتِ وَتَوَاصَوْاْ بِٱلْحَقِّ وَتَوَاصَوْاْ بِٱلصَّبْرِ ۞

We call to witness *that age when man as a whole would be in a state of loss, except those who believe and do righteous deeds and deliver Truth* in a manner that is also truthful. *They exhort patience* while they themselves exercise patience. (Ch. 103: Al-Asr: 2-4)

Again:

ثُمَّ كَانَ مِنَ ٱلَّذِينَ ءَامَنُواْ وَتَوَاصَوْاْ بِٱلصَّبْرِ وَتَوَاصَوْاْ بِٱلْمَرْحَمَةِ ۞

Then he should have been of those who believe and exhort one another to exercise patience while they do the same themselves and they exhort one another to be considerate and merciful to others while they themselves are considerate and merciful. (Ch. 90: Al-Balad: 18)

SURVIVAL OF THE FITTEST

According to the Holy Quran, the survival and ultimate victory of a Message depends entirely upon the potency of its arguments and not on the material force it can employ. The Holy Quran is very clear and specific on this subject. It declares that even if the most powerful forces are employed to annihilate Truth and support falsehood, such efforts would invariably be defeated and frustrated. Reason will always prevail over the crude force of material weapons. For instance, it is stated in the Holy Quran:

قَالَ ٱلَّذِينَ يَظُنُّونَ أَنَّهُم مُّلَٰقُواْ ٱللَّهِ كَم مِّن فِئَةٍ قَلِيلَةٍ غَلَبَتْ فِئَةً كَثِيرَةً بِإِذْنِ ٱللَّهِ وَٱللَّهُ مَعَ

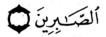

. . . . . . But those who knew for certain that they would one day meet Allah said: How many a small party has triumphed over a large party by Allah's command! And Allah is with the steadfast. (Ch. 2: Al-Baqarah: 250)

The concept of the supremacy of Islam has to be understood in the context of the afore-mentioned divine command.

In another part of a verse of the Holy Quran, it is stated:

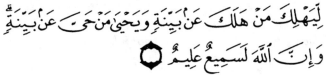

. . . . . . Allah is well pleased with them and they are well pleased with Him. They are Allah's party. Take note, it is Allah's party who will prosper. (Ch. 58:Al-Mujadila: 23)

During the Battle of Badr (the first battle in the history of Islam), the might of Meccan idolators was pitched against a small number of Muslims - overwhelmingly outnumbered, outclassed in weaponry and equipment, and forced to fight a defensive battle for the preservation of their ideology rather than for their personal survival. Commenting upon this, the Holy Quran declares:

. . . . So let him perish who is condemned to perish by the verdict of manifest logic and let him survive who is worthy of survival by virtue of manifest logic. (Ch. 8: Al-Anfal: 43)

45

This is the everlasting principle which has played the most important role in the evolution of mankind, Survival of the fittest is the essence of this Message. That, in fact, is the methodology of the evolution of life.

FREEDOM OF SPEECH

Freedom of speech and expression is vital to the spread of a Message as well as to restore the dignity of man. No religion is worthy of any consideration unless it addresses itself to the restoration and protection of human dignity.

In view of what has passed, it should become apparent that it is impossible for a religion like Islam to deny freedom of speech and expression. On the contrary, Islam upholds this principle in such a manner and with such boldness as is seldom witnessed in any other ideology or religion in the world. For instance, the Holy Quran declares:

وَقَالُواْ لَن يَدۡخُلَ ٱلۡجَنَّةَ إِلَّا مَن كَانَ هُودًا أَوۡ نَصَـٰرَىٰ تِلۡكَ أَمَانِيُّهُمۡ قُلۡ هَاتُواْ بُرۡهَـٰنَكُمۡ إِن كُنتُمۡ صَـٰدِقِينَ ۝

They say, 'None shall ever enter Heaven unless he be a Jew or a Christian.' These are their vain desires. Say, 'Produce your proof, if you are truthful.' (Ch. 2: Al-Baqarah: 112)

Again:

أَمِ ٱتَّخَذُواْ مِن دُونِهِۦٓ ءَالِهَةً قُلۡ هَاتُواْ بُرۡهَـٰنَكُمۡ هَـٰذَا ذِكۡرُ مَن مَّعِيَ وَذِكۡرُ مَن قَبۡلِيٓ بَلۡ أَكۡثَرُهُمۡ لَا يَعۡلَمُونَ ٱلۡحَقَّ فَهُم مُّعۡرِضُونَ ۝

46

Have they taken gods beside Him! Say, 'Bring forth your proof. Here is the Book of those with me, and those before me!' Nay, most of them know not the truth and so they turn away from it. (Ch. 21: Al-Anbiya: 25)

And:

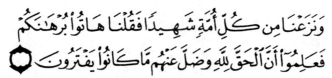

We shall draw from every people a witness and We shall say to them, 'Bring your proof.' Then will they know that the truth belongs to Allah and that which they used to forge will be lost unto them. (Ch. 28: Al-Qasas: 76)

And:

Or have you a clear authority? Then provide your Book if you are truthful. (Ch. 37: Al-Saffat: 157-158)

LIBERTY AND EMANCIPATION IN THE CONTEXT OF THE CONTEMPORARY WORLD

Liberty and emancipation are the two important slogans which are influencing the entire world with varying intensity and different connotations in different parts of the world. There is no doubt, whatsoever, that man is gaining greater awareness and consciousness in the importance and value of liberty. There is a pressing need felt everywhere in the world for emancipation, but from what? Is it from the yoke of foreign rule; dictatorship; fascism; theocratic or other regimes with totalitarian philosophies; oppressive democracies and corrupt bureaucracies; the economic stranglehold of the poor countries by the rich; ignorance; superstition; or fetishism?

Islam champions the cause of liberty from all these maladies but not in a manner as to cause disorder, chaos and indiscriminate vengeance causing suffering to the innocent.

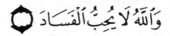

Is the message of Islam: *And God does not like disorder. (Ch.2: Al-Baqarah: 206)*

Islam like every other religion emphasises the role of balanced freedom in a spirit of give and take. The concept of absolute freedom is hollow, weird, and unreal in the context of society.

Sometimes, the concept of freedom is so misconceived and misapplied that the beauty of the cherished principle of freedom of speech gets transformed into the ugliness of freedom to abuse, hurl insults and to blaspheme.

BLASPHEMY

Islam goes one step further than any other religion in granting man the freedom of speech and expression. Blasphemy is condemned on moral and ethical grounds, no doubt, but no physical punishment is prescribed for blasphemy in Islam despite the commonly held view in the contemporary world.

Having studied the Holy Quran extensively and repeatedly with deep concentration, I have failed to find a single verse which declares blasphemy to be a crime punishable by man.

Although the Holy Quran very strongly discourages indecent behaviour and indecent talk, or the hurting of the sensitivity of others, with or without rhyme or reason, Islam does not advocate the punishment of blasphemy in this world nor vests such authority in anyone.

Blasphemy has been mentioned five times in the Holy Quran.

1) For instance, this subject is mentioned in generality:

وَقَدْ نَزَّلَ عَلَيْكُمْ فِى الْكِتَٰبِ أَنْ إِذَا سَمِعْتُمْ ءَايَٰتِ اللَّهِ يُكْفَرُ بِهَا وَيُسْتَهْزَأُ بِهَا فَلَا تَقْعُدُوا مَعَهُمْ حَتَّىٰ يَخُوضُوا فِى حَدِيثٍ غَيْرِهِ إِنَّكُمْ إِذًا مِّثْلُهُمْ إِنَّ اللَّهَ جَامِعُ الْمُنَٰفِقِينَ وَالْكَٰفِرِينَ فِى جَهَنَّمَ جَمِيعًا ۝

He has already revealed to you in the Book that, when you hear the Signs of Allah being denied and mocked at, sit not with them until they engage in a talk other than that; for in that case you would be like them. Surely, Allah will assemble the hypocrites and the disbelievers in Hell, all together. (Ch. 4: Al-Nisa: 141)

وَإِذَا رَأَيْتَ الَّذِينَ يَخُوضُونَ فِى ءَايَٰتِنَا فَأَعْرِضْ عَنْهُمْ حَتَّىٰ يَخُوضُوا فِى حَدِيثٍ غَيْرِهِ وَإِمَّا يُنسِيَنَّكَ الشَّيْطَٰنُ فَلَا تَقْعُدْ بَعْدَ الذِّكْرَىٰ مَعَ الْقَوْمِ الظَّٰلِمِينَ ۝

When thou sees those who engage in vain discourse concerning Our Signs, then turn thou away from them until they engage in a discourse other than that. And if Satan cause thee to forget, then sit not after recollection, with the unjust people. (Ch. 6: Al-An'am: 69)

What a beautiful response to the utter ugliness of blasphemy! Not only does Islam disallow any human being to take the punishment of the blasphemer into his or her own hands, but declares that people should register their protest against blasphemy by staging a walkout from an assembly of men where religious values are being mocked and ridiculed. Suggestions of any positive measures aside, not even a permanent boycott of the blasphemer is prescribed by the Holy Quran. On the contrary,

49

the Holy Quran makes it amply clear that this boycott is only to last for the period during which the act of blasphemy is being committed.

2) Again, blasphemy is mentioned in Surah (chapter) Al-An'am where, hypothetically, the question of blasphemy is discussed not only with regard to God but also idols and imaginary objects of worship besides God. One is overwhelmed by the beauty of Quranic teachings when one reads:

وَلَا تَسُبُّواْ ٱلَّذِينَ يَدْعُونَ مِن دُونِ ٱللَّهِ فَيَسُبُّواْ ٱللَّهَ عَدْوًۢا بِغَيْرِ عِلْمٍ كَذَٰلِكَ زَيَّنَّا لِكُلِّ أُمَّةٍ عَمَلَهُمْ ثُمَّ إِلَىٰ رَبِّهِم مَّرْجِعُهُمْ فَيُنَبِّئُهُم بِمَا كَانُواْ يَعْمَلُونَ ۝

Revile not those whom they call upon beside Allah, lest they, out of spite, revile Allah in their ignorance. Thus unto every people have We caused their doing seem fair. Then unto their Lord is their return; and He will inform them what they used to do. (Ch. 6: Al-An'am: 109)

It is the Muslims who are addressed in this verse. They are strictly prohibited from blaspheming the idols and imaginary gods of the idolators. It is also pointed out that if one does so, others may, by way of retaliation, indulge in blasphemy against God. In this hypothetical discussion of blasphemy against God and idols on equal terms, no physical punishment is prescribed in either case.

The moral of this teaching is rich in profound wisdom. If one commits a crime against one's spiritual sensibilities, the aggrieved party has a right to pay back in the same coin regardless of the nature of his beliefs and his being right or wrong. Neither is permitted to retaliate in different terms. One can safely conclude from this that spiritual offence should be avenged by spiritual means just as a physical offence is avenged by physical retaliation—but without transgression.

3) Blasphemy is mentioned in the Holy Quran in relation to Mary and Jesus, peace be upon them.

وَبِكُفْرِهِمْ وَقَوْلِهِمْ عَلَى مَرْيَمَ بُهْتَانًا عَظِيمًا ۝

For their disbelief and for their uttering against Mary a grievous calumny. (Ch. 4: Al-Nisa: 157)

This verse refers to the historical stance of the Jews contemporary to the times of Jesus Christ[as]. According to this verse, the Jews committed a grave blasphemy by declaring Mary, on whom be peace, to be unchaste and alleging Jesus, on whom be peace, to be a child of questionable birth.

The Arabic word *Buhtanan Azeema* (translated above as 'a grievous calumny') expresses condemnation of this folly on the part of the Jews in the strongest term. Yet, surprisingly, no physical punishment is prescribed.

4) It is interesting to note that while the Jews are condemnd by the Quran for committing an act of blasphemy against Mary and Jesus (peace be on them), at the same time the Christians, in their turn, are censured for committing blasphemy against God by claiming that a son was born to God through a human wife. In the following verse, the Holy Quran declares it as an enormity. Yet no corporal punishment of any sort is advocated nor is the right delegated to any human authority to punish blasphemy against God.

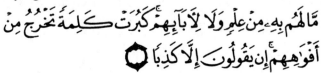

No knowledge have they thereof, nor had their fathers.
Monstrous is the word that comes out of their mouths. They
speak naught but a lie. (Ch. 18: Al-Kahf: 6)

5) In the end, let me come to the most sensitive area—more sensitive in the sense that the Muslims of today are more sensitive to blasphemy against the Holy Founder[sa] of Islam than blasphemy against anything else — even God!

Yet there is a case of blasphemy so serious that it is recorded in the Holy Quran itself, which speaks of Abdullah bin Ubayy bin Salul, known in the history of Islam as the Chief of Hypocrites.

Once returning from an expedition, Abdullah bin Ubayy declared in the company of others that the moment they returned to Madinah, the Noblest would expel the Meanest among the Medinites.

يَقُولُونَ لَبِن رَّجَعْنَآ إِلَى ٱلْمَدِينَةِ لَيُخْرِجَنَّ ٱلْأَعَزُّ
مِنْهَا ٱلْأَذَلَّ وَلِلَّهِ ٱلْعِزَّةُ وَلِرَسُولِهِ وَلِلْمُؤْمِنِينَ وَلَٰكِنَّ
ٱلْمُنَٰفِقِينَ لَا يَعْلَمُونَ ۞

They say, 'If we return to Madinah, the most exalted
will, surely, drive out therefrom the most mean, while true
honour belongs to Allah and to His Messenger and the believers;
but the hypocrites know not. (Ch. 63: Al-Munafiqun: 9)

Everyone understood the implied insult to the Holy Prophet, may peace and blessings of Allah be upon him. They were seething with indignation and rage to the extent that, if permitted, they would have most certainly put Abdullah bin Ubayy to the sword.

52

It is reported authentically that tempers were running so high at this incident that no less a person than the son of Abdullah bin Ubayy himself approached the Holy Founder[sa] of Islam seeking permission to kill his father with his own hands. The son argued that if anyone else did so, he might later on, in ignorance, entertain the thought of revenge against his father's killer. For centuries, the Arabs were accustomed to take revenge at even the smallest insult hurled at them or their close relative. Perhaps, this custom was what the son had in mind. But the Holy Prophet, may peace and blessings of Allah be upon him, refused to grant his request nor did he permit anyone else from among his Companions to punish the hypocrite, Abdullah bin Ubayy, in any manner whatsoever. (Narrated by Ibn Ishaq: *Al-Seera tun Nabawiyya* by Ibn Hashim, pt. III; p. 155)

Having returned to Madinah after the expedition, Abdullah bin Ubayy continued to live in peace. When he died at last, a natural death, of course, to the surprise of everyone, the Holy Prophet[sa] gave Abdullah's son his own shirt so that he could enshroud his father's body for burial - a singular act of blessing, indeed, which must have left the other Companions yearning to barter it from the son at the cost of all their possessions. Not only that, the Holy Prophet decided to lead his funeral prayer. This decision must have deeply disturbed many of his Companions who could never forgive Abdullah for the grievous offence mentioned above. Yet, it fell to the lot of Umar, who later succeeded the Prophet[sa] as the second Caliph to give voice to their suppressed uneasiness.

It is reported that as the Holy Prophet[sa] was proceeding to the funeral, Umar suddenly stepped forward and stood in the way begging the Prophet[sa] to change his decision. In doing so, Umar reminded the Prophet[sa] of the verse of the Holy Quran in which reference is made to some known hypocrite on whose behalf intercession would not be accepted even if the Holy Prophet[sa] prayed for them seventy times. Incidentally, the number seventy should not be taken too literally because, according to Arab usage, it was only employed to indicate a large number.

However, the Holy Prophet[sa] smiled and responded: Stand aside, Umar. I know better. If I know God would not forgive him even if I seek forgiveness seventy times, I would seek forgiveness for him more than seventy times. The Prophet then led the funeral prayer. *(Bukhari II, Kitab Al-Janaiz p. 121, and ibid Bab-al-Kafn pp. 96-97).*

This is a fitting rebuttal to those who are crying themselves hoarse in demanding death for the blasphemer who dares to insult the Holy Founder[sa] of Islam and nothing but death.

Such a religion must have a claim to establish inter-religious peace in the world.

INTER-RELIGIOUS COOPERATION

In inter-religious relationships Islam goes one step further by declaring:

وَلَا يَجْرِمَنَّكُمْ شَنَآنُ قَوْمٍ أَن صَدُّوكُمْ عَنِ ٱلْمَسْجِدِ ٱلْحَرَامِ أَن تَعْتَدُواْ وَتَعَاوَنُواْ عَلَى ٱلْبِرِّ وَٱلتَّقْوَىٰ وَلَا تَعَاوَنُواْ عَلَى ٱلْإِثْمِ وَٱلْعُدْوَٰنِ وَٱتَّقُواْ ٱللَّهَ إِنَّ ٱللَّهَ شَدِيدُ ٱلْعِقَابِ ۝

. . . And let not the enmity of a people that they hindered you from access to the Sacred Mosque, incite you to treat them with inequity. Instead help each other in good things of life and in all such things as are based on the fear of Allah. Do not, however, help one another in the sinful things and transgression . . . (Ch. 5: Al-Ma'idah: 3)

The Quran does not permit Muslims to treat with injustice even such enemies as had committed aggression against them due to religious enmity.

We now turn to the category of those non-believers who were not known to have taken any active part in hostilities against Muslims. Referring to them, the believers are told in the Holy Quran:

عَسَى اللَّهُ أَن يَجْعَلَ بَيْنَكُمْ وَبَيْنَ الَّذِينَ عَادَيْتُم مِّنْهُم مَّوَدَّةً وَاللَّهُ قَدِيرٌ وَاللَّهُ غَفُورٌ رَّحِيمٌ ۝ لَّا يَنْهَىٰكُمُ اللَّهُ عَنِ الَّذِينَ لَمْ يُقَٰتِلُوكُمْ فِى الدِّينِ وَلَمْ يُخْرِجُوكُم مِّن دِيَٰرِكُمْ أَن تَبَرُّوهُمْ وَتُقْسِطُوٓا إِلَيْهِمْ إِنَّ اللَّهَ يُحِبُّ الْمُقْسِطِينَ ۝

It may be that Allah will bring about love between you and those of them with whom you are now at enmity; and Allah is All-Powerful and Allah is Most Forgiving, Merciful. Allah forbids you not, respecting those who have fought against you on account of your religion; and who have not driven you out of your homes, that you be kind to them and deal equitably with them; surely, Allah loves those who are equitable. (Ch. 60: Al-Mumtahanah:8-9)

Muslims are also taught to invite the People of the Book and to cooperate with them in spreading the Message of the Unity of God — a belief shared with them. The import of the verse below is to emphasise the point of commonality and chalk a mutual programme for the benefit of mankind rather than to highlight the areas of differences resulting in discord.

قُلْ يَٰٓأَهْلَ الْكِتَٰبِ تَعَالَوْا إِلَىٰ كَلِمَةٍ سَوَآءٍ بَيْنَنَا وَبَيْنَكُمْ أَلَّا نَعْبُدَ إِلَّا اللَّهَ وَلَا نُشْرِكَ بِهِ شَيْئًا وَلَا يَتَّخِذَ بَعْضُنَا

بَعۡضًا أَرۡبَابًا مِّن دُونِ ٱللَّهِ فَإِن تَوَلَّوۡاْ فَقُولُواْ ٱشۡهَدُواْ بِأَنَّا مُسۡلِمُونَ ۝

Say, 'O People of the Book! Come to a word equal between us and you—that we worship none but Allah, and that we associate no partner with Him, and that some of us take not others for Lords besides Allah' But if they turn away, then say, 'Bear witness that we have submitted to God.' (Ch. 3: Al-Imran: 65)

CONCLUSION

Before examining any meaningful role that the bona fide religions of the world can play in providing peace to man in all areas of human activity, it is highly essential to critically examine the role of religions in establishing peace within the various sections of their own adherents and also to adjudge whether religions - as long as they exist - can ever learn to live at peace with each other. Judging from the growing influence of materialism and the emphasis of society as a whole shifting from spiritual to carnal and sensual pleasures, one may be led to believe that religion should be discarded and ignored as an unimportant factor.

I regret to disagree with such a conclusion because unless we reform religious attitudes, internally and externally, religion will continue to play a very strong negative role, rather than a beneficial positive role, in our efforts to achieve global peace. Religion, which should have played a leading role in establishing peace, removing misunderstanding between adherents of different sects and religions, cultivating decency, and promoting the principle of live and let live, has unfortunately, in the contemporary times, played a very minor and insignificant role, if any at all, in the promotion of peace anywhere in the world. Yet in creating disorder and bloodshed and in causing misery and immense suffering, it still is a very potent and dynamic force which should not be under-estimated at all. No global peace can be visualised without addressing this vital problem and redressing its faults.

Internally, religious sentiments can be strongly excited and activated to spread misery and suffering amongst a section of its adherents which, unfortunately, happens to belong to a minority sect within that religion.

The entire Muslim history is full of such ugly and despicable episodes where Islam, the religion of peace, was itself employed to shatter the peace of innocent believers, who, of course, believed in Islam but not in the way and style as others would have them. In fact, a study of Islamic history proves beyond a shadow of doubt that Islam has been misemployed for the persecution of Muslims themselves. The 'holy wars' that the Muslims fought against the Crusaders are far outnumbered and outweighed by the 'holy wars' that Muslims fought against Muslims during the last fourteen centuries.

The chapter is not closed. What has been happening in Pakistan vis-a-vis Ahmadiyya Muslims and not too infrequently against the Shi'ite minority, is enough to bring the focus of attention to the fact that this heinous problem which should have died long ago lives on.

In Christianity, persecution of Christians at the hands of Christians may appear to be a far cry buried under the debris of European and American history, but a study of the religion-political strife in Ireland appears to prove otherwise. Also there are potential dangers of sectarian strife within Christianity in other parts of the world which at present are preoccupied with other strifes and feuds.

In inter-religious relationships, the Hindu-Muslim riots in India, or Muslim-Christian strife in Nigeria or Jewish-Muslim hostilities in the Middle East and elsewhere, and also an undercurrent of politically and economically fragile Judeo-Christian relationship, are all but a few signs of latent dangers which lie like dormant volcanoes in the subterranean religious world.

The importance of reforming the attitudes to such problems cannot be over-emphasised.

To recapitulate the Islamic approach as to how such problems should be resolved, we conclude by pointing out that:

1) All religions of the world, whether they believe in Islam or not, must conform to the underlying Islamic principle of not permitting the use of force and coercion in any manner as an instrument in resolving inter-sectarian and inter-religious strife. The choice of religion, the freedom to profess, propagate, practise and exercise, or to denounce or to cease to believe or change one's belief must be protected absolutely.

2) Even if other religions cannot agree with the Islamic concept of universality of truth and even if, for instance, from the vantage point of Judaism, Christianity, Buddhism, Confucianism, Hinduism, Zoroastrianism, etc. other religions are all false and have nothing to do with God, then despite this negation of truth elsewhere, all religions must conform to the Islamic principle of showing respect and reverence to the Founders and holy personages of other faiths. In pursuance thereof, they do not have to compromise their principles. It is simply a matter of fundamental human rights. The right of every

58

human being that his religious sensibilities and sentiments shall not be violated and offended, must be recognised.

3)It should be remembered that the above principle cannot be enforced by any national or international law. It should be understood in conjunction with the principle that blasphemy does not warrant man-made punishment but that it should be decried and discouraged by promoting public opinion for condemning such acts as indecent, imprudent and loathsome.

4) Inter-faith conferences on the pattern introduced by the Ahmadiyya Muslim Community in the earlier part of this century, should be widely encouraged and promoted. The soul and spirit of such conferences can be summed up by the following characteristics:

a) All speakers should be encouraged to highlight the good points and attractive and distinctive features of their respective faiths without maligning other faiths.

b) Indeed, speakers, preferably, belonging to one faith should genuinely try to discover the good features of other faiths, speak on them and explain why they are impressed by them.

c) Speakers belonging to different faiths should pay tribute to the nobility and character of the leaders of other faiths. For instance, a Jewish speaker could speak on the distinctive features of the Holy Prophet, Mohammad which can be appreciated by all human beings without compromising their religious dogmas. Similarly, a Muslim speaker could speak of Krishna[as], Hindu speaker on Jesus Christ[as], a Buddhist on Moses (may peace and blessings of God be upon them all), and so on and so forth. During the third decade of this century, such conferences were held to great benefit and growing popularity by the Ahmadiyya Community to improve Hindu-Muslim relationships in India.

d) Without prejudice to what has been proposed in (c), the sanctity of religious dialogue must be protected between sects and faiths. Inter-religious exchange of views must not be condemned as attempts to sabotage religious peace. It is the manner of dialogue, which, if wrong, should be condemned and not the dialogue itself. The free flow of ideas is the most important of fundamental human rights, essential for the survival of the fittest. It may not be compromised at any cost.

e) To narrow the areas of differences and enlarge the possibility of agreements, it is highly essential that all religions accept the principle of limiting their debates with followers of other faiths to the sources of their respective religions. The Quranic declaration that all religions are the same at their sources should not be treated lightly. It comprises a world of wisdom which should be examined and explored by all religions to their own advantage as well as to the advantage of mankind as a whole.

5) Cooperation in all good plans and schemes for the mutual benefit of mankind must be promoted and encouraged. For instance, philanthropic projects could be undertaken jointly between Christians and Muslims and Hindus and Jews etc.

Only then can we hopefully realise the time old Utopian dream of past sages and thinkers, namely that of uniting man under one flag in all spheres of human activity—whether they be religious, social, economic or political fields and all that really matters.

II
SOCIAL PEACE

1. Contemporary social order
2. Two climates of social order
3. Vanity of materialistic society and its ultimate destination
4. Rejection of life to come
5. Four characteristics of materialistic society
6. Accountability
7. Islamic social climate
8. Fundamentals of an Islamic society
9. Chastity
10. Segregation of sexes
11. The dawn of a new age in women's rights
12. Equal rights for women
13. Polygamy
14. Care of the aged
15. The future generation
16. Wasteful vain pursuits discouraged
17. Bridling of desires
18. Building of trust and inviolability of trusts and treaties
19. Eradication of evil - a collective responsibility
20. Do's and don'ts
21. Rejection of racialism

Verily Allah enjoins justice and the doing of good to others; and giving like kindred; and forbids indecency and manifest evil, and wrongful transgression. He admonishes you that you may take heed. (Ch. 16: Al-Nahl: 91)

Know that the life of this world is only a sport and a pastime, and an adornment and a source of boasting among yourselves, and rivalry in multiplying riches and children. This life is like the rain, the vegetation produced whereby rejoices the tillers. Then it dries up and thou seest it turn yellow; then it becomes broken piece of straw. And in the Hereafter, there is severe punishment and also forgiveness from Allah and His pleasure. And the life of this world is nothing but temporary enjoyment of deceitful things. (Ch. 57: Al-Hadid: 21)

Let us now turn to the question of Islam's role in providing social peace for contemporary society.

CONTEMPORARY SOCIAL ORDER

Unfortunately religious influence on moral behaviour is fast being lost in society. To aggravate the situation further, a strong urge for liberation from religious obligations is in motion and gaining momentum almost everywhere in the contemporary world. Yet, there is also panic born out of the growing lack of security and disorderliness in social behaviour running parallel to the trends to disregard religious and ethical codes. Belief in a living God, Who has shaped not only the destiny of human beings but Who also has a right to determine the patterns of their day to day life is rapidly eroding.

The Holy Quran summarises this condition as:

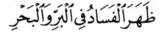

Disorder has inundated land and sea(Ch. 30: Al-Rum:42)

Christianity, being the predominant religion of the West, had, until the turn of this century, a strong and effective hold on the moral behaviour of its adherents in the West. Alas, not so any more.

Instead a civilization has evolved due to the interplay of scientific socialism, rapid scientific development and material progress, forcing Christianity to beat a retreat, step by step, and adopt a progressively diminishing role in moulding social behaviour.

Moral behaviour, therefore, in the West today is as little or as much Christian in its character as the moral behaviour in most

63

Muslim countries is Islamic. The same, unfortunately, is the state of social and moral behaviour elsewhere in the world.

There are so many Buddhists and Confucianists and Hindus in the world today but, unfortunately very little of Buddhism, Confucianism or Hinduism can be observed.

Water water everywhere but not a drop to drink.

If religious or traditional codes of ethics are wanting in a society, morality will lose all relevance to a generation which no longer blindly accepts its traditional heritage as sound and valid. Such a generation is bound to pass through a critical transitional period of emptiness. This in turn would generate a new urge for inquiry. The process of inquiry may or may not lead to the discovery of a better and more satisfying code of conduct. It may, on the other hand, end up in total chaos or a state of moral anarchy. Unfortunately, as I see things, it is the latter option which seems to be the choice of modern society.

A wind of change is blowing across societies of the world, be they eastern or western, religious or secular. It is an evil wind which is polluting the entire world climate.

The modern world seems to be far more aware and conscious of the rising level of pollution in the material atmosphere than the rapidly rising level of pollution in our social environment.

The Holy Quran, obviously speaking of such an age, declares:

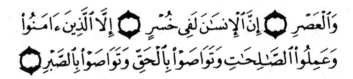

We bring to witness that age when man as a whole would be in a state of loss, except for those few who believe and do good deeds and exhort others with truth to accept truth, and

admonish others with patience to be patient. (Ch. 103: Al-Asr: 2-4)

Exploitation, duplicity, hypocrisy, selfishness, oppression, greed, the mad pursuit of pleasure, indiscipline, corruption, theft, robbery, violation of human rights, fraud, treachery, lack of responsibility, and want of mutual respect and trust have become the hallmark of the modern societies. The thin veneer of civilization can no longer hide the ugliness which is becoming more and more apparent. However, it would be wrong to say that these threatening signs of human failings were absent in past ages. In fact, many civilizations in the past had also suffered the same maladies before their chapters in the book of human history were finally closed. It would be wrong to single out any one particular region of the world which had been beset by moral evils.

Societies are beginning to crumble everywhere alike. As against the countries governed by totalitarian philosophies, the rising consciousness of individual liberty in the so-called free world is in itself becoming a lop-sided trend which is largely responsible for growing social misbehaviour.

In the countries governed by totalitarian philosophies, this progressive rise of consciousness of individual freedom is at present engaged in a grim battle of liberation of the individual from complete totalitarian control. Unless there is a counter-revolutionary upsurge in the powerful extreme left of the armed forces, this trend for greater freedom has every likelihood of winning the battle very soon. What may happen afterwards does not augur well for the moral prospects of emancipated youths in the erstwhile communist countries.

Almost two generations have grown to adulthood in the void of a godless society, with nothing to guide and discipline moral behaviour. Apart from the lack of an in-built code of moral values vested in religious ideologies, the danger of vain, playful pleasure-seeking and irresponsible trends flooding from the West on the youth in the USSR and Eastern Europe, can produce devastating effects on their moral behaviour in years to come.

At the same time, one cannot fail to note that the experience of living without religion for many decades has not only bequeathed ill to contemporary society but has also brought some clear advantages. The socialist revolution of Russia severed the ties of the socialist world not only with religion but with religious dogmas and views which themselves were corrupted and distorted. Be it Christianity or Islam, whatever sects the Christians or Muslims belonged, there was a medievalism about the concept of their respective religions which had created in many areas of belief, a parallax between religious doctrines and the realities of nature. Both could not be true at one and the same time. It took a special training of minds to view the discrepancies between the religious views and facts of nature and yet not feel disturbed. To live with paradoxes is, perhaps, not easy except when paradoxes are bred into a people, generation after generation. Gradually, the point is reached in time when religious communities can somehow live with paradoxes without noticing their presence.

Among other things, what the socialist revolution did to their people was to wash them clean of ideological dogmas and cure them of the strabismus and myopia.

This, in turn, has gifted them with a sort of innocence which can only be achieved when there is total lack of hypocrisy. It is too early to say whether this state of innocence can be turned to their moral advantage in the difficult time of struggle ahead. But one thing is certain. They are far more amenable to receiving the

Message of truth and accepting it without prejudices than any other people in the world today.

Alas! The same cannot be said about the rising trends of individualism in the so-called 'free' people living in the world today. One can do practically anything by justifying freedom in the name of individual liberty. Being the leaders in this trend, America is largely and profoundly influencing not only the First World European countries but also the people of the Second and Third World. The echo of this distorted concept of individual liberty rendering one free from the discipline of moral life is being heard far across the ideological curtains of scientific socialism.

The gays, lesbians, drug addicts, skin-heads, punks and criminals of all sorts, all continue to grow in numbers and strength. Their audacity to defend their behaviour by simply asking their admonisher, '*Why not?*', has become the ominous challenge to contemporary society.

TWO CLIMATES OF SOCIAL ORDER

The Holy Quran describes two social climates:
    a) one in which evil is free to flourish, and
    b) the other in which the growth of evil is strongly, inhibited.

If you take up Islamic moral teachings piecemeal, it would be very difficult for the western mind to understand the philosophy of its Message. This is because moral teachings must be studied as parts of a social climate. One must look at them in totality. You cannot understand the autumnal season just by looking at a fallen dry leaf or some foliage changing its colour. One has to visualise and feel the whole atmosphere and temperament of autumn to know what autumn is and what it does to plant life. Likewise, one swallow does not a summer make. Whereas autumn discourages life, spring encourages it. It is not just a change in temperature but a transformation in the whole atmosphere when the very wind seems to breathe life. Social systems are also like seasons with their own qualities and influences.

VANITY OF MATERIALISTIC SOCIETY AND ITS ULTIMATE DESTINATION

Islam deals with this subject in exactly the same manner. First, let me describe a society which, according to the Quran, is unIslamic.

اَعْلَمُوٓاْ أَنَّمَا الْحَيَوٰةُ الدُّنْيَا لَعِبٌ وَلَهْوٌ وَزِينَةٌ وَتَفَاخُرُ بَيْنَكُمْ وَتَكَاثُرٌ فِى الْأَمْوَالِ وَالْأَوْلَدِ كَمَثَلِ غَيْثٍ أَعْجَبَ الْكُفَّارَ نَبَاتُهُ ثُمَّ يَهِيجُ فَتَرَىٰهُ مُصْفَرًّا ثُمَّ يَكُونُ حُطَامًا وَفِى الْأَخِرَةِ عَذَابٌ شَدِيدٌ وَمَغْفِرَةٌ مِّنَ اللَّهِ وَرِضْوَانٌ وَمَا الْحَيَوٰةُ الدُّنْيَآ إِلَّا مَتَاعُ الْغُرُورِ ۝

Know that the life of this world is only a sport and a pastime, and an adornment, and source of boasting among yourselves, and of rivalry in multiplying riches and children. It is like the rain, the vegetation produced whereby rejoices the tillers. Then it dries up and thou sees it turn yellow; then it becomes worthless stubble. And in the Hereafter there is severe punishment for the wicked and also forgiveness from Allah, and His pleasure for the righteous. And the life of this world is nothing but temporary enjoyment of delusive things. (Ch. 57: Al-Hadid: 21)

Again, referring to the vanity of material life, the Holy Quran has this to say:

وَٱلَّذِينَ كَفَرُوٓاْ أَعْمَٰلُهُمْ كَسَرَابٍ
بِقِيعَةٍ يَحْسَبُهُ ٱلظَّمْـَٔانُ مَآءً حَتَّىٰٓ إِذَا جَآءَهُۥ لَمْ يَجِدْهُ شَيْـًٔا
وَوَجَدَ ٱللَّهَ عِندَهُۥ فَوَفَّىٰهُ حِسَابَهُۥ ۗ وَٱللَّهُ سَرِيعُ ٱلْحِسَابِ ۝

As to those who disbelieve, their deeds are like a mirage in a desert. The thirsty one thinks it to be water until, when he comes up to it, he finds it to be nothing. And he finds Allah near him, Who fully pays him his account; and Allah is swift in reckoning. (Ch. 24: Al-Nur: 40)

The Holy Quran depicts this as a mirage which tantalises the thirsty person by ever-running away from him until be becomes so exhausted that he can pursue it no more. That is when he is punished. He is made to realise that this is the goal of emptiness and void which he had been following all along. Suddenly, the mirage stops running away and permits him to catch up only to make him understand the bitter meaning of pursuing nothingness. That is the punishment meted out to those who pursue the vanity of life, and that, according to the Holy Quran, is how all such societies end up.

As against this, religion advocates an ideology which declares that life on this earth is not the be - all and end - all of things but that there is a life to come hereafter.

If we do not die a permanent death here but continue to survive in one form or another, as Islam and many other religions would have us believe; if life on earth cannot be taken separately from the life Hereafter; and if both lives must be understood as the continuation of the one to the other, then it will be extremely unwise to ignore the role of social influences on a person here on earth. Evil, immoral and unhealthy influences are bound to give birth to an unhealthy soul in the life to come.

REJECTION OF LIFE TO COME

This is no place to discuss the Islamic philosophy about life after death in detail but let it suffice here to mention that, according to Islam, the way we lead our lives here on earth influences our souls in a manner as sometimes, certain diseases of a pregnant mother influence her child in the embryonic stage. The child may be so congenitally handicapped that it may prove to be a hell for it to live with its disabilities among healthy children in a state of utter helplessness. The torment would become more bitter and profound with the maturity of its consciousness. This, in a nutshell, according to Islam, is how we shape our own heaven or hell.

In this context, it should have become clear that any social order which promotes irresponsible, disorderly and evil behaviour, no matter how attractive or enticing it may seem to the casual observer, must be rejected.

It is all right for the believers to say things and make such claims as are otherworldly in nature. After all, who has returned from the so-called otherworld to testify to such claims or stand witness against them? Why not be content with a bird in hand than to barter it for two in the bush? This is the materialistic answer to the Islamic philosophy regarding how society should be shaped and on what principles it should be based.

The Islamic philosophy encompasses the life here on earth and the life in the Hereafter as a continuous flow broken momentarily on death, which, infact, is only a transformational stage of one life to another. As against this, the materialistic philosophy visualises life as only a short, accidental span of consciousness which drowns into nothingness at the moment of death. Therefore, the social system has only to cater for the needs related to this short span of life. The individual is answerable to the society only as long as he lives and only for that aspect of life which is visible and detectable; that which is hidden in the form of his thoughts, intentions, plans, conspiracies and evil crimes subtly perpetrated, goes undetected and unquestioned.

Again, the crimes against society are only adjudged as crimes when it is established beyond a reasonable shadow of doubt that a crime had been committed. There is the possibility of the miscarriage of justice. In such a social order, the dispensation of justice is not only superficial and limited but also becomes conducive to offences against society. It promotes the pursuit of vested interests and encourages extreme selfishness on the part of the individual.

It is also interesting to note that in a godless or semi-godless society where the concept of answerability after death is rejected entirely or treated so lightly and vaguely as to practically render it meaningless, it is very difficult indeed to find a definition of crime which is fully supported in a sound moral philosophy. It is very difficult to conceive that members of a godless society will be truly convinced of the wrong they commit when they break a law. After all, what is law? Is it the word of a despot or an absolute ruler, the decision of totalitarian regimes, or the dictate of a democratic majority? To a common man, which of the above should appear to be a just legislation based on sound moral philosophy? What moral philosophy indeed?

If he does not owe his existence to any Being, or if he has no fear of being questioned regarding his conduct during his earthly life in the life to come, since, according to him, there is no life Hereafter, then the answers to the questions raised above, from his vantage point, could be very different from the requirements of a responsible society. He has only this short life to live. He needs society only for his own benefit. He submits to the superior authority of the society only out of necessity. If he can run away with some self-appropriated benefit and snatch a few moments of pleasure here and there while remaining clever enough to escape detection, why not? What so-called 'moral' inhibition could stop his hand?

This psychological attitude towards crime begins to develop and become stronger with the passage of time in godless and materialistic societies.

This exactly has been mentioned in the Holy Quran as the essence of the materialistic society.

The disbelievers declare:

$$إِنْ هِىَ إِلَّا حَيَاتُنَا الدُّنْيَا نَمُوتُ وَنَحْيَا وَمَا نَحْنُ بِمَبْعُوثِينَ ۝$$

> *There is no life other than our present life; we shall die here and it is only here that we shall live and we shall not be raised again i.e., we reject the concept of life after death or life elsewhere. (Ch. 23: Al-Mu'minun: 38)*

Then, again, the disbelievers mockingly address earlier Prophets by asking them:

$$وَقَالُوٓا أَءِذَا كُنَّا عِظَامًا وَرُفَاتًا أَءِنَّا لَمَبْعُوثُونَ خَلْقًا جَدِيدًا ۝$$

They say, 'When we shall have become bones and turned to dust, shall we really be raised again into a new form of creation?' (Ch. 17: Bani-Israel: 50)

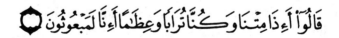

$$قَالُوٓا أَءِذَا مِتْنَا وَكُنَّا تُرَابًا وَعِظَامًا أَءِنَّا لَمَبْعُوثُونَ ۝$$

They say, 'Do you really mean to assert that when we are dead and have become mere dust and bones, shall we indeed be raised again?' (Ch. 23: Al-Mu'minun: 83)

This, according to the Holy Quran, is central to all evils of a materialistic society. That is why so much stress is laid on the life to come and on a Day of Reckoning.

In one of the Traditions, Ibn Masud relates that the Holy Prophet[sa] drew a rectangle and in the middle of it he drew a line lengthwise the upper end of which protended beyond the rectangle. Across this middle line, he drew a number of short lines. He indicated that the figure represented man, that the encircling rectangle was death, the middle line stood for his desires and the short lines across it were the trials and tribulations of life. He said: If one of these misses him, he falls a victim to one of the others. *(Bukhari)*. In another tradition, death is described as the terminator of pleasure. *(Tirmidhi)*

FOUR CHARACTERISTICS OF MATERIALISTIC SOCIETY

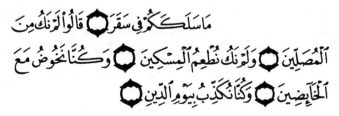

'What has brought you into the Fire of Hell?' They will say. 'We were not of those who worshipped God, nor did we feed the poor. And we indulged in vain talk with those who indulge therein. And we used to deny the Day of Judgement.' (Ch. 74; Al-Muddaththir: 43-47)

73

The features of a godless and materialistic society could not have been summed up more precisely and comprehensively. These are:

1. Failure to perform worship.
2. Failure to feed the poor.
3. Indulgence in vain pursuits.
4. Denial of the Day of Reckoning or accountability.

Before proceeding further, let us remove a confusion which makes it difficult to truly diagnose the state of a society. Even in societies where the belief in God seems to be strong and prominent and the belief in the Hereafter is an integral part of their faith, such evils flourish as cannot be logically conceived to exist among believers of God and life after death with full accountability.

The question then arises as to why such societies believe in a God and the Hereafter, yet in all other characteristics remain materialist through and through? The answer to this question is not difficult to find when we examine, in depth the nature of the beliefs. In fact, just a remote theosophical belief in a God cannot influence the social academic in nature and is never translated into responsible godly behaviour. How can genuine belief in a God cohabit with lies, falsehood, extreme selfishness, usurpation of the rights of the others, corruption and cruelty? The concept of God in such societies is only cosmetic, too unreal and airy fairy to play an active role in the after life, and accountability is reduced only to a pale shadow of a distant possibility. At every moment of choice, immediate interests always dominate and displace any consideration for the life to come.

When we speak of materialistic societies, we do not only mean societies which have uprightly rebelled against the ideas of God and life after death. Most theistic and atheistic societies may

74

appear to be diametrically opposed in their idealogies, yet, for all practical purposes, they have very close similarities.

ACCOUNTABILITY

The Holy Quran, on the other hand, declares:

$$لِّلَّهِ مَا فِي ٱلسَّمَٰوَٰتِ وَمَا فِي ٱلْأَرْضِ وَإِن تُبْدُوا۟ مَا فِيٓ أَنفُسِكُمْ أَوْ تُخْفُوهُ يُحَاسِبْكُم بِهِ ٱللَّهُ فَيَغْفِرُ لِمَن يَشَآءُ وَيُعَذِّبُ مَن يَشَآءُ ۗ وَٱللَّهُ عَلَىٰ كُلِّ شَىْءٍ قَدِيرٌ ۝$$

Everything which you find *in the heavens and in the earth belongs to God.* He is the Master. He has the right to shape your destinies and your social behaviour. *Whether you conceal what is in your hearts or declare it, He would bring you to book* and question you regarding your evil thoughts and evil doings, *then will He forgive whomsoever He considers fit* to be forgiven *and punish whomsoever He considers fit* to be punished *and Allah has the power to do all that He wills. (Ch. 2: Al-Baqarah: 285)*

The Holy Quran adds:

$$وَلَا تَقْفُ مَا لَيْسَ لَكَ بِهِۦ عِلْمٌ إِنَّ ٱلسَّمْعَ وَٱلْبَصَرَ وَٱلْفُؤَادَ كُلُّ أُو۟لَٰٓئِكَ كَانَ عَنْهُ مَسْـُٔولًا ۝$$

Follow not that of which thou hast no knowledge. Verily, the ear and the eye and the heart - all these shall be called to account. (Ch. 17: Bani-Israel: 37)

Here, by 'heart', the Holy Quran means the ultimate life force which is behind every human act. *Fu'wad,* in the Holy Quran, means that ultimate decisive will in man which operates the brain as one operates computers. So that ultimate will is the source of all evil and good and it is that will in the form of a new life after death which, in addition to the ear and the eyes, shall be held answerable.

Let us now study the features of godless societies at a closer range. It so happens that atheism and disbelief in the Hereafter lie vague and undetected in a semi-conscious state. In beliefs, apparently one may continue to subscribe to the existence of God and the belief in the Hereafter, but for all practical purposes, they seem to be non-existent, Sometimes it takes a crisis to bring these concealed realities to one's conscious mind. Sometimes, even generations can live without truly realising the fickleness and fragility of their beliefs. It is at such times that atheism and disbelief in the Hereafter, which had lain undetected and unchallenged, begin to surface. In society already given to indiscriminate and incontinent pursuit of pleasure, the conscious rejection of God and the Hereafter brings the process of moral decay and erosion of values to a rapid head.

The direction of civilization, regardless of which region of the world or which era of human history, is always from the coarse to the refined. Human basic psychological urges, which work as underlying motive forces of human behaviour, remain unchangeable. What changes is the response to those changes. For instance, one's hunger can be satiated by eating meat or vegetables. The quality and freshness of meat and vegetable varies. One can have them cooked and seasoned in so many ways or take them raw if one so prefers.

As society develops, responses to the fundamental urges begin to evolve and become more and more refined and sophisticated. This process goes on and on, though its pace may be determined to a large extent by economic and political factors of the people.

But the vanguard of a society always moves on — sometimes slowly, sometimes at a faster pace.

When a civilization ripens or matures, over-sophistication and some other detrimental phenomenon begin to reverse the tide of this progressive trend. In decadent societies, the direction is reversed from the refined to the coarse.

This is a subject of wide application and requires detailed study. I regret that it is beyond the scope of today's address but I would like to elaborate a few points.

When societies begin to degenerate or become top-heavy and lopsided with over-sophistication, they begin to topple down and return to the same crude animal answer to their urges. This may not be visible in every social and cultural activity, but it is almost always pronounced in human relation and style in the pursuit of pleasure. A brief study of man in his responses to sex will demonstrate the case in point.

Around the basic instinct to reproduce through sexual regeneration, pleasures are associated by nature in the entire animal Kingdom. What we find different in human society is a gradual departure from the mere satiation of crude desires to a gradually more refined attitude to the fulfilment of animal urges.

Nature never desired sex as an ultimate object. The ultimate object has always been reproduction and propagation of species. Sex was only secondary to it. When societies become decadent, the role is almost reversed.

The gradual development of the institution of marriage, the rites associated with this institution and the taboos regarding the inter-play of male and female sexes, may be considered by a sociologist to be a phenomenon resulting from a natural growth of society and unrelated to religion. But, whether the growth is directed from on high or a random phenomenon moving forward

77

by itself, there is no denying the fact that gradually the responses to satisfy the fundamental urge become more and more sophisticated and involved.

Growing promiscuousness in male and female relationships is again symptomatic of the same malady. It is not just a permissive, liberal attitude towards sexual relationships but there is, indeed, much more that goes with it to change the entire atmosphere of this extremely important sphere of human interest and activity. Debate about the legitimacy or illicitness of such relationships are looked down upon as a thing of the past. Of course, there are many staunch religious-minded groups which go on discussing this issue. But during their discussions on the media, one cannot fail to observe that such old-fashioned, rigidly religious-minded people are being reduced to a minority of insignificance.

It is becoming much more fashionable in the West to consider sex as a natural urge which should be responded to without any inhibitions. A traditional coyness associated with talk amongst women is becoming a thing of the past. Nakedness, exposure, display, unabashed discussion and confession are considered only as public expressions of truth.

Nobody seems to take the trouble to extend the same argument to other natural human urges. Is it not a natural animal urge, common to humans as well, to possess that which one likes? Is it not, again a natural animal urge to feel angered and agitated and to release these emotions in the wildest possible terms? A weaker dog would be impelled by the same urges as the stronger but whereas the stronger would bite, the weaker one would bark at the least.

What are those taboos in society - the codes of civil behaviour, the concept of decency, etc - which keep interfering with the free expression of natural urges? Why must sex be the only motive force which should be given a free licence to express itself without regard to tradition, norms, decency, appropriateness, and the question of belonging or otherwise?

What we observe today is a phenomenon which has to be carefully discerned and analysed. What we call permissiveness in sexual relationship is being expressed in the form of a growing tendency to steal and rob in other areas of human activity, and to injure and hurt others. The uninhibited pursuit of pleasure with perverted tastes emanates from the same decadent tendencies which are demolishing the noblest edifices of civilization and returning the mode of life back to square one.

Not only do we observe a prolific growth of rites, taboos and do's and don'ts imposed upon individuals by societies, but also we find an indulgence in romance and courtship playing a vital role in this area. Poetry, literature, art, music, styles, fashions, displays, love of fragrance, and growth of decent and cultivated behaviour are all by-products, if not entirely, at least to a degree, of the same fundamental urge in the form of social responses.

A time may come when a future generation begins to rebel against and reject the achievements of society attained after thousands of years of progress. This rebellion may not take the form of the total rejection of everything. Yet the discerning eye cannot fail to notice the movement in this direction. Hippyism, bohemianism, sadism, growing violence associated with sex and the return of sexual behaviour to its original, beastly, crude aspects are but a few examples of the reversal of trends mentioned before.

One only has to venture out to watch a group of rebellious, unkempt youths living in their communes to realise what is happening to the younger generation. Filth and stench seems to have replaced cleanliness and fragrance. Immaculate dress has given way to shabby, `couldn't-care-less' clothes. Gone are the days when a minute spec on one's attire could cause immense embarrassment. Worn out jeans, specially torn to reveal the flesh underneath, are becoming far more valuable than a new pair of trousers. Of course, not all of society shows such extreme signs of dissatisfaction with the past or traditional heritage, but when a disease sets in, the entire body may not always be ulcerated. A few ulcers appear here and there and these reveal the underlying diseased state or malady. Irresponsibility begins to grow. Indiscipline and disorderliness begin to be the order of the day. More signs of decadence begin to surface in different areas of human interest.

The pursuit of pleasure in every sphere of life requires change and novelty to provide a greater kick. Things which used to satisfy in the past no longer do now. Smoking and traditional intoxicants fail to provide the kick which the progressively restless society requires. Drugs of all sorts begin to appear and no measure whatsoever taken to suppress the menacing trend of drug-addiction is enough. Yet, the drug addict requires a still greater kick. So a stronger, more addictive and lethal drug like *crack* is invented.

In the area of music, the same trends have gradually set in during the last few decades of this century. A study of the development of music over recent centuries, as against the rapid and decibel eruptive changes witnessed during the last few decades of this century, provides interesting and intriguing data for comparison.

I do not personally know much of music and should be pardoned if some of my remarks are considered alien to the realities of the world of music. My intuition would make me believe, however, that the progressive development of music, during the last few centuries in the West, has been in the direction of the sublime, exquisite and noble. Such music brought peace to the mind and heart simultaneously. The best music was that which identified and submerged completely with the latent music of human mind and soul. Harmony and peace were the ultimate goals which the evolution of music pursued. Of course, there were passages in the works of great composers and artistes which created images of volcanic eruptions, typhoons, thunderbolts and a sense of commotion which tallied with the external phenomenon of nature. Its memories were stored and preserved indelibly in the memorising mechanism of life. At times, its climax reached such crescendos as if the whole universe was about to burst apart. Yet the audience sat motionless, drowning itself in the deluge of music, without moving a muscle or batting an eyelid, until, suddenly pin-drop silence fell. Only then would the hall explode into tremendous applause. Even the most powerful music, highly charged with emotion, would not turn the listener into a violent, eruptive, and rebellious being. The message of all music was sublime, peaceful and harmonious. The best in man was brought out and awakened; the worst was banished.

Alas! During the last few decades, we observe a different phenomenon altogether. The ears of the contemporary generation are deafened with music capable of arousing coarse and rudimentary passions of life. A disturbed and restless generation finds itself only attuned to such music as makes them go mad. The more violent the music, the more popular it would be. Again, I should be excused for any observation born out of my ignorance of the world of classical and popular music, but of one thing I am sure and it is that violence, rebellion, madness and vandalism etc. are fast corrupting the noble human faculties.

Professor Bloom, who must be credited with some knowledge of western music, seems to agree with me in his book, *The Closing of the American Minds* when he laments the erosion of the sensibilities of adolescents of the contemporary age who, in his words, are brutalised by constant exposure to rock music which he dismisses as junk food for the soul.

There are many visible and palpable signs of this diseased state of society which are gradually making the life of man more disturbed and lacking in contentment, satisfaction, peace and security. Man may deny the existence of God as he pleases but he cannot deny the existence of an all-powerful nature which knows well how to punish crimes committed against it.

In all materialistic societies, the major factors responsible for progressive growth and proliferation of evil are about the same. Some discussion has already preceded; so, we shall briefly enumerate the responsible factors to serve as reminders. These factors are:

(a) growing atheism;

(b) an enfeebling of the belief in a real powerful God Who takes live interest in human affairs and the way human beings shape their conduct;

(c) a progressive weakness in the beliefs in traditional and ethical values; and,

(d) a growing tendency to forget the end and to treat the means as ends in themselves.

This is a situation which prevails in all the so-called 'civilized' or 'advanced' societies of the world. Slowly, as moral and ethical values continue to wither, they begin to influence the legislative and executive process of governments. When there is no God—made law to be accepted, and absolute ethical values and noble traditions are challenged and defied daily, any legislation to discipline moral behaviour also becomes lax and more accommodating. The very platform on which laws pertaining to moral behaviour are founded, begins to slip away.

A comparative study of legislation in this area over the last few centuries would effectively prove the case in point. Gone are the days of Oscar Wilde when homosexuality was considered a crime by society which would most mercilessly punish it. Gone are the days of chastity not being just a virtue but a social trust which, if violated, would be brought to account. This softening on crime is no longer seen as alarming. That is the problem.

The definition of crime itself is undergoing fundamental change. That which was considered a crime yesterday is no longer so. That which was concealed for fear of shame or reprimand is disclosed and displayed with great pride. If this philosophy was sound and worthy of survival then all the religious, ethical and moral philosophies may be considered obsolete and unwanted. They no longer serve any purpose in the contemporary age.

The driving force in nature, common to both the animate and inanimate world, is the universal and all-powerful principle of crime and punishment and goodness and reward. In the inanimate world, this principle can be discerned to be operational in the unconscious operation of the laws of nature. In the animate world, evolution prior to the creation of man, was driven by the same principle which acquired a semi-conscious or semi-dormant state. As one travels through the lowest rungs of evolutionary stages up to man, the journey seems to be from the less conscious to the more conscious. In evolutionary terms, the principle of crime and punishment and goodness and reward is described as survival of the fittest. Throughout the whole evolutionary process, this remains the driving and motive force which constantly pushes evolution forward and upward.

It is inconceivable that when this process had reached its consummation in man, the best of creation, and consciousness had acquired horizons beyond the wildest fancies of sub-human fancies, suddenly the principle of crime and punishment should be lifted and rendered obsolete. If there is a higher goal for creation, there has to be some accountability without which the whole exercise would be rendered meaningless.

It is extremely surprising that sometimes the greatest of intellectuals and visionaries fail to see an obvious and self-evident truth like this. Such is the case of Albert Einstein, the architect of the theory of relativity, who observes:

> *I cannot imagine a God who rewards and punishes the object of his own creation, whose purposes are modelled after our own- a God, in short, who is but a reflection of human frailty. (Albert Einstein)*

If there is a God, the Lord Creator Whose existence Albert Einstein could not deny, and if all the scientific laws operating in His creation are devised, created and governed by the same creative Supreme Being, it is inconceivable for Him to abandon the ultimate object of His creation by lifting the principle of crime and punishment and leaving man to wander in the chaos of undisciplined and unaccountable behaviour.

As far as the second part of his observation is concerned, it is obvious that he failed to understand not only the role of crime and punishment in the progressive development of creation, but also completely misunderstood the meaning of man having been *created in the image of God.*

Man is *created in the image of God* not as a perfect model of God on earth. Were that so, the world would become more than a heaven on earth and all human beings would be exactly alike. It is debateable, of course, whether such a place would be worthy of being called heaven or boredom, where there is no variety, change or difference between odour, colour and hue- instead a calm, multitudinous sea of colourless identical drops. That is not the meaning and purpose of man having been *created in the image of God.*

This phrase is rich in profound wisdom and speaks of the potential with which man has been endowed. It speaks of the ultimate noble goal which man must constantly endeavour to achieve. That goal is to be as perfect as man can possibly be, by acquiring godly attributes and emerging more like God. It is not a fixed goal which one can reach and then, basking in the glory of having become *the image of God,* stay put there. As God is unlimited or limitless in His attributes, so every journey to Him remains limitless. The perfection in this context only means moving towards perfection from a lower order of things to a higher order of things.

God is the Most Perfect, the Most Just, the Most Gracious, Ever Merciful, All-Seeing, All-Knowing, The Lord Creator and Master of the Day of Judgement. All praise belongs to God. The Holy Quran states:

هُوَ ٱللَّهُ ٱلَّذِى لَآ إِلَٰهَ إِلَّا هُوَ عَٰلِمُ ٱلۡغَيۡبِ وَٱلشَّهَٰدَةِ

هُوَ ٱلرَّحۡمَٰنُ ٱلرَّحِيمُ ۝ هُوَ ٱللَّهُ ٱلَّذِى لَآ إِلَٰهَ إِلَّا هُوَ

ٱلۡمَلِكُ ٱلۡقُدُّوسُ ٱلسَّلَٰمُ ٱلۡمُؤۡمِنُ ٱلۡمُهَيۡمِنُ ٱلۡعَزِيزُ

ٱلۡجَبَّارُ ٱلۡمُتَكَبِّرُ سُبۡحَٰنَ ٱللَّهِ عَمَّا يُشۡرِكُونَ

۝ هُوَ ٱللَّهُ ٱلۡخَٰلِقُ ٱلۡبَارِئُ ٱلۡمُصَوِّرُ لَهُ ٱلۡأَسۡمَآءُ ٱلۡحُسۡنَىٰ

يُسَبِّحُ لَهُۥ مَا فِى ٱلسَّمَٰوَٰتِ وَٱلۡأَرۡضِ وَهُوَ ٱلۡعَزِيزُ ٱلۡحَكِيمُ ۝

Allah is He beside Whom there is no god, Knower of the unseen and the seen. He is the Most Gracious, the Ever Merciful. Allah is He beside Whom there is no god, the Sovereign, the Most Holy, the Source of Peace, the Bestower of Security, the Protector, the Mighty, the Subduer, the Exalted. Holy is Allah, far above that which they associate with Him. *He is Allah, the Creator, the Maker, the Fashioner. His are the most perfect names. All that is in the heavens and the earth glorifies Him. And He is the Mighty, the Wise.* (Ch.59 Al-Hashr:23-25)

It is such a God Who created this universe. He does not suffer from human frailties. The Holy Quran repeatedly asks the believers to reflect on His Signs. For instance:

تَبَـٰرَكَ ٱلَّذِى بِيَدِهِ ٱلْمُلْكُ وَهُوَ عَلَىٰ كُلِّ شَىْءٍ قَدِيرٌ ۝ ٱلَّذِى خَلَقَ ٱلْمَوْتَ وَٱلْحَيَوٰةَ لِيَبْلُوَكُمْ أَيُّكُمْ أَحْسَنُ عَمَلًا وَهُوَ ٱلْعَزِيزُ ٱلْغَفُورُ ۝ ٱلَّذِى خَلَقَ سَبْعَ سَمَـٰوَٰتٍ طِبَاقًا مَّا تَرَىٰ فِى خَلْقِ ٱلرَّحْمَـٰنِ مِن تَفَـٰوُتٍ فَٱرْجِعِ ٱلْبَصَرَ هَلْ تَرَىٰ مِن فُطُورٍ ۝ ثُمَّ ٱرْجِعِ ٱلْبَصَرَ كَرَّتَيْنِ يَنقَلِبْ إِلَيْكَ ٱلْبَصَرُ خَاسِئًا وَهُوَ حَسِيرٌ ۝

Blessed is He in Whose hand is the kingdom and He has the power to do all that He wills, *Who has created death and life that He might try you — which of you is best in conduct; and He is the Mighty, the Most Forgiving, Who has created the seven heavens in order*, one above the other. *Thou canst not discover a flaw in the creation of the Gracious One. Then look again: Seest thou any disparity? Look again, and yet again, thy sight will return to thee frustrated and fatigued.* (Ch.67 Al-Mulk:2-5)

86

Having understood the significance of the words *the image of God*, when one looks back at the entire forces of the creation of the universe—from the time of the Big Bang to the present day—the entire journey of creation from the unconscious to the conscious, in fact, is a journey to become *the image of God* and to develop in man godly attributes.

ISLAMIC SOCIAL CLIMATE

Islam, on the other hand, designs to create a climate which is as different from the one described above as spring is from autumn.

Within the Islamic concept of society, Islam moderates, disciplines and trims natural desires which, if left uncontrolled, would play havoc with the gamut of human emotions. It discourages or prohibits the fulfilment of desires which can, in the final analysis, result in more misery than pleasure in the society.

At the same time, Islam cultivates new tastes and develops the ability to derive pleasure and satisfaction from acts which may appear colourless, insipid and tasteless to the uncultured and untrained. Tastes are modified and coarse sensual cravings are trained and refined and turned into aspirations for the sublime.

But the question is how can we determine that the prevalent and contemporary social trends are unhealthy for a society? To me, the answer seems to be a simple one. The health of a society should be judged by the same symptoms as the health of an individual. When someone is in pain, restless, abnormal or sub-normal in his reactions or when anxiety seems to displace one's content and peace of heart and mind, it does not require an exceptionally wise man or highly-proficient physician to adjudge or diagnose such an unhealthy person as being seriously ill. All these symptoms are manifest in contemporary society.

How true were the words of Jesus[as] when he said:

By their fruits you will recognise them. Never do people gather grapes from thorns or figs from thistles, do they? Likewise every good tree bears fine fruit, but every rotten tree produces worthless fruit; a good tree cannot bear worthless fruit, neither can a rotten tree produce fine fruit. (Matthew 7: 16-18: New World Translation)

People are crying themselves hoarse against the bitterness of the fruit today, but somehow they do not want to replace the tree with a better one. They fail to see that it is not the tree which is at fault nor the fruit it bears.

The Islamic social order stands for the uprooting of the evil tree and the planting of a healthier one instead.

According to the Holy Quran, when Adam[as] was forbidden to eat the fruit of the tree, this is precisely what was meant:

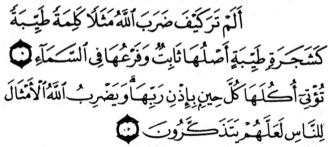

Dost thou not see how Allah sets forth the similitude of a good word? It is like a good tree, whose root is firm and whose branches reach into heaven. It brings forth its fruit at all times by the command of its Lord. And Allah sets forth similitudes for men that they may reflect. (Ch. 14: Ibrahim: 25-26)

Here, the tree is just a symbol. The Quran clearly speaks of an unhealthy philosophy as against a healthy one in the same symbolic language. The evil tree and the condition of the disbeliever are described in the next two verses:

وَمَثَلُ كَلِمَةٍ خَبِيثَةٍ كَشَجَرَةٍ خَبِيثَةٍ ٱجْتُثَّتْ مِن فَوْقِ ٱلْأَرْضِ
مَا لَهَا مِن قَرَارٍ ۝ يُثَبِّتُ ٱللَّهُ ٱلَّذِينَ ءَامَنُوا بِٱلْقَوْلِ ٱلثَّابِتِ
فِي ٱلْحَيَوٰةِ ٱلدُّنْيَا وَفِي ٱلْأَخِرَةِ وَيُضِلُّ ٱللَّهُ ٱلظَّٰلِمِينَ
وَيَفْعَلُ ٱللَّهُ مَا يَشَآءُ ۝

And the case of an evil word is like that of an evil tree, which is uprooted from above the earth and has no stability. Allah strengthens the believers with the word that is firmly established, both *in the present life and in the Hereafter, and Allah lets the wrongdoers go astray. And Allah does what He wills. (Ch. 14: Ibrahim: 27-28)*

The 'word' is used in this context in the connotation of a philosophy, system, and order just as the same 'word' is also used in its much wider connotation in the opening verse of John:

In the beginning the Word was and the Word was with God, and the Word was God. (John: 1:1)

Evil philosophies and orders are bound to meet the fate of an evil tree which fails to pass the test of survival of the fittest and is ultimately uprooted and tossed from place to place by the raging tempest.

On the other hand, the example of a healthy system and order of things is like that of a healthy tree which is firmly rooted in this earth but whose lofty stems and twigs reach out into a pure heavenly atmosphere. It is nourished by heavenly light and it bears good wholesome fruit in every season. The Quran describes the believers as having a firm belief in God; their entire ethical and moral structure is securely and firmly founded in this belief. This gives a quality of absoluteness to the Islamic concept of morality and ethics which does not permit discrimination on any known plane of social, religious or racial divisions.

The guiding principle applicable to all human activity is expressed in the following verse of the Holy Quran:

$$وَلِلَّهِ غَيْبُ ٱلسَّمَٰوَٰتِ وَٱلْأَرْضِ وَإِلَيْهِ يُرْجَعُ ٱلْأَمْرُ كُلُّهُۥ فَٱعْبُدْهُ وَتَوَكَّلْ عَلَيْهِ وَمَا رَبُّكَ بِغَٰفِلٍ عَمَّا تَعْمَلُونَ ۝$$

To Allah belong the hidden things of the heavens and the earth, and to Him shall the whole affair be referred. So worship Him and put thy faith in Him alone. And thy Lord is not unmindful of what you do. (Ch. 11: Hud: 124)

Likewise:

$$أَلَا لَهُ ٱلْخَلْقُ وَٱلْأَمْرُ تَبَارَكَ ٱللَّهُ رَبُّ ٱلْعَٰلَمِينَ ۝$$

. . . . . . *Verily, His is the creation and the command. Blessed is Allah, the Lord of the worlds. (Ch. 7: Al-A'raf: 55)*

All Islamic philosophies start and end with the absolute authority of God, the Lord Creator of the universe.

FUNDAMENTALS OF AN ISLAMIC SOCIETY

The Quranic verse which is most central to this issue is as follows:

$$إِنَّ ٱللَّهَ يَأْمُرُ بِٱلْعَدْلِ وَٱلْإِحْسَٰنِ وَإِيتَآئِ ذِي ٱلْقُرْبَىٰ وَيَنْهَىٰ عَنِ ٱلْفَحْشَآءِ وَٱلْمُنكَرِ وَٱلْبَغْيِ يَعِظُكُمْ لَعَلَّكُمْ تَذَكَّرُونَ ۝$$

90

Verily God enjoins justice - and more than justice; to give people more than their dues - *and to serve humanity with beneficent treatment* as if they belong to you (like your near, kith and kin) *and God prohibits the display of evil* - as observed nowadays so often on television, radio and streets of many societies of the world - *and forbids all that is considered wrong* not by religions but by human conscience, *and everything that leads to rebellion and chaos. God admonishes you - may you benefit from this admonishment. (Ch. 16: Al-Nahl:91)*

The first part of this verse is applicable more to the economic sphere than the social order. It paints a clear image of the Islamic concept of justice, fair play and benevolence in treating the less fortunate sections of society. The second part applies to the social image of a society which Islam is committed to create.

In this part, God forbids all that is considered wrong by universal standards, like indecent behaviour, affront, insult and indeed all social evils which, without reference to any religious teachings, are condemned by the general consensus of human society at large. *Like suicide bombings?*

Similarly, Islam strictly rejects and condemns every tendency, behaviour and attitude which may lead to disorder, rebellion and violence. The word 'rebellion' should be understood in the connotation of any unjustified attempt to overthrow an established order. But that is not all. Whenever the Arabic word BAGHIYI is used in the Holy Quran, it is applicable not only to an armed or political uprising but also to a rebellion in society against its noble traditions, ethical standards, religious teachings and moral value.

In the end, a society is clearly warned that this admonition is for man's own benefit. This completes the picture of the essential features of an Islamic social order. It may be added that the first part of this verse is also deeply intertwined with the Islamic social teachings. A society which is insensitive to the sufferings of other human beings and is not always inclined to serve the cause of humanity, cannot be described as an Islamic society howsoever it may adhere to other aspects of Islamic social teachings.

Let us now turn to some other features of Islamic society envisaged in the Holy Quran.

Islam emphasises integrity, loyalty, faithfulness and promotes all such measures as would create peace of mind and heart. It takes preventive measures against the society becoming lopsided in its pursuit of pleasure. Hence, any behaviour, howsoever innocent as it may appear in the beginning, which is likely to lead towards unrestrained permissiveness in the society, is discouraged. The damage done to society is immense and manifold. Such societies are bound to end up in the state of promiscuousness we find in the world today.

In such societies, the unrestricted tendency to pursue pleasure leads, among other things, to the erosion and ultimate destruction of family ties. Contrary to this, Islam cherishes and zealously guards all fatherly, motherly, brotherly, sisterly and filial relationships. Islam wants to promote friendships which are more platonic than sensual.

CHASTITY

Beginning with a plan for women in society, it is essential, according to Islam, to take all such measures to promote chastity, fidelity, restraint and clean living.

An emphasis on chaste living, well-insulated against the dangers of a short circuiting of sexual urges is an important feature of Islamic society. This aspect of Islamic social teachings is extremely important for the protection and survival of the family system. This is the dire need of the hour.

Islam seeks to widen the unit of family rather than to squeeze it to a bare minimum: a family in which the human capacity to love and the desire to be loved is satiated not by the mere fulfilling of sexual urges, but by more sophisticated and refined friendship and association such as naturally prevails between close and distant blood relations.

It is surprising how the wise men of modern society fail to notice human weakness once sex-related pleasures are permitted to play an unbridled role in the society; indeed, they flourish at the expense of other refined values and draw their blood like parasites.

Sigmond Freud, no doubt, was the product of such a society. He began to analyse every human motivation through the coloured eyeglass of sex. To him, the most pious child-mother relationship was sex-related. Even the father-daughter relationship had no sanctity but was sex-oriented or sex-generated. Almost everything that man did, irrespective of him being aware of it or not, was for the deeply subconscious sex urges. I wonder if in the time of Freud, society had achieved the degree of promiscuity which prevails today, but, it was enough to give birth to a completely sex-dominated understanding of the human psyche. But if Freud was right, it is even more essential not to permit society to play incautiously with such dangerous forces as may cause a short circuiting.

Alas! The present climate of modern societies would not even attempt to understand the nature and features of the Islamic social climate. Whether man agrees or does not agree with the concept of God playing a role in human affairs and shaping man's destiny, and whether man is willing to modulate his social behaviour in accordance with the revealed word of God or not, one thing is most certain - man can neither defeat the Act of God (i.e., Nature) nor the Word of God (i.e., the revealed Truth). Both the Act and Word must be found in harmony with each other to be considered valid. Any social behaviour which man adopts in direct contradiction of the Word of God is bound to end in disaster.

Man cannot have unlimited and unrestricted pleasure however he may desire it. All he can do is to swap certain values and options. A society which seeks to escape responsibility or the realities of life with the help of opiates and drugs; a society which is obsessed by sex, vain excitement and exhilaration; a society where the tastes are wilfully perverted to suit an artificially created market for new instruments and toys of pleasure which are fit only to create excitement and thirst for more; a market masterminded by powerful syndicates whose sole purpose is to amass wealth; such a society chooses all this at the cost of nobler human values, peace of mind and security in a society as a whole. You cannot possess both simultaneously. You cannot have your cake and eat it.

The emphasis of Islam is exactly the opposite. Pleasure indeed - but not at the cost of peace of mind and the security of society as a whole. All such tendencies which if unchecked, are likely to lead to a gradual disintegration of family life and promote selfishness, irresponsibility, vulgarity, crime and violence, are strongly discouraged.

The climates created by the two philosophies are poles apart.

It astounds me how some people believe that by raising ambitions or giving free reign to desires in a society, they can ever hopefully promise peace of mind. No society in the world, however economically sound it may be, can support unlimited and unbridled generation of lustful desires.

Even in the richest societies of the world, there are always haves and have nots. Those who are deprived of the most basic amenities of life make a much larger section of the society than the comparatively smaller number of those who can afford to pay for what they like. Even that is questionable because it seems that with the growth of wealth, desires also rise and perhaps even the richest cannot fully realise all their dreams. But the case of the comparatively poorer majority is worse. They cannot even have access to the basic amenities of life, not to speak of the luxuries the affluent society can afford. It is the poor with whose emotions and desires modern media plays havoc. Day in and day out, it brings to their squalid dwellings, rosy images of a glorious lifestyle with palatial homes, fabulous gardens, fleets of luxury cars, helicopters, private planes and an army of attendants. The lifestyle of Hollywood and Beverley Hills with revelries, dances, merry-making parties, or the life in casinos, gambling houses, or all that soap operas can conjure up, are temptations to which the poorest have access. Yet few, even amongst the richest, can ever dream of achieving this heaven on earth. Such people would most certainly loose interest in their poor coarse surroundings. The home and hearth would no longer have any appeal to them. Lack of culture and civilisation stand juxtaposed to this rosy vision, and, in this context, the realities of their own life begins to lose all meaning. If this be the ultimate achievement of a society fed on vain pleasures and unreal visions, warmth and the peace of home and hearth all become increasingly illusionary. Then there would be nothing left for them to live for in the future.

It would take more than one measure to restore the traditional family unit so essential to bind its members together with mutual trust, reliance and warmth generating peace. But, perhaps, we are already too late to talk of this.

Islam has a clear message. It has a well-defined plan to protect, guard and preserve a universal family system or to rebuild it wherever it has been totally demolished.

According to Islam, discipline must be inculcated through conviction and understanding in every sphere of social activity, and lost balances must be restored.

SEGREGATION OF SEXES

People in the West grossly misunderstand the Islamic social system of PARDAH (lit. veil) seen as the segregation between the two sexes. This misunderstanding partly arises out of a misapplication of the true teachings of Islam in many parts of the Muslim world and the negative role of the Western media. It has become a rule with Western media to associate the ugliness of behaviour wherever it occurs with Islam, but to refrain from associating Jewish, Christian, Buddhist or Hindu behaviour to their respective religions.

The Islamic injunction of segregation is certainly not born out of a narrow-minded attitude of the past dark ages. In fact, the question of promiscuousness or otherwise in a society, has no relationship whatsoever to the advancement or backwardness of time. Societies throughout history have either ridden along the crest or descended to the troughs of social or religious waves.

The concept of Women's Lib is not at all a progressive trend of human society. There is strong evidence that both in the remote past as well as in the closer period of human history, women as a class have held a very powerful and dominant position in human society in different parts of the world.

Free and uninhibited intercourse between the male and female section of the society is nothing new and novel. Civilizations came and went. Behaviour patterns kept oscillating between one style and another. The myriads of social tendencies have been falling and settling down into different patterns only to go through new experimentation and formation at each twist of the kaleidoscope. Yet, no trend has ever been fixed by which we could conclude with certainty that throughout history, society travelled from segregation to promiscuity or from confinement to comparative emancipation and liberation of women.

THE DAWN OF A NEW AGE IN WOMEN'S RIGHTS

It is only fitting here to focus our attention to that dark period of time in the history of Arabia when Islam came to be born, through divine instructions, as we Muslim believe, or as the personal teachings of Muhammad[sa], as the non-Muslim would have it. Whatever the view of some theologians, Islamic teachings regarding the segregation of sexes did not represent Arab behaviour at all.

The society in Arabia at that time was extremely paradoxical in its attitude towards women. On the one hand, sexual permissiveness, the free mixing of men and women and mad orgies of wine, women and song were the highlights of Arab society. On the other hand, the birth of a girl was considered to be a matter of disgrace and extreme shame. Some 'proud' Arabs are even reported to have buried their new-born daughters with their own hands to escape this ignominy.

Women were treated as chattels and were deprived the right to oppose their husbands, fathers or other male members of the family. However, there were exceptions to the rule.

Occasionally, a woman of outstanding leadership quality would play a significant role in the affairs of the tribe.

Islam changed all that, not as a natural progressive outcome of social tensions but as an arbiter of values. A social system was dictated from on high which was unrelated to the normal forces which shape a society.

Through the teachings of segregation, sexual anarchy was brought to a sudden halt. Order between male and female relationship was established on the basis of deep moral principles. The status of women was simultaneously raised to such high standards that they could no longer be treated as helpless commodities. They were given an equal share in the affairs of life. Whereas previously they were distributed as chattels of inheritance, now they could inherit not only the estate of their fathers but also of their husbands, children and next of kin. They could now stand up to their husbands and talk back to them. They could reason with them and, of course, had the full right to disagree. They could not only be divorced but they had equal rights to divorce their husbands if they so pleased.

As mothers, they were treated with such profound respect in Islam as is hard to find a similar example in other societies of the world. It was the Holy Founder of Islam[sa] who was to stand for the rights of women by declaring under divine instructions, that:

Paradise lies under the feet of your mothers.

He was not only referring to a promise to be fulfilled in life after death, but to the social paradise which was promised to a people who showed profound respect and reverence to their mothers, and were dedicated to please them and provide every possible comfort to them.

The teaching of segregation should be understood in this context. It was not the outcome of any male superiority but was designed to establish the sanctity of the home; to create greater trust between man and wife; bring temperance to basic human urges; and, to harness and discipline them so that, instead of being released as powerful demons in the society, they play a constructive role just as harnessed forces play a role in nature.

Segregation is grossly misunderstood when it is conceived as an imposition of restriction on female members of the Muslim society from fully participating in all spheres of human activities. This is not true.

The Islamic concept of segregation is only to be understood in the context of measures to protect the sanctity of female chastity and the honour of women in society so that the dangers of violating these objectives are minimised.

Free mixing of both sexes and clandestine affairs between men and women are strongly discouraged. Men and women are both advised to abstain not only from casting covetous eyes at each other, but to abstain from such visual or physical contacts as may lead to uncontrollable temptations. Women are expected to cover themselves decently and are advised not to behave in a manner as to attract untoward attention from wayward men. The use of cosmetics and ornaments are not forbidden but they should not be worn when appearing in public to attract attention.

We fully understand that in the present mood of societies all over the world, this teaching appears to be rather harsh, restrictive and colourless. However, a deeper study of the entire Islamic social system may lead one to believe this judgement to be hasty and superficial. This teaching should, therefore, be understood as an integral part of the entire Islamic social climate.

The role which women play in the Islamic social system is certainly not of concubines in harems nor of a society imprisoned in the four walls of their homes, barred from progress and deprived of the four walls of the light of knowledge. This ugly picture of the Islamic social system is only painted by internal or external enemies of Islam or by scholars who grossly misunderstand the Islamic way of life.

The only thing which Islam would not endorse would be to turn women into play things, to be exploited or left at the mercy of male vulgarity. Islam does not promote such attitudes towards women.

Merely because society as a whole has become more and more demanding, it is sheer cruelty to women if it necessitates that they must always remain conscious of their looks, appearances, and the way they are dressed and made up. Feminine charms are always on display. Even selling an article of food or daily needs, such as a washing powder, requires advertisements with female models. Artificial, stylish and expensive ways of life are presented as essentials for a woman to realise her dreams. Such a society cannot remain balanced, sober and healthy for long.

According to Islam, women must be emancipated from exploitation and playing a role of being mere instruments of pleasure. They must have more time to themselves to discharge their responsibilities towards their homes and the future generation of mankind.

EQUAL RIGHTS FOR WOMEN

You hear so much about *Women's Lib* and women's rights, etc. Islam speaks of a comprehensive fundamental principle which covers all situations:

$$وَلَهُنَّ مِثْلُ الَّذِى عَلَيْهِنَّ بِالْمَعْرُوفِ ۚ وَلِلرِّجَالِ عَلَيْهِنَّ دَرَجَةٌ ۗ$$

$$وَاللَّهُ عَزِيزٌ حَكِيمٌ ۝$$

. . .*And they* (the women) *have rights similar* and equal *to those* (of men) *over them in equity*; i.e., for women, there are exactly equal rights as for men, as men have rights upon women. There is thus total equality and there is no difference whatsoever between the fundamental human rights of women and men. *But men have a degree of advantage over them. And Allah is Mighty and Wise.* (Ch. 2: Al-Baqarah: 229)

In another part of a verse of the Holy Quran, it is stated:

$$الرِّجَالُ قَوَّامُونَ عَلَى النِّسَاءِ بِمَا فَضَّلَ اللَّهُ بَعْضَهُمْ$$

$$عَلَىٰ بَعْضٍ وَبِمَا أَنْفَقُوا مِنْ أَمْوَالِهِمْ$$

Men are appointed guardians over women because of that in respect of which *Allah has made some of them excel others despite the fact that they spend of their wealth. . . (Ch. 4: Al-Nisa: 35)*

From the Arabic word *QAWWAMUN* (guardians made responsible to keep their wards on the right path), some medieval-minded Ulemas (doctors of religion) deduce and claim the superiority of men over women whereas the verse only refers to an advantage that the breadwinner has over his dependants. As such, the guardian is better qualified to exert moral pressure on the wards to continue to remain on the right path. As far as basic human rights are concerned, it does not in any way refer to women being unequal or to men's superiority over women. The last part of the verse refers to the above mentioned advantage and makes it manifestly clear that despite this advantage, the

101

fundamental rights of women are exactly equal to those of men. The Arabic letters *WA* is to be translated as `despite the fact that`' or `while`' and in this context seems to be the only correct translation.

POLYGAMY

In the West it is quite common to confront a speaker on the subject of Islam with the question: does Islam permit one to marry four times and keep four wives simultaneously? I have had vast experience in addressing many public and select gatherings of intellectuals in the Western world. Seldom do I remember an occasion when this question was not raised.

More often than not a lady would stand up, and, of course, with due apologies, innocently enquire whether Islam permits four wives or not. Obviously, everybody knows the answer. But, perhaps, this is the only aspect of Islam which is so widely known in the West. The other well-known aspect is terrorism, but terrorism has nothing to do with Islam. (See *'Murder in the Name of Allah'* by the Speaker).

What sort of equality between man and woman does Islam propound when man is permitted to have four wives and a woman can keep only one husband? This is another form of the same question which I believe is only used as a ploy to wipe out any good impression about Islam which may have been built by the speaker. In less formal assemblies, wherein civilities and courtesies are not meticulously adhered to, the same enquiry attains the nature of mockery rather than that of a simple question.

Many decades ago when I was at the SOAS (School of Oriental and African Studies), University of London, a Pakistani student was plagued by an English fellow student with the same question repeatedly and somehow it never failed to elicit laughter. Once, I remember, he was pushed, perhaps too far, and he suddenly turned back and asked the young Englishman: Why do you object to us having four mothers when you have no objections against having forefathers (four fathers, sic.) A pun on the word four, which effectively turned the table against the teaser.

Apparently, it was a joke, but when you examine it closely, you will discover more than a joke, for it refers to a tragic situation prevailing in societies and offers a befitting case for comparing the attitude of Islam with that of modern society. It is not only a matter for carefree student assemblies but even the serious-minded highly respected members of society do not consider it unkind and discourteous to express their disapproval of this injunction with a joke.

Not long ago, I received a letter from a senior judge in Frankfurt, whom I personally know to be a very wise, open-minded, courteous and well-meaning person. He, too, objected to the Islamic provision on limited polygamy and could not suppress the temptations to drive the point home with the help of a crude joke, or, at least so I thought. For a fleeting moment I thought of returning the compliment of his joke with the joke about forefathers, but discretion had the better of me.

The brief answer I sent him was to the effect that first this provision in Islam of marrying more than once is not a generality. It pertains to certain situations when it becomes necessary for both preserving the health of society and the rights of women to have this provision available.

The Holy Quran is a logical Book. As such, it could not have instructed Muslims to achieve the impossible. God has created men and women in almost equal numbers - with a few pluses and minuses here and there. How could a rational religion like Islam, which repeatedly emphasises the fact that there is no inconsistency between the Act of God and the Word of God, preach something so glaringly unnatural and unrealistic, which, if attempted, would create grave situations of imbalance, insurmountable difficulties and frustrations. Imagine a small country of one million men of marriageable age and almost the same number of women. If this provision was taken to be an injunction to be followed to the letter of the law by all, then, at best, 250,000 men will marry one million women and 750,000 men will be left without a wife.

Yet, among all the religions of the world, Islam stands out in its emphasis on marriage for every man and woman. The Holy Quran describes the relationship between a husband and wife as based on love by nature and providing a source of peace for each other:

$$وَٱلْمُحْصَنَٰتُ مِنَ ٱلْمُؤْمِنَٰتِ وَٱلْمُحْصَنَٰتُ$$

$$مِنَ ٱلَّذِينَ أُوتُوا۟ ٱلْكِتَٰبَ مِن قَبْلِكُمْ إِذَآ ءَاتَيْتُمُوهُنَّ أُجُورَهُنَّ$$

$$مُحْصِنِينَ غَيْرَ مُسَٰفِحِينَ وَلَا مُتَّخِذِىٓ أَخْدَانٍ$$

. . . *And* lawful for you are *chaste believing women and chaste women from among those who were given the Book before you, when you give them their dowers, contracting valid marriages, not committing fornication, nor taking secret paramours* . . . *(Ch. 5: Al-Ma'idah: 6)*

At the same time, the Quran rejects celibacy declaring it to be a man-made institution (e.g. see Ch. 57:28). There is nothing to be gained from shutting oneself from the rest of the world or from punishing oneself by denying natural desires. The institution of marriage is well established in Islam, but time does not permit me to digress and discuss the various requirements of choosing marriage partners, the remedies available and the regulations of divorce, etc.

To return to polygamy, it is evident from a study of the Holy Quran that a special situation of a post-war period is being discussed. It is a time when a society is left with a large number of orphans and young widows, and the balance of male and female population is severely disturbed. A similar situation prevailed in Germany after the Second World War. Islam not being the predominant religion of Germany, Germany was left with no solution for the problem. The strictly monogamous teaching of Christianity could offer no relief. As such, the people of Germany had to suffer the consequence of these imbalances. There was a large number of virgins, dejected spinsters and young widows for whom it was impossible to get married.

Germany was not the only country in the vast continent of Europe to experience such social problems of extremely dangerous and gigantic proportions. It was too great a challenge for the post-war Western society to stem the tide and check the growth of moral degradation and promiscuity which so naturally and exuberantly thrived on the prevailing imbalances.

As can be plainly seen by every unbiased person, the only answer to all such problematic disturbances, is to permit men to marry more than once. This is not proposed as a solution to satiate their sensual desires but to meet the genuine requirements of a large number of women. If this very logical and realistic solution is rejected, the only alternative left for society is to rapidly degenerate into a growingly corrupt and permissive society.

Alas! That seems to have been the option taken by the West.

When you re-examine more realistically and unemotionally the two attitudes, you cannot fail to notice that it is not a question of equality between men and women but it is simply a choice between responsibility and irresponsibility.

Islam only permits marriage more than once with the proviso that men accept the challenge of such difficult and specific situations with full responsibility and mete out the full measure of justice and equality to the second, third or fourth wives as well:

وَإِنْ خِفْتُمْ أَلَّا تُقْسِطُوا فِي ٱلْيَتَٰمَىٰ فَٱنكِحُوا

مَا طَابَ لَكُم مِّنَ ٱلنِّسَاءِ مَثْنَىٰ وَثُلَٰثَ وَرُبَٰعَ فَإِنْ خِفْتُمْ أَلَّا تَعْدِلُوا

فَوَٰحِدَةً أَوْ مَا مَلَكَتْ أَيْمَٰنُكُمْ ذَٰلِكَ أَدْنَىٰ أَلَّا تَعُولُوا ۝

Should you apprehend that you will not be able to deal fairly with orphans, then marry of other women as may be agreeable to you, two or three, or four; but if you apprehend that you will not deal justly and equally between them, then marry only one, or out of those over whom you have authority. That is the best way for you to obviate injustice. (Ch. 4: Al-Nisa: 4)

The alternative is much uglier. An excessive number of women left without marriage cannot be blamed for attempting to entice and allure married men in societies which are not deeply religious. After all, women are humans too. They have their own emotions and unfulfilled desires. Whilst the psychological traumas of war has enhanced the urge for finding someone to turn to, a life without security of marriage and home, with no life partner and no hope for children is a life which is empty. The future is as blank and bleak as the present.

If such women are not lawfully accommodated and assimilated on the principle of give and take, it can play havoc with the peace of society. They will, anyhow, illegally share the husbands of married women. The outcome is bound to be preposterous. Loyalties will be split. Married women will begin to lose faith in their husbands. Suspicions will grow. The increasing lack of mutual trust between husband and wife will rock the foundation of many homes. For unfaithful men to live with a sense of crime and guilt will further generate psychological complexes and propensity towards more crime. The noble concept of love and loyalty would be among the prime victims. Romance would begin to lose sublimity and descend to commonplace, transient infatuation.

Those who talk of equality in every sphere forget that the issue of equality becomes irrelevant in those areas where male and female are built differently.

It is only women who can give birth to children. It is they alone who can go through more than nine months of nourishing the seed of human generation for the future. It is women again who can look after their babies, at least during the early period of infancy and childhood, as no man ever could. Because of the long and extremely intimate blood relationships with their offspring, it is the women who have far more powerful psychological bonding with the children as compared to men.

If social and economic systems ignore this constitutional difference between man and woman and the corresponding difference in the role of the two sexes in society, then such a socio-economic system is bound to fail to produce a state of healthy equilibrium. It is mainly because of these constitutional differences between male and female that Islam proposes correspondingly different roles for each.

A woman must be kept free, as far as possible, from the responsibility of earning bread for the family. In principle, that responsibility must fall on the shoulders of men. Yet, there is no reason why women should be debarred from playing their part in turning the wheel of economy provided that they find themselves free to do so, i.e., without neglecting their prime responsibility of human reproduction, family care and concomitant involvements. This is exactly what Islam proposes.

Again, women in general have a weaker and comparatively frail constitution. Yet, surprisingly, they have been provided by God with tougher potentials in their physique. These attributes are mainly due to the presence of an extra half chromosome in their cells which is responsible for the difference between men and women. This is obviously provided to meet the extra challenge placed on them during pregnancy, childbirth and the lactation period. All the same, this potential does not make a woman outwardly stronger and tougher. They should not be relegated to hard menial tasks in the productive economic field merely in the name of equality or any other name. This also requires that they should be treated with more tenderness and kindness. Women should have a lesser load to bear in daily life and should not be forced to bear equal load with men in public activities.

It emerges from the above that if the task of the running of a home is a special area of responsibility to be assigned to either man or woman, a woman has obviously much greater merit than a man to perform such responsibilities. Additionally, by nature women have been assigned the responsibility of looking after the children. Such responsibility can only be partly shared with men.

Women must be granted the right to remain at home far more than men; if, at the same time, they are absolved of the responsibility of earning their livelihood, the free time available to them must be employed for their own sake or for the sake of society as a whole. That is how the concept of '*a woman's place is in the home*' is born. There is no question of their being tied to their aprons or imprisoned in the four walls of the home. In no way does Islam infringe the rights of women to go out in their spare time to perform any task or to participate in any healthy pursuit they may choose, providing, again, that they do not jeopardise the interests and rights of the future generation of mankind entrusted to them. Among other reasons, this is why over-socialising or the free mixing of sexes is strongly discouraged by Islam. For Islam to propose that the home is the centre of a woman's activities is a very wise and practical solution to most ills of modern times. When women shift their interests away from the home it has to be at the cost of family life and the neglect of children.

To build a family life around the pivotal figure of a mother requires the strengthening of other blood relationships and the restoration of a genuine affinity with kith and kin. Even though each unit may live separately, this larger family concept is supported and promoted by Islam for many reasons, some of which are as follows:

1) It prevents imbalances from occurring in society.

2) If strong love and affection were promoted in the family between brothers and sisters, father and daughters, mother and sons, etc., it would naturally lead to the consolidation and protection of a healthy family unit. This natural bonding is further strengthened by a system of relationships surrounding it in the form of genuine affinity and closeness between aunts, uncles, nieces, nephews, cousins, grandchildren and grandparents. New avenues of seeking warmth and healthy pleasure, derived from the consciousness of belonging, would open up for this larger family system.

3) The institution of family in such cases is less likely to be fragmented. To share a common roof in the name of a family would no longer be as meaningless as we generally find today. The members of the family would continue to gravitate towards the central beacon of family elders; most family activities would rotate around this axis. There would be no lone individuals, forgotten, dejected and relegated to the attic or basement of social order, or, knocked out of families as useless articles.

This exactly is the Islamic concept of homes and families which is regarded as the most important central unit in society. It is mainly because of this difference in attitudes that today we find in the modern societies of the world a much greater incidence of abandoned, old, or disabled parents considered as burdens on families.

CARE OF THE AGED

The responsibility for care of the aged is gradually shifting to the state. Care of the aged represents a heavy burden on the national economy. However much a state is ready to spend, it can never buy them peace and contentment. The most terrible feeling of having been rejected, left out and abandoned, and the most painful realisation of a growing void of loneliness within, are problems beyond the reach of many to resolve. To consider that a comparatively remote relative would ever be taken care of by the rest of the family has become almost impossible to imagine.

In such societies, the need for homes for the aged grows with the passage of time. Yet, it is not always possible for a state to apportion enough money to provide for them even the minimum requirements of a decent life. Physical ailments are much easier to cure or alleviate, but the deep psychological traumas from which a considerable number of elderly members of modern societies are suffering, are far more difficult to treat.

In predominantly Muslim countries, however much values may have deteriorated, this condition which prevails in the rest of contemporary society, is unthinkable. It is considered a disgrace and dishonour for the old and aged to be treated with such disrespect and callousness. It is a matter of shame for most Muslims to hand over the responsibilities of elderly relatives to the state even if the state is willing to look after them.

As such, the role of a Muslim woman amidst her home and family is far from over with the coming of age of the children. She remains deeply bonded to the past as well as to the future. It is her kind and humane concern, and her innate ability to look after those who stand in need of care, which comes to the rescue of the older members of society. They remain as precious and respected as before and continue to be integral members of the family. The mother plays a major part in looking after them and providing them with her company, not as drudgery and tedium, but as a live natural expression of human kinship. Thus, when she grows older she can rest assured that such a society will not eject her nor leave her abandoned as a relic of the past.

Of course, there are exceptions in every society and there are old remnants of the past considered as tiresome burdens in some Muslim families living under the influences of the modern trends. But on the whole, Muslim societies are relatively free of homes for abandoned parents unlike other societies.

This reminds me of a joke which may make some people laugh yet move some others to tears. Once a child observed with much pain and unease the ill-treatment of his grandfather at the hands of his father. He was gradually transferred from a well-provided and comfortable main bedroom to smaller and less convenient accommodation until it was finally decided to remove the grandfather to the servant's quarters. During an exceptionally severe winter, the grandfather complained of his room being too chilly and his quilt being too thin to make him feel warm and comfortable. The father started looking for an extra blanket from a stock of old, useless rags. Observing this, the child turned to his father and requested: 'Please do not give all the rags to grandpa. Keep some for me so that I may be able to give them to you when you grow old.'

In this innocent expression of a child's displeasure is concentrated all the agony of the older generation in modern times.

In Muslim societies, it is as rare to find such exceptions, as it is rare and becoming more rare to find exceptions in modern societies amongst relatives in their treatment of the old. Muslims are taught:

وَقَضَىٰ رَبُّكَ أَلَّا تَعْبُدُوٓا إِلَّآ إِيَّاهُ وَبِٱلْوَٰلِدَيْنِ إِحْسَٰنًا إِمَّا يَبْلُغَنَّ عِندَكَ ٱلْكِبَرَ أَحَدُهُمَآ أَوْ كِلَاهُمَا فَلَا تَقُل لَّهُمَآ أُفٍّ وَلَا تَنْهَرْهُمَا وَقُل لَّهُمَا قَوْلًا كَرِيمًا ۞ وَٱخْفِضْ لَهُمَا جَنَاحَ ٱلذُّلِّ مِنَ ٱلرَّحْمَةِ وَقُل رَّبِّ ٱرْحَمْهُمَا كَمَا رَبَّيَانِى صَغِيرًا ۞

Thy Lord has commanded, 'Worship none but Him, and show kindness to parents. If one of them or both of them attain old age with thee, never say unto them any word expressive of disgust nor reproach them, but always address them with excellent speech. And lower to them the wing of humility out of

112

tenderness.' And say, 'My Lord, have mercy on them even as they nourished me when I was a little child'. (C.17: Bani-Israel: 24-25)

These verses are the most significant on this subject. After the Unity of God, human beings should, through their attitude of love, affection and kindness, give priority over all other things to their parents who have reached an old and difficult age.

Further, the verses speak of situations when the behaviour of one or both of the parents becomes extremely trying and sometimes offensive. In response to that, not even a mild expression of disgust or disapproval should pass one's lips. On the contrary, they should be treated with profound respect.

The emphasis on the most excellent relationship between one generation and another guarantees that no generation gaps appear. Such gaps always interrupt the transmission of traditional moral values.

Islamic social philosophy, therefore, teaches that no generation should permit a gap to appear between it and the outgoing generation and between it and the future generation. Generation gaps are totally alien to Islam.

As stated earlier, the family concept in Islam is not limited to members of a single home. The following verse instructs Muslims to spend not only on their parents, but also their kith and kin who are mentioned next to parents in order of preference so that their sense of dignity is not injured and mutual love is promoted.

وَٱعۡبُدُواْ ٱللَّهَ وَلَا تُشۡرِكُواْ بِهِۦ شَيۡـًٔا وَبِٱلۡوَٰلِدَيۡنِ
إِحۡسَٰنٗا وَبِذِى ٱلۡقُرۡبَىٰ وَٱلۡيَتَٰمَىٰ وَٱلۡمَسَٰكِينِ وَٱلۡجَارِ

بِذِى ٱلۡقُرۡبَىٰ وَٱلۡجَارِ ٱلۡجُنُبِ وَٱلصَّاحِبِ بِٱلۡجَنۢبِ
وَٱبۡنِ ٱلسَّبِيلِ وَمَا مَلَكَتۡ أَيۡمَـٰنُكُمۡۗ إِنَّ ٱللَّهَ لَا يُحِبُّ مَن
كَانَ مُخۡتَالًا فَخُورًا ۝

Worship Allah and associate naught with Him, and show kindness to parents, and to kindred, orphans, the needy and to the neighbour who is a kinsman and the neighbour who is a stranger, and the companion by your side and the wayfarer and those who are under your authority. Surely, Allah loves not the arrogant and the boastful. (Ch.4: Al-Nisa: 37)

The Holy Quran declares that you must be mindful of kindness to your parents.

If contemporary society learns the lesson from these injunctions, many problems which it faces today and which represent a blemish on an advanced society, would cease to exist. No homes for the aged would be needed, except for some aged people who, unfortunately, have no close relative to look after them. But in an Islamic society, the love between parents and children is so repeatedly emphasised that it is impossible for a child to abandon his parents when they grow old for the sake of his or her own pleasure.

THE FUTURE GENERATION

As for the future generation, the Holy Quran educates society in a unique way. It teaches that to achieve the best of relationships between you and your children, it is highly essential that the relationships between you and your wife should also be excellent.

In this regard, the verse cited earlier (*Ch. 4: Al-Nisa: 35*), which refers to guardians (QAWWAMUN), lays a very heavy responsibility on the shoulders of a husband. If his conduct is not conducive to the creation of an ideal atmosphere for a healthy family life, he would have failed in his responsibility to act as a guardian (QAWWAM). It should be remembered that the best example of *QAWWAM* was the Holy Founder of Islam[sa] himself. He was neither harsh nor dictatorial nor in any way offensive or over-assertive in relation to his family. To keep them on the right path was a grave responsibility, but the way that he discharged this responsibility serves as an excellent living example for all times to come for all those who want to investigate and comprehend the real meaning of the epithet *QAWWAM*.

In a famous Tradition, Abu Hurairah relates that the Holy Prophet[sa] said:

The most perfect of believers in the matter of faith is he whose behaviour is best; and the best of you are those who behave best towards their wives. (Tirmidhi)

If the parents really want their children to grow up into members of a righteous society, they should remember that mutual relationships between husbands and wives are going to play an important role in the making or breaking of the character of their children.

The Holy Quran teaches:

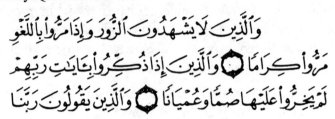

هَبْ لَنَا مِنْ أَزْوَجِنَا وَذُرِّيَّتِنَا قُرَّةَ أَعْيُنٍ وَاجْعَلْنَا
لِلْمُتَّقِينَ إِمَامًا ۝

Those who bear not false witness, and when they pass by anything vain, they pass by with dignity; and those who, when they are reminded of the Signs of their Lord, fall not down thereat deaf and blind; and those who say, 'Our Lord, grant us of our wives and children the delight of our eyes, and make us a model for the righteous.' (Ch. 25: Al-Furqan: 73-75)

This prayer possesses a unique charm and is filled with profound wisdom. Both partners in marriage are taught to pray for each other and their children that God may always provide them deep satisfaction and happiness from one another as well as from the children and to make their children the forerunners and leaders of a God-fearing, righteous generation.

It only takes one to apply this teaching to oneself to fully realise the significance of this verse. When you desire something vaguely, it may not influence your conduct significantly, but when you pray for it earnestly, then your conduct is bound to be influenced by that prayer. To illustrate this further, there are many amongst us who desire to be truthful but seldom is this desire translated into practice. Those who earnestly pray to God that He should make them become truthful, are influenced far more in their conduct by their prayer than those merely wishing for something vague. A genuine effort is made in moulding one's behaviour for the better. A person would be acting very oddly indeed after such a prayer if he treats his wife and children in a manner inconsistent with the prayer.

Turning exclusively to the younger generation and their rights and obligations, the Holy Quran admonishes:

يَـٰٓأَيُّهَا ٱلَّذِينَ ءَامَنُوا۟ ٱتَّقُوا۟ ٱللَّهَ وَلْتَنظُرْ نَفْسٌ مَّا قَدَّمَتْ لِغَدٍ وَٱتَّقُوا۟ ٱللَّهَ إِنَّ ٱللَّهَ خَبِيرٌۢ بِمَا تَعْمَلُونَ ۞

O ye who believe! Fear Allah and let every soul look to what it sends forth for the morrow. And fear Allah; verily Allah is Well-Aware of what you do. (Ch. 59: Al-Hashr: 19)

The Quran warns the parents that if they fail to discharge the responsibility due to their offspring and leave behind a generation which is not beyond censure in its conduct, then the parents will be held answerable before God.

Again, the parents are warned not to murder their own children in the sense that the parents become instrumental and responsible in some way in destroying their character. (*e.g. Ch.6: Al-An'am: 152*)

Not only one's own children but that the younger generation as a whole must be treated with love, kindness and respect is the strong word of advice given by the Holy Prophet of Islam, may peace and blessings of Allah be upon him:

أَكْرِمُوا أَوْلَادَكُم

Always be kind to your children. (Ibn Majah: Bk:'Adab; Ch. Birul Walad)

One cannot help observing that this is exactly what the contemporary world needs today. There is a serious debate going on in Britain, nowadays, regarding possible legislation which would make parents vicariously responsible, in the eyes of the law, for crimes committed by their children and thus as delinquents dealt with by juvenile courts. It is strongly felt that had the parents discharged their responsibility to discipline their

117

children more seriously, there would be much less crime seen in the streets of Great Britain. But the question is how far punitive and restrictive measures can improve the quality of society when there is no background of religious ethics at work in every sphere of life?

WASTEFUL, VAIN PURSUITS DISCOURAGED

The Holy Quran goes on developing this subject of society by declaring:

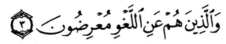

And who shun all that which is vain. (Ch. 23: Al-Mu'minun: 4)

Those who are wise, shun the waste of their energies in useless and meaningless pursuits.

To find time for light entertainment is neither bad nor prohibited in Islam. But if the entertainment begins to exert a negative influence on society as a whole, it is certainly not recommended. Moreover, if instead of providing a genuine outlet for the stresses of life, entertainment becomes an objective in itself, it would be condemned as LAGHW (vain and wasteful) in the Quranic terminology. When entertainment begins to interfere in the daily pursuits of life or takes a toll upon one's time which could be better spent otherwise, it too would be classified as vain according to the Arabic word LAGHW.

Television has done immense good for society. But children sit all day long with their eyes glued to the box. After returning from work, men continue to sit before the screen no matter what the TV programme might be. In doing so, they neglect their responsibilities to their children, wives, friends and society as a whole. TV has indeed become a modern curse. So much time is wasted in this age in watching television that it will be rather difficult and challenging for one to correctly weigh its pros and cons. But that is not all.

By screening films on crime, TV often presents the image of crime in a manner which instead of creating a sense of repulsion in the hearts of children, achieves the opposite. Even in programmes exclusive for children, it is not uncommon to find popular characters causing mischief by devising ingenious pranks that play havoc with the peace at home. However amusing and entertaining such programmes may be, they are certainly not educational. No doubt, many a difficult child is born out of watching such programmes. The child grows with the potential of becoming a would-be criminal.

In the programmes for adults, innovative methods of committing crime are inadvertently taught. A leisurely life of fun and playfulness portraying what life should be is painted so rosily that it leaves a false impression on the mind. Alas! Little do they realise the distance between fantasy and realities and between what should be and what is.

The pursuit of vain pleasures forbidden in the Holy Quran is not that minor or inconsequential as most may consider it to be. This and many other modes of entertainment play an important role in the creation of an atmosphere where the level of frustration continues to rise. One wonders when the point of saturation may be reached.

BRIDLING OF DESIRES

The Holy Quran requires the bridling of desires: envy may not be permitted to give birth to inordinate, insatiable desires.

This teaching contains a very important message regarding discipline and the trimming of desires. Islam, of course, is not a religion of escapism or denial by monasticism or asceticism whereby man is required to negate all his natural desires to achieve *Nirvana* or deliverance from material bondage. According to the philosophy of *Nirvana*, it is the desires which bind us to matter and enslave us to materialism. The simple answer is to deny oneself all desires.

Islam rejects this philosophy as man-made, unnatural and inadequate to resolve problems. The concept of *Nirvana* is closer to death than peace. Islam has a completely different solution to offer. To kill desires is no answer, according to Islam, to solve the riddle of life.

Among many measures suggested to create social peace is the admonition that man should discipline and curtail his desires and keep them in check. Otherwise, it would be impossible for any man to achieve peace through the satiation of desire. As stated earlier, desires always run faster than one can pursue them. Small as these measures may appear, they are potentially very effective and important. For instance, the Holy Quran states:

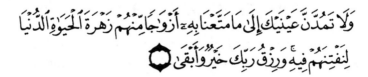

Strain not thy eyes after what We have bestowed on some classes of them to enjoy for a short time—the splendour of the present world—that We may try them thereby. And the provision of thy Lord is better and more lasting. (Ch. 20: Ta-Ha: 132)

The Holy Quran prohibits thinking ill of others, or to be nosy and inquisitive or to back-bite:

يَـٰٓأَيُّهَا ٱلَّذِينَ ءَامَنُوا ٱجْتَنِبُوا كَثِيرًا مِّنَ ٱلظَّنِّ إِنَّ بَعْضَ ٱلظَّنِّ إِثْمٌ
وَلَا تَجَسَّسُوا وَلَا يَغْتَب بَّعْضُكُم بَعْضًا أَيُحِبُّ أَحَدُكُمْ أَن
يَأْكُلَ لَحْمَ أَخِيهِ مَيْتًا فَكَرِهْتُمُوهُ وَٱتَّقُوا ٱللَّهَ إِنَّ ٱللَّهَ تَوَّابٌ
رَّحِيمٌ ۝

O ye who believe! avoid much suspicion; for suspicion in some cases is a sin. And spy not on one another, neither back-bite one another. Would any of you like to eat the flesh of his dead brother? Certainly you would loathe it. And fear Allah, surely, Allah is oft-returning with compassion and is *Merciful. (Ch. 49: Al-Hujurat: 13)*

BUILDING OF TRUST AND INVIOLABILITY OF TRUSTS AND TREATIES

In the Islamic society, the building of trust plays a very important role. The inviolability of trusts and international treaties is considered fundamental to the concept of unity in Islamic society. Believers are described in the Holy Quran as:

وَٱلَّذِينَ هُمْ لِأَمَـٰنَـٰتِهِمْ وَعَهْدِهِمْ رَٰعُونَ ۝

Who are watchful of their trusts and their covenants. (Ch. 23: Al-Mu'minun: 9)

ERADICATION OF EVIL-A COLLECTIVE RESPONSIBILITY

The responsibility of educating people is not entrusted to governments but collectively to the people themselves to do good deeds and to abstain from evil.

121

In more developed societies, it is the job of refuse collectors to gather unwanted waste from homes and streets for disposal. In poorer countries, the housewife simply throws away the junk and refuse on to the streets till the streets become littered with filth and are no longer fit as passageways. Of course it is the responsibility of the inmates to clean the houses but there has to be some system of keeping the streets and pathways clean.

It is tragic that though the West has learned the importance of this social responsibility of keeping places frequented by the public clean, it has yet to recognise the dire need of acquiring the responsibility to purge society from the criminal human waste which daily spills over from homes to streets and public places.

Islam treats this question more comprehensively. The primary stress is on the elders of the family to minimise the social waste so that more goodness than evil is contributed towards society.

Secondly, Islam fixes the responsibility on society to launch, individually as well as collectively, a holy war against evil, not with the help of the sword and restrictive legislation, but more so by constant admonition, advice and wise counsel. Admonition and persuasion with patience is the best instrument, according to the Quran, to cleanse the society of social evils:

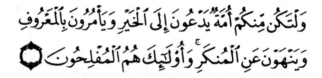

Let there be among you a body of men who are always devoted to admonishing people to do good and who *invite to goodness, and enjoin equity and dissuade* people from indulging in *evil. And it is they who shall prosper,* (i.e. such societies shall survive. The word 'Muflihoon' here could also be translated as those who are fittest for survival). *(Ch. 3: Al-Imran: 105)*

It should not be inferred from the aforementioned verse that the Islamic approach of the maintenance of public health and well-being is entirely non-governmental and the state has no part to play in it. Of course, the areas of legislation and its application are the prerogatives of states. But what I have been trying to emphasise is merely the fact that according to Islam, the state machinery alone is inadequate to suppress, discourage or minimise crime. Once criminal tendencies are permitted to grow and flourish in homes and societies in general, the best a government can do is to wipe out the symptoms from time to time. The root cause of evil is far too deep for the long arm of the law to reach. It is the primary job of families, religious leaders and leaders of public opinion in every society to eradicate evil.

Keeping this and many other similar verses in view, the Holy Prophet, may peace and blessings of Allah be upon him, once declared that the people before you came to a tragic end because they disobeyed authority and were given to transgression. They did not restrain one another from the iniquity that they committed. Then he continued: *Indeed, by Allah, you must enjoin good and forbid evil; seize the hand of the wrong-doer and persuade him to act justly; establish him firmly on the right, else Allah will involve the hearts of some of you with the hearts of others and will curse you as He cursed them. (Abu Daud and Tirmidhi: Riadhus Saleheen 198 p.50)*

According to the Prophet[sa], one of the more serious signs of decline of a people is that they lose the courage to show their displeasure at the public display of indecency and misconduct. The Holy Prophet, may peace and blessings of Allah be upon him, draws the parallel between such a society and travellers on a boat in the following tradition:

Nu'man ibn Bashir relates that the Holy Prophet[?] said: The case of those who observe the limits set by Allah and those who are careless about them is like passengers on a ship who cast lots to determine who should occupy the upper deck and who the lower and settled accordingly. Those who occupied the upper deck had no direct access to water. To fetch water, they had to repeatedly climb down thus disturbing the occupants of the lower deck. Once they suggested to the occupants of the lower deck that if they had no objection, they could bore a hole through the bottom of the ship to gain direct access to water. Now if the occupants of the lower deck were to leave the others to carry out their design, they would all perish together, but if they were to stop them from carrying it out, they would all be saved. (Bukhari: Riadhus Saleheen 189 p.48)

I am afraid this parable applies to a large degree to the contemporary societies of the world.

DO'S AND DON'TS

Some verses from the Holy Quran on other social responsibilities which promote peace are:

وَعِبَادُ ٱلرَّحْمَٰنِ ٱلَّذِينَ يَمْشُونَ عَلَى ٱلْأَرْضِ هَوْنًا وَإِذَا خَاطَبَهُمُ ٱلْجَٰهِلُونَ قَالُوا سَلَٰمًا

The servants of the Gracious God are those who walk on the earth in a dignified manner, and when the ignorant address them, they say, 'Peace!'. (Ch.25: Al-Furqan: 64)

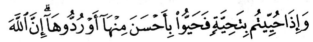

وَإِذَا حُيِّيتُم بِتَحِيَّةٍ فَحَيُّوا بِأَحْسَنَ مِنْهَآ أَوْ رُدُّوهَآ إِنَّ ٱللَّهَ

124

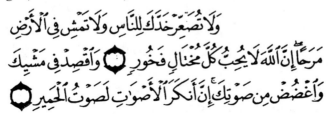

كَانَ عَلَىٰ كُلِّ شَىْءٍ حَسِيبًا ۞

When you are greeted with a prayer, greet ye with a better prayer or at least return it. Surely, Allah takes account of all things. (Ch.4:Al-Nisa:87)

وَلَا تُصَعِّرْ خَدَّكَ لِلنَّاسِ وَلَا تَمْشِ فِى ٱلْأَرْضِ مَرَحًا إِنَّ ٱللَّهَ لَا يُحِبُّ كُلَّ مُخْتَالٍ فَخُورٍ ۞ وَٱقْصِدْ فِى مَشْيِكَ وَٱغْضُضْ مِن صَوْتِكَ إِنَّ أَنكَرَ ٱلْأَصْوَٰتِ لَصَوْتُ ٱلْحَمِيرِ ۞

Turn not thy cheek away from men in pride nor walk in the earth haughtily; surely, Allah loves not any arrogant boaster. And walk thou at moderate pace and restrain thy voice; verily the most disagreeable sound is the bray of a donkey. (Ch.31: Luqman: 19–20)

The character which Islam attempts to inculcate amongst Muslims is in itself inhibitive to the growth of irresponsible behaviour and crime. Islam creates a healthy soil which discourages the growth of parasites and weeds.

This objective is achieved by very detailed and comprehensive teachings of do's and don'ts which run into many hundreds. The central core of this teaching is common to almost all religions. Instead of highlighting the doctrinal differences between one religion and another, I set some of them before you with the relevant Quranic (Chapter: Verse) reference:

DO'S:
Chastity: 17:33; 23:6–8; 24:31, 34, 61; 25:69; 33:36; 70:30–32.
Cleanliness: 2:223; 4:44; 5:7; 22:30; 74:5–6.
Controlling anger: 3:135.

Cooperation: 5:3.

Courage: 2:178; 3:173–175; 9:40; 20:73–74; 33:40; 46:14.

Doing good: 2:196; 3:135; 5:94; 7:57.

Enjoining good and forbidding evil: 3:111.

Excelling in doing good: 2:149.

Faithful discharge of trusts: 2:284; 4:59; 23:9; 70:33.

Feeding the hungry: 76:9; 90:15–7.

Forgiveness: 2:110; 3:135,160; 4:150; 5:7,90; 14:8; 39:8,67; 46:16.

Giving of true evidence: 4:136; 5:9; 25:73.

Good treatment of employees: 4:37.

Good treatment of neighbours: 4:37.

Good treatment of relatives: 2:178; 16:91; 30:39.

Gratefulness: 2:153,173,186,244; 3:145; 5:7,90; 14:8; 39:8,67; 46:16.

Humility: 6:64; 7;14,56,147; 16:24,30; 17:38; 28:84; 31:19–20;40:36.

Justice: 5:9; 6:153; 16:91; 49:10.

Making peace between people: 4:115; 49:10.

Patience: 2:46, 154,156,178; 11:12; 13:23; 16:127–128; 28:81;29:61; 39:11; 42:44; 103:4.

Perseverance: 13:23; 41:31–33.

Purity: 2:223; 5:7; 9:103,108; 24:22; 33:34; 74:5; 87:15; 91:10-11.

Self Control: 4:136; 7:202; 18:29; 30:30; 38:27; 79:41–42.

Sincerity: 39:3–4; 98:6; 107:5–7.

Truthfulness: 4:136; 5:120; 9:119; 17:82; 22:31; 25:73; 33:25,36,71; 39:33.

Unselfishness: 2:208,263; 11:52; 59:10; 64:17; 76:9-10; 92:20-21.

DON'TS

Adultery: 17:33.
Arrogance: 2:35,88; 4:174; 7:37 & c.
Backbiting: 49:13.
Boasting: 57:24.
Defamation: 49: 12.
Derision: 49:12.
Despair: 39:54.
Envy: 113:6.
Extravagance: 7:32; 17:27–28.
Following that of which one has no knowledge: 17:37.
Haughtiness: 17:38; 23:47; 31:19.
Giving short measure: 83:2–4.
Nicknaming: 49:12.
Niggardliness: 4:38; 47:39; 57:2–5; 59:10; 64:17.
Perfidy: 4:106,108; 8:28,59.
Suspicion: 49:13.
Telling lies: 22:31; 25:73.
Theft: 5:39.

Islam invites leaders of all religions to join hands in an effort to promote and inculcate goodness and to admonish against the committing of evil deeds.

Were this to happen, the world would be better for it.

REJECTION OF RACIALISM

Of all the curses which infest the contemporary age, racialism is the one that holds the greatest danger to world peace.

The Holy Quran reminds not only Muslim but all mankind:

يَـٰٓأَيُّهَا ٱلنَّاسُ ٱتَّقُوا۟ رَبَّكُمُ ٱلَّذِى خَلَقَكُم مِّن نَّفْسٍ وَٰحِدَةٍ وَخَلَقَ مِنْهَا

زَوْجَهَا وَبَثَّ مِنْهُمَا رِجَالًا كَثِيرًا وَنِسَاءً ۚ وَاتَّقُوا اللَّهَ الَّذِى تَسَاءَلُونَ بِهِ وَالْأَرْحَامَ ۚ إِنَّ اللَّهَ كَانَ عَلَيْكُمْ رَقِيبًا ۝

O ye people! Fear your Lord, Who created you from a single soul and created therefrom its mate, and from the two spread many men and women; and fear Allah, in Whose name you appeal to one another, and fear Him particularly respecting ties of relationship. Verily, Allah watches over you. (Ch.4: Al-Nisa:2)

No one has superiority over others. Similarly, the Holy Quran states:

يَا أَيُّهَا النَّاسُ إِنَّا خَلَقْنَاكُم مِّن ذَكَرٍ وَأُنثَىٰ وَجَعَلْنَاكُمْ شُعُوبًا وَقَبَائِلَ لِتَعَارَفُوا ۚ إِنَّ أَكْرَمَكُمْ عِندَ اللَّهِ أَتْقَاكُمْ ۚ إِنَّ اللَّهَ عَلِيمٌ خَبِيرٌ ۝

O mankind, We have created you from a male and a female; and We have made you into tribes and sub-tribes for the sake of easy recognition. Verily, the most honourable among you, in the sight of Allah, is the most righteous among you. Surely, Allah is All-Knowing, All-Aware. (Ch.49: Al-Hujurat:14)

And:

يَا أَيُّهَا الَّذِينَ آمَنُوا لَا يَسْخَرْ قَوْمٌ مِّن قَوْمٍ عَسَىٰ أَن يَكُونُوا خَيْرًا مِّنْهُمْ وَلَا نِسَاءٌ مِّن نِّسَاءٍ عَسَىٰ أَن يَكُنَّ خَيْرًا مِّنْهُنَّ ۖ وَلَا تَلْمِزُوا أَنفُسَكُمْ وَلَا تَنَابَزُوا بِالْأَلْقَابِ ۖ بِئْسَ الِاسْمُ الْفُسُوقُ بَعْدَ الْإِيمَانِ ۚ وَمَن لَّمْ يَتُبْ فَأُولَٰئِكَ هُمُ الظَّالِمُونَ ۝

128

O ye who believe! Let not one people deride another *people,
haply they may be better than they, nor let* one group of *women*
deride other *women, haply they may be better than them. And
do not defame your people nor call* one another *by nick-names.
It is* indeed *bad* to fall back into the *malpractice* of ignorant
days *after having believed; and those who repent not, such are
the wrongdoers. (Ch.49: Al-Hujurat:12)*

Apparently, contemporary society seems to be moving away
from racialism and apartheid and is becoming more conscious of
the horrors related to them. But if you examine the issue more
carefully and in depth, you will begin to realise that racialism
exists everywhere.

One major difficulty is the definition of 'racialism'. It can
appear different from various perspectives. It is difficult to draw
hard and fast lines between racialism, consciousness of class or
religious superiority, tribalism, fascism, imperialism and
nationalism. The most tragic and inhumane treatment of the
Jews at the hands of Christians in Western Europe for more than
a thousand years may be considered buried in the past, but the
recent beastly treatment of the Jews during the 30s and 40s at
the hand of Nazis is too fresh in our memories to be forgotten.
Therefore, the moment we hear the word 'racialism', our minds
are inadvertently turned to anti-Semitism and the long history of
the ill-treatment of the Semitic race at the hands of the gentiles.

This is a very limited understanding of racialism, of course. It is
so limited that the other connotations of the same scenario
completely miss our attention. We hardly stop to think of
extremists among the Jews looking at the gentiles with the same
horrid prejudices of which they themselves have been the
targets.

But that is not all. There is much more to racialism than meets
the eye. Racialism, though not clearly identified as such, does

exist under different guises, nationalism being one of them. Again, religious, tribal and regional prejudices are but a few examples where racialism is found at work under different names. The prejudices of white races against non-whites are also forms of racialism, but it is unjust to blame only the whites for harbouring prejudices against people who do not share their colour and complexion. There also exists black racialism, yellow racialism and the racialism of such people who cannot be so clearly defined into white, black or yellow but lie somewhere in between.

The essence of racialism is class prejudice. Perhaps this is the best definition of racialism. Whenever people begin to act prejudicially against another class of people on the pretext of their own class interests, racialism uncoils and raises its ugly and venomous head. No discretion is exercised in the expression of such hatred; no individual merit is taken into account; and, generality becomes the law.

Not many centuries ago, the western hemisphere was divided mainly along the plane of Christianity versus Islam. Whatever role the Jews played during that age of strong religious prejudices towards the Muslim east is relatively obscure. What is known, however, is the fact that the Jews were a part of Christian Europe, which hated and mistrusted Muslim nations around the Mediterranean and were apprehensive of Muslim expansion westwards.

During that period of intense hostilities between Christians and Muslims, there was an added element of racialism based on a difference in colour. At that time, the Muslims of Indonesia, Malaysia, China and India remained totally aloof and unconcerned. The conflict looked more like that of a Turko-Arab axis versus Christian Europe in general.

Although this history seems to be buried and forgotten, I can see it raising its head again. Human problems never seem to die permanently howsoever deeply buried they may appear. Returning to the present age, as long as the world was polarised by the two superpowers and their allies, it was vital for the interest of the West not to stir such issues or permit them to be stirred. But ever since the dawn of the new era of the East-West relationship, a dark knight from the medieval ages is also about to cast its sinister shadow.

There is a real danger of revival of the historic Christian-Muslim religio-political rivalries in the new climate created by the momentous changes in the USSR and Eastern Europe. This could be further fanned by consideration of vested interests on both sides. I am afraid that in this regard, the clergy of both Christianity and Islam are very likely to play a sinister role in aggravating the situation and further destroying the prospects of peace and harmony between Muslims and Christians. If this happens, it would certainly be of advantage to the cause of Israel. Israel cannot be conceived in the role of a disinterested and uninvolved observer.

Again, there are politico-economic dividing lines which are giving birth to a new type of racialism i.e., the racialism between the rich North and the poorer South and the East and West best expressed by:

East is East and West is West

And never the twain shall meet.

The recent rapprochement and detente between the superpowers may revive the historic religio-political controversies and rivalries between the Christian occident and the Muslim orient. It should not at all be surprising if East and West begin to drift further apart as a result of the new imperialism and a broadly based racialism which is bound to be born out of the recent detente between the superpowers.

According to the universally accepted terminology, I may appear to be outstepping the definition of racialism and extending it to areas which are not understood to have any racial implications. But my observation is based on a detached and deeper study of human motives which give birth to racialism. As long as the underlying motive forces remain the same, whether you name a certain expression of distorted human behaviour as racialism or call it by any other decent and civilised name, essentially the malady remains the same.

Racialism, in the broader sense, has to be understood as group prejudices as opposed to considerations of absolute justice and fair play.

The rapid waning of polarisation between the American and Russian blocs has ushered us into a completely new era in which we are moving towards global readjustments rather than the disappearance of divisions. As ideological divisions fade, divisions already marked on different planes in international relations are bound to grow and become more sharply defined. The age-old traditional division between the occident and the orient was reduced to a comparatively insignificant second place during the era of heightened capitalist-socialist rivalries. That being no longer so, the East-West division will once again emerge as the most pronounced dividing line between the developed nations of the West and the underdeveloped nations of the East.

The emancipated East European countries as well as Russia will gradually shift and ultimately merge with capitalist states adopting the same attitudes towards the Third World. Although new rivalries would result from a competition to capture and monopolise foreign markets, as a whole, the West will emerge as a much larger political-economic unit than ever before with the ultimate assimilation of the Eastern bloc. This will bring into greater relief and emphasis the traditional division between the occident and the orient.

Add to this the birth of neo-socialism, where nations will replace the individual and classes of individuals. The have-all and have-not polarisation will, therefore, not be between the rich of one nation and their interplay with the poor of another country. For some years to come, this catastrophic polarisation may be kept subdued and blunt but ultimate large scale confrontation cannot be averted forever.

I have deep-seated fears that we are entering a new era of global racialism of the most heinous type which may be further aided and abetted by a section of the Zionists' political leadership. If Benjamin Beit-Hallahmi of the University of Haifa and author of *The Israeli Connection: Whom Israel Arms and Why* (published 1988 by I.B. Tauris & Co. Ltd, London) is to be taken seriously, and if the evidence he has produced of the well-formed and well-defined political philosophy of the Zionists, is to be considered authentic it augurs ill indeed for the prospects of world peace.

The following picture of the role played and of that yet to be played by Israel in global affairs emerges:

David Ben-Gurion, Israel's founding father, said in January 1957, 'From the point of view of our existence and security, the friendship of one European country is more valuable than the view of all the people of Asia. [Medzini, 1976; p.75 (p.5)].

. . . . Israel's own concern for regaining its superiority against the Arabs has come to coincide with the American goal of halting imperial decline. (p.205).

What the modern right winger loves is the Israeli—tall, tough, armed with an Uzi and killing dark-skinned natives in a triumph over the forces of Third World radicalism. That is how Argentine generals, Paraguayan colonels, and Afrikaner brigadiers have come to love Israelis. (p.218)

The new *down with the Third World* rhetoric developing in the United States since the 1970's was tied to Israel, and its champions such as Daniel Patrick Moynihan and Jean Kirkpatrick have regarded Israel as an ally and an inspiration. (p.222).

Vladimir Jabotinsky, the leader of right wing Zionism before World War II, was quite blunt about the alliance between Zionism and imperialism . . . . Zionism has the *unshakeable resolve to keep the whole Mediterranean in European hands . . . . In every East-West conflict, we will always be on the side of the West, for the West has represented a more superior culture than the East over the last thousand years after the destruction of the Baghdad caliphate by the Mongols . . . . . and we today are the most prominent loyal bearers of the culture . . . . . We can never support the Arab movement which is at present opposed to us, and we are heartily pleased at every mishap to this movement . . . . .* [Brenner, 1984 pp.75–77 (p.227)].

The idea of liberation for Third World group threatens the very essence of Zionism. Concepts of human rights are too dangerous for the Israeli political system . . . . . . The injustice done to the Palestinians is so clear and so striking that it cannot be openly discussed and any discussion of what

Israel has been doing in the Third World is certain to lead to an examination of the rights of Palestinians. . . . . . (Israelis) are quick to denounce the rest of the world as hypocritical when issues of human rights and universal justice are discussed. In that they are quite similar to white South Africans. (p.236–237).

From Manila in the Philippines to Tegucigalpa in Honduras to Windhoek in Namibia, Israel's emissaries have been involved in a continuous war, which is truly a world war. And what enemy is Israel fighting? It is the population of the Third World which cannot be allowed to win its revolution. (p.243).

Israel's prognosis looks good only as long as the Arab world, and the rest of the Third World, remains divided and weak. Any change in this picture bodes ill. (p.247).

What Israel has been exporting is the logic of the oppressor, the way of seeing the world that is tied to successful domination. What is exported is not just technology, armaments, and experience, not just expertise but a certain frame of mind. (p.248).

It is strongly hoped that against this battle-cry of Zionism, the voice of the more sober section of Israel's leadership will prevail. Of all the Israeli writers who can perhaps be described to be moderate and logical, Harkabi appears to be a typical example. He does not only disapprove of the hawkish attitude of Zionist extremists but also genuinely considers it to be suicidal for the ultimate Zionist interest itself. The views expressed by Harkabi are not shared equally by other Jewish thinkers and intellectuals. Harkabi, for instance, takes a more pragmatic and realistic view to the same problem. Particularly, his 'land for peace' proposal opens an avenue of hope for the Arabs.

I firmly believe that discrimination and any effort to divide mankind on any plane may yield short-lived dividends for some, but, in the long run the consequences are bound to be evil for all concerned. In this contemporary scenario, Islam has a very positive message and an effective role to play.

Racialism and class hatred are denounced by Islam in the strongest terms. To create disorder in any form is abhorred. The verses of the Holy Quran quoted earlier are a few of the many on this subject.

The character of the Holy Prophet[sa] of Islam, is described as:

The Light of God which belongs neither to the East nor to the West, i.e., equally shared by both.

اَللّٰهُ نُوْرُ السَّمٰوٰتِ وَالْاَرْضِ مَثَلُ نُوْرِهٖ كَمِشْكٰوةٍ فِيْهَا مِصْبَاحٌ اَلْمِصْبَاحُ فِيْ زُجَاجَةٍ اَلزُّجَاجَةُ كَاَنَّهَا كَوْكَبٌ دُرِّيٌّ يُّوْقَدُ مِنْ شَجَرَةٍ مُّبٰرَكَةٍ زَيْتُوْنَةٍ لَّا شَرْقِيَّةٍ وَّلَا غَرْبِيَّةٍ يَّكَادُ زَيْتُهَا يُضِيْءُ وَلَوْ لَمْ تَمْسَسْهُ نَارٌ نُوْرٌ عَلٰى نُوْرٍ يَّهْدِى اللّٰهُ لِنُوْرِهٖ مَنْ يَّشَاءُ وَيَضْرِبُ اللّٰهُ الْاَمْثَالَ لِلنَّاسِ وَاللّٰهُ بِكُلِّ شَيْءٍ عَلِيْمٌ ۝

Allah is the Light of the heavens and of the earth. His light is as if there were a lustrous *niche, wherein is a lamp contained in a crystal* globe, *the globe as bright as a glittering star. The lamp is lit with the oil of a blessed tree, an olive, neither of the East not of the West. The oil would well-nigh glow forth even though no fire were to touch it. Light upon light! Allah guides to His light whomsoever He wills. And Allah sets forth parables for men and Allah knows all things full will. (Ch. 24: Al-Nur: 36)*

He is further introduced as:

A Mercy (and source of blessings) for the whole world (and the whole of mankind). (Ch.21: Al-Anbiya:108)

I am astounded to see many medieval-minded Muslim scholars, erroneously referred to as fundamentalists, subscribe to the view that Muslims must confront non-Muslims in an armed struggle and remain at war with them till either they are exterminated or they accept Islam. Islam, as found in the Holy Quran, has nothing whatsoever to do with this distorted and corrupt notion of a 'holy war'. As many verses have been quoted in the section dealing with religious peace, there is no need to repeat them.

Let me conclude by reaffirming that Islam truly advocates and suggests measures to bring mankind together through a peaceful process with the object of establishing world peace and the unification of mankind.

As far as the attitude of the Holy Founder of Islam is concerned, the following excerpts from the Last Sermon (known as the Farewell Sermon) he delivered before his demise in front of the largest assembly of mankind he ever addressed should suffice:

O men, lend me an attentive ear for I know not whether I will stand before you again in this valley and address you as I address you now. Your lives and your possessions have been made immune by God to attacks by one another until the Day of Judgement. God has appointed for everyone a share in the inheritance. No testament shall now be admitted which is prejudicial to the interests of a rightful heir. A child born in any house will be regarded as the child of the father of that house. Whoever contests the parentage of such a child shall be liable to punishment under the Law of Islam. Anyone who attributes his birth to someone else's father, or falsely claims someone to be his master, God, His angels and the whole of mankind will curse him.

O men, you have some rights against your wives, but your wives also have some rights against you. Your right against them is that they should live chaste lives, and not adopt ways which may bring disgrace to the husband in the sight of his people . . . . . . But if the behaviour of your wives is not such as would bring disgrace to their husbands, then your duty is to provide for them food and clothing and shelter, according to your own standard of living. Remember, you must always treat your wives well. God has charged you with the duty of looking after them. Woman is weak and cannot protect her own rights. When you married, God appointed you trustees of those rights. You brought your wives to your homes under the law of God. You must not, therefore, abuse the trust which God has placed in your hands.

O men, you still have in your possession some prisoners of war. I advise you, therefore, to feed them and to clothe them in the same way and style as you feed and clothe yourselves. If they do anything wrong which you are unable to forgive, then pass them on to someone else. They are part of God's creation. To give them pain or cause them suffering can never be right . . . . .

O men, what I say to you, you must hear and remember. All Muslims are as brethren to one another. All of you are equal. All men, whatever nation or tribe they may belong to, and whatever station in life they may hold are equal. (Raising his hands, and joining the fingers of the one hand with those of the other, he added). *Even as the fingers of the two hands are equal, so are human beings equal to one another. No one has any right, any superiority to claim over another. You are as brothers. O men, your God is One and your ancestor is one. An Arab possesses no superiority over a non-Arab, nor does a non-Arab over an Arab. A white man is in no way superior to a black nor for that matter, is a black man better than a white, but only to the extent to which he discharges his duty to God and man. The most honoured among you in the sight of God is the most righteous among you . . . . . .*

Even as this month is sacred, this land inviolate, and this day holy, so has God made the lives, property and honour of every man sacred. To take any man's life or his property, or attack his honour, is as unjust and wrong as to violate the sacredness of this day, this month, and this territory. What I command you today is not meant only for today. It is meant for all time. You are expected to remember it and to act upon it until you leave this world and go to the next to meet your Maker . . . .

What I have said to you, you should communicate to the ends of the earth. Maybe those who have not heard me may benefit by it more than those who have heard. (Sihah Sita, Tabari, Hisham, Khamis and Baihaqi)

The passage is very powerful and self-evident. But particularly noteworthy is the reminder by the Holy Prophet, may peace and blessings of Allah be upon him, that we are children of the same father. This in fact, has the evident connotation that different religions should not be permitted to divide the universal brotherhood of mankind originating from a single parenthood.

III

SOCIO-ECONOMIC PEACE

1. Introduction
2. Economic justice under capitalism, socialism and Islam
3. Spending in a good cause even in adversity
4. Spending in the cause of the poor
5. Gratitude
6. No human reward for favours
7. Begging
8. What can be given in charity?
9. Giving openly and discretely
10. Social responsibilities
11. An example from early Islam
12. Extended boundaries of expenditure
13. Service to others
14. Prohibition of drinking and gambling

The case of those who spend their wealth to seek the pleasure of Allah and to strengthen their souls is like the case of a garden on elevated ground. Heavy rain falls on it so that it brings forth its fruit twofold. And if heavy rain does not fall on it, then light rain suffices. And Allah sees what you do. (Ch. 2: Al-Baqarah: 266)

Beautified for men is the love of desired things—women and children, and stored-up heaps of gold and silver, and pastured horses and cattle and crops. That is the provision of the present life; but it is Allah with Whom is an excellent home. (Ch. 3: Al-Imran: 15)

INTRODUCTION

Islam also has a word of advice concerning the areas where the horizons of society and economy meet. If these teachings are implemented, they can turn our dusks and dawns into twilights of exceptional beauty.

ECONOMIC JUSTICE UNDER CAPITALISM, SOCIALISM AND ISLAM

Economic justice is a beautiful slogan. Whereas attempts have been made to monopolise it to the exclusion of the others, the slogan is common to both the capitalist society of the free market economy as well as the scientific social doctrine of dialectical materialism: both talk of justice. But, with due apologies, I must express my dismay in that both have failed to do full justice to the golden principle of economic justice; but more of this, later.

The Islamic concept of absolute justice is all-prevailing and all-pervading. It covers every aspect of Islamic teaching. But that is not all. Islam goes one step further.

In scientific socialism, an attempt is made to level-off the economic soil so completely and perfectly that there are no ups and downs left. If watered, such soil will get its share equally. There is no question of any demand from the have-nots nor any threat to the have-alls from the less fortunate sections of society to forcibly 'rob' them of their 'surplus wealth'.

In the capitalist society they talk more of equal opportunities, level playing fields and free economies than of equal distribution of wealth. Thus, there is always room for the demand of rights and the creation of pressure groups such as trade unions etc., which seek the most out of the government or other capitalists for the sake of the employee and the labourer who always live under a sense of deprivation.

If scientific socialism is implemented ideally, there is no need left for any section of society to make demands. Either that society would be rich enough to equitably distribute national wealth according to the needs or it would be so poor as to have failed to fulfil their needs leaving every member of the society sharing his or her misery equally. Either way, it would end up as a society where demand no longer has a meaningful role to play.

The capitalist system on the other hand is demand-oriented. The less fortunate section of society must be given the right to express its dissatisfaction and a free opportunity to be heard: hence the need for the formation of pressure groups and strikes, industrial strife, lockouts etc.

Islam attempts to create an attitude whereby the governments and the wealthy are constantly reminded that it is in their own ultimate interest to establish an equitable economic system. They are also constantly exhorted to be on the look out for the rights of others. The weak and poor should not be denied their fundamental economic rights such as freedom to choose one's profession, equal access to opportunities and the basic requirements of life. The lack of this very special attitude has already caused much misery, pain and disorder in the history of human struggle for survival. There is thus greater emphasis in Islam on 'giving' than on 'taking' or 'keeping'. The governments and the wealthy must constantly be on the lookout lest there be a section of society which is deprived of the fundamental human right to live decently. A truly Islamic state would have felt the need and taken appropriate measures for its fulfillment. Before grief turns into cries and protest and before

144

the need threatens peace and order, the cause of grief must be removed and the need fulfilled.

Apparently, in this respect, Islam shares its character with the socialist society but, in fact, the similarity is only superficial. Islam achieves its goal but not through the same coercive means prescribed by scientific socialism.

Time does not permit me to describe in detail how Islam endeavours to achieve this lofty goal but we can briefly mention that the Islamic approach to this issue is not lifeless and mechanical like the philosophy of dialectical materialism. The Islamic social system remains deeply wedded to the innate laws of the human psyche.

Among other things, Islam creates an atmosphere where the demand for one's own rights gives way to regard for the rights of others. The level of consciousness and sensitivity to the suffering of fellow human beings is raised to a degree whereby members of society as a whole are concerned more about what they owe to society than what society owes to them.

'Give the labourer more than his dues' is the Holy Prophet's repeated reminder to his followers. *'Pay him what he has earned before his sweat has dried out. Do not put those who serve under you to such tasks as you cannot perform yourself. As far as possible, feed your servants with whatever you feed your family. Provide them with similar clothing. Do not transgress against the meek in any way, or you will be held responsible before God. Lest you succumb to false pride, occasionally make your servants sit on the same table with you and serve them.'* (Various Ahadith)

SPENDING IN A GOOD CAUSE EVEN IN ADVERSITY

Human dignity is emphasised in the strongest terms in every sphere of life. The following verses of the Holy Quran present the code of ethics regarding the needs of the poor and needy and how these should be fulfilled.

God's reward for forgiveness is for:

اَلَّذِينَ يُنفِقُونَ فِى ٱلسَّرَّآءِ وَٱلضَّرَّآءِ وَٱلْكَـٰظِمِينَ ٱلْغَيْظَ وَٱلْعَافِينَ عَنِ ٱلنَّاسِ وَٱللَّهُ يُحِبُّ ٱلْمُحْسِنِينَ ۝

Those who spend in prosperity and adversity, and those who suppress anger and pardon men; and Allah loves those who do good. (Ch.3: Al-Imran:135)

SPENDING IN THE CAUSE OF THE POOR

The concept of alms generally understood in the world is double-edged. On the one hand, it pays compliment to the qualities of excellence to the donor of the alms. On the other, it creates an embarrassing, if not disgraceful, image of the recipient. The very act of receiving alms degrades his status. Islam revolutionises this concept.

A fascinating analysis is made of why some people are very poor and some rich in the following verse of the Holy Quran:

وَفِىٓ أَمْوَٰلِهِمْ حَقٌّ لِّلسَّآئِلِ وَٱلْمَحْرُومِ ۝

A part of *their wealth comprises that* which should by right have *belonged to the one who asked for help, beggar, and the one who could not*, the poor. *(Ch. 51: Al-Dhariyat: 20)*

146

The point generally missed is usage of the word HAQ (lit.right) which speaks volumes about the attitude of the one who gives alms as well as the attitude of the one who receives alms. The one who gives is reminded that what one gives to the poor, in reality, did not belong to one. Something has to be very wrong with an economy where some people are left destitute or compelled to beg for their living. In a healthy economic system, there should be no destitutes. There is no genuine need to beg for one's survival. The message delivered to the recipient of alms reminds him that there is no need for him to be embarrassed or to suffer from any complexes because, in fact, God has granted him the fundamental right to survive decently and honourably. So, whatever your apparent benefactor is giving to you, is your own right which somehow had got transferred to the donor.

As already mentioned earlier, God's teachings are directly related to human nature. Any injunction which is likely to disturb the equilibrium is counter-balanced by corrective measures.

GRATITUDE

In the case discussed above, there was of course, an inherent danger that some people would become ungrateful to their benefactors: instead of expressing gratitude for any favours they received from others, they may end up by saying that what one has given us was our right. There is no need for us to be grateful to such a person at all. If this tendency were to be promoted, then, it would be at the cost of courteous and decent behaviour.

Turning to the recipient of favours, the Holy Quran repeatedly reminds him of his duty to be grateful and to express his gratitude for even the smallest favour shown to him. The believer is repeatedly told that God does not love the ungrateful e.g.

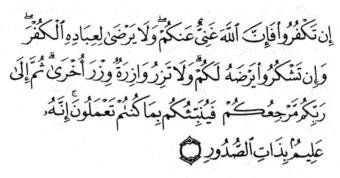

If you are ungrateful, surely Allah is Self-Sufficient, being independent of you; and He is not pleased with ingratitude in His servants; but if you are grateful, He likes it in you. No one shall bear the burden of another. Then to your Lord is your return; and He will inform you of that which you used to do. Surely, He is Well-Aware of whatever passes in your thoughts. (Ch. 39: Al-Zumar: 8)

Further emphasising the importance of a grateful disposition, the Holy Founder[sa] of Islam reminds the believers:

مَنْ لَمْ يَشْكُرِ النَّاسَ لَمْ يَشْكُرِ اللهَ

One who is not grateful to human beings is not grateful to God either.

The implication is that anyone who is ungrateful to fellow human beings, even if he were grateful to God, his gratitude will not be accepted by God. So decency, courtesy and gratitude are not discouraged by the Message of the Holy Quran as contained in the earlier verse *(Al-Zumar: 8)*. It is only a quiet message to the recipient of favours that he should not suffer from any complex and his dignity should remain uninjured. The inference

148

would be that to express gratitude is not against the dignity of man; on the contrary, it elevates it further.

Turning to the donor, Islam inculcates a completely different attitude. It is considered against dignity and modesty to accept gratitude as if one deserved it. This tendency is found to be a part of civilized behaviour everywhere in the world, but there is one fundamental difference between this universal mannerism and Islamic teachings of noble conduct. Islam instructs the donor to serve mankind for a higher and nobler cause than merely to satisfy a natural urge or earn good reputation by benevolent acts. Islam repeatedly reminds man to do acts of goodness for the sake of God and only to win His pleasure and earn His favours.

From this it becomes obvious that when a true Muslim donates something to anyone in need, in truth, he does not do it for his own sake or anyone else's sake, but only for the sake of pleasing his Creator Who initially bestowed on him everything he possesses.

In the light of this principle, whatever he spends on others is by way of an expression of gratitude to his Lord and not by way of any favour to anyone. This sublime attitude has its roots in one of the earliest verses of the Holy Quran which reminds the believers:

$$\text{وَمِمَّا رَزَقْنَـٰهُمْ يُنفِقُونَ ۝}$$

. . . From what we had provided them, they spend a part thereof in Our cause. (Ch.2: Al-Baqarah: 4)

Therefore, it is not out of mere courtesy that a true believer rejects gratitude but he genuinely believes that if a recipient of his favours owes gratitude to anyone, it is only to God and not to him. True believers, who really understand the meaning of faith, feel extremely embarrassed whenever their favours are returned with thanks. The Holy Quran declares:

They feed, for love of Him, the poor, the orphan, the prisoner, even when they themselves stand in need saying: 'We feed you for Allah's pleasure only. We desire no reward nor thanks from you'. (Ch. 76: Al-Dahr:9–10)

Just to feed people is not enough; you should feed them when you yourself know the meaning of hunger and suffering and you share in their pain, expecting no reward or thanks in return.

The beauty of this verse is dazzling. If the believers were taught to show a superficial and condescending attitude by just refusing to accept gratitude and posing as humble men, there was every danger that this would promote hypocrisy. When we say, 'No, thanks', in fact, we are conscious of the fact that by doing so, our image is further enhanced in the eyes of the person under favour.

The Islamic teaching is much more sublime. The benefactor is reminded that he cannot sell his commodities twice over to different parties. An act of goodness can either be done to win the pleasure of God or to win public favour. According to this verse, one cannot entertain both intentions simultaneously.

When the refined faithful servant of God tells the needy that his intentions were indeed to please God, it also reminds him at the same time that God is his real benefactor. So whatever inferiority complex may have been born is wiped out.

NO HUMAN REWARD FOR FAVOURS

In Islam, to be courteous to others should not be a superficial habit acquired out of values of civilization but should be deeply rooted in the belief in God. All alms given to the needy should be given without any ulterior motive of getting any return from the recipient.

وَلَا تَمْنُن تَسْتَكْثِرُ ۝

Bestow not favours seeking to get more in return. *(Ch.74:Al-Muddaththir:7)*

Once a favour is shown to anyone, Islam would require him to forget it, as if nothing had happened. To exult over one's act of goodness and to rub in one's favours are declared suicidal and self-annihilatory to the very act of goodness. On the contrary, the true believer behaves as described in the following verses which compare the correct behaviour with the incorrect one most comprehensively:

مَّثَلُ ٱلَّذِينَ يُنفِقُونَ أَمْوَٰلَهُمْ فِى سَبِيلِ ٱللَّهِ كَمَثَلِ حَبَّةٍ
أَنۢبَتَتْ سَبْعَ سَنَابِلَ فِى كُلِّ سُنۢبُلَةٍ مِّاْئَةُ حَبَّةٍ وَٱللَّهُ يُضَٰعِفُ
لِمَن يَشَآءُ وَٱللَّهُ وَٰسِعٌ عَلِيمٌ ۝ ٱلَّذِينَ يُنفِقُونَ أَمْوَٰلَهُمْ
فِى سَبِيلِ ٱللَّهِ ثُمَّ لَا يُتْبِعُونَ مَآ أَنفَقُواْ مَنًّا وَلَآ أَذًى لَّهُمْ
أَجْرُهُمْ عِندَ رَبِّهِمْ وَلَا خَوْفٌ عَلَيْهِمْ وَلَا هُمْ يَحْزَنُونَ ۝
قَوْلٌ مَّعْرُوفٌ وَمَغْفِرَةٌ خَيْرٌ مِّن صَدَقَةٍ يَتْبَعُهَآ
أَذًى وَٱللَّهُ غَنِىٌّ حَلِيمٌ ۝ يَٰٓأَيُّهَا ٱلَّذِينَ ءَامَنُواْ لَا تُبْطِلُواْ

151

صَدَقَـٰتِكُم بِٱلْمَنِّ وَٱلْأَذَىٰ كَٱلَّذِى يُنفِقُ مَالَهُۥ رِئَآءَٱلنَّاسِ وَلَا يُؤْمِنُ بِٱللَّهِ وَٱلْيَوْمِ ٱلْأَخِرِ ۖ فَمَثَلُهُۥ كَمَثَلِ صَفْوَانٍ عَلَيْهِ تُرَابٌ فَأَصَابَهُۥ وَابِلٌ فَتَرَكَهُۥ صَلْدًا ۖ لَّا يَقْدِرُونَ عَلَىٰ شَىْءٍ مِّمَّا كَسَبُوا ۗ وَٱللَّهُ لَا يَهْدِى ٱلْقَوْمَ ٱلْكَـٰفِرِينَ ۝

The case of those who spend their wealth in the cause of Allah is like that of a grain of corn which grows seven ears, in each ear there are a hundred grains. And Allah multiplies it even more for whomsoever He pleases. Allah is Bountiful, All-Knowing. Those who spend their wealth for the cause of Allah, then follow not up that which they have spent with taunt or injury, have their reward with their Lord. And they shall have no fear, nor shall they grieve. A kind word and forgiveness are better than charity followed up by injury. And Allah is Self-Sufficient, Forbearing. O ye who believe, render not vain your alms by reminding the recipient of your favours or causing him any inconvenience in return for what you have done for him. As such, his case will be like him who spends his wealth to be seen of men, and he believes not in Allah and the Last Day. His example is like that of a smooth rock covered with earth, on which heavy rain falls, washing it clean and leaving it bare, smooth and hard. Such people shall not secure aught of that which they earn. And Allah guides not the disbelieving people. (Ch.2: Al-Baqarah: 262-265)

Likewise:

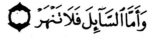

Chide not him who seeks thy help. (Ch. 93: Al-Duha: 11)

152

BEGGING

Even beggars should be treated with respect. Do not speak harshly to a beggar. Although, begging is discouraged, the right to beg when one is in dire need is guaranteed. Not only that, no one is permitted to injure the self-respect of those who are compelled to beg.

In early Islam, despite the fact that the self-respect of even the beggar had been fully safeguarded, society as a whole had not failed to understand that not to beg was certainly better than to beg. Once the Holy Founder[sa] of Islam highlighted this comparison by stating:

اَليَدُ العُليَا خَيرٌ مِنَ اليَدِ السُّفلَى

The hand of the donor is better than that of the receiver.

As a result of this a considerable number of Muslims preferred to die in poverty than to beg for survival. To cater for their needs, the Holy Quran reminds society as a whole that among you there are people striving in the path of Allah who have no way out of their poverty.

لِلْفُقَرَاءِ الَّذِينَ أُحْصِرُوا فِى سَبِيلِ اللَّهِ لَا يَسْتَطِيعُونَ ضَرْبًا فِى الْأَرْضِ يَحْسَبُهُمُ الْجَاهِلُ أَغْنِيَاءَ مِنَ التَّعَفُّفِ تَعْرِفُهُم بِسِيمَاهُمْ لَا يَسْئَلُونَ النَّاسَ إِلْحَافًا وَمَا تُنفِقُوا مِنْ خَيْرٍ فَإِنَّ اللَّهَ بِهِ عَلِيمٌ ۝

These alms are for the poor who are detained in the cause of Allah and are unable to move about in the land. The

153

ignorant considers them to be free from want merely because they desist from begging. Thou shalt know them by their appearance; they do not beg of men with importunity. And whatever you spend of your wealth on such people of that Allah is Fully-Aware. (Ch.2: Al-Baqarah:274)

This principle becomes very clear from the following verse:

مَّآ أَفَآءَ ٱللَّهُ عَلَىٰ رَسُولِهِۦ مِنْ أَهْلِ ٱلْقُرَىٰ فَلِلَّهِ وَلِلرَّسُولِ وَلِذِى ٱلْقُرْبَىٰ وَٱلْيَتَـٰمَىٰ وَٱلْمَسَـٰكِينِ وَٱبْنِ ٱلسَّبِيلِ كَىْ لَا يَكُونَ دُولَةًۢ بَيْنَ ٱلْأَغْنِيَآءِ مِنكُمْ وَمَآ ءَاتَىٰكُمُ ٱلرَّسُولُ فَخُذُوهُ وَمَا نَهَىٰكُمْ عَنْهُ فَٱنتَهُوا۟ وَٱتَّقُوا۟ ٱللَّهَ إِنَّ ٱللَّهَ شَدِيدُ ٱلْعِقَابِ ۝

Whatever Allah has given to His Messenger as spoils from the people of the towns is for Allah, and for the Messenger, and the near of kin, and the orphans, and the needy and the wayfarer, that it may not circulate only among those of you who are rich. And whatsoever the Messenger gives you, take it; and whatsoever he forbids you, abstain from that. And fear Allah; surely, Allah is severe in retribution. (Ch. 59: Al-Hashr:8)

The Holy Prophet of Islam, may peace and blessings of Allah be upon him, also mentions this principle in a Tradition partly translated as:

عَن حَكِيم بِن حِزَامٍ رَضِيَ اللهُ عَنهُ، عَنِ النَّبِي صَلَّى اللهُ عَلَيْهِ وَسَلمَ قَالَ: اَلَيَدُ الْعُلْيَا خَيْرٌ مِنَ الْيَدِ السُّفْلَى، وَأُبدَأ بِمَن تَعُولُ وَخَيرُ الصَّدَقَةِ

عن ظَهْرِ غِنًى. ومَنْ يَسْتَعْفِفْ يُعِفِّهِ اللهُ وَمَنْ
يَسْتَغْنِ يُغْنِهِ اللهُ.

Narrates Hakim bin Hizam: The Holy Prophet[sa] said, 'The upper hand is better than the lower hand (i.e., he who gives in charity is better than he who takes it). One should start giving first to his dependants. The best object of charity is that which is given by a wealthy person (from the wealth left after his expenses). Whoever abstains from asking others for some financial help, Allah will give him and save him from asking others, Allah will make him self-sufficient.'

You have an upper hand in service, i.e. to give alms and serve others and not to be on the receiving end of alm and favours.

WHAT CAN BE GIVEN IN CHARITY?

Apart from the manner in which you give, what you give is also important. If you give something of which you yourself will be ashamed to receive from anyone else, this will not fall within the definition of alms, according to the Holy Quran. It will be more like throwing something in the dustbin.

يَـٰٓأَيُّهَا ٱلَّذِينَ ءَامَنُوٓا۟ أَنفِقُوا۟ مِن طَيِّبَـٰتِ مَا كَسَبْتُمْ وَمِمَّآ
أَخْرَجْنَا لَكُم مِّنَ ٱلْأَرْضِ وَلَا تَيَمَّمُوا۟ ٱلْخَبِيثَ مِنْهُ تُنفِقُونَ
وَلَسْتُم بِـَٔاخِذِيهِ إِلَّآ أَن تُغْمِضُوا۟ فِيهِ وَٱعْلَمُوٓا۟ أَنَّ ٱللَّهَ غَنِىٌّ
حَمِيدٌ ۝

O ye who believe spend of the good things that you have earned, and of that which We produce for you from the earth; and do not select out of it for charity that which is worthless,

155

*which you yourself would not take without extreme
embarrassment and a sense of shame. And know that Allah is
Self-Sufficient, Worthy of Highest Praise. (Ch. 2: Al-Baqarah:
268)*

لَن يَنَالَ اللَّهَ لُحُومُهَا وَلَا دِمَآؤُهَا وَلَٰكِن يَنَالُهُ ٱلتَّقُوىٰ مِنكُمْ

The flesh of the sacrificial animals reaches not Allah, nor their
blood, but it is your righteousness that reaches Him . . .(Ch. 22:
Al-Hajj: 38)

GIVING OPENLY AND DISCRETELY

Islam leaves both options open: to spend publicly or privately.
The Holy Quran teaches:

وَمَآ أَنفَقْتُم مِّن نَّفَقَةٍ أَوْ نَذَرْتُم مِّن نَّذْرٍ فَإِنَّ ٱللَّهَ
يَعْلَمُهُ وَمَا لِلظَّٰلِمِينَ مِنْ أَنصَارٍ ۝ إِن تُبْدُواْ
ٱلصَّدَقَٰتِ فَنِعِمَّا هِىَ وَإِن تُخْفُوهَا وَتُؤْتُوهَا ٱلْفُقَرَآءَ
فَهُوَ خَيْرٌ لَّكُمْ وَيُكَفِّرُ عَنكُم مِّن سَيِّئَاتِكُمْ
وَٱللَّهُ بِمَا تَعْمَلُونَ خَبِيرٌ ۝

*Whatsoever you spend in the cause of Allah or vow as an
offering, surely Allah knows it well; and the wrongdoers shall
have no helpers. If you give alms openly that is indeed good,
but if you give them secretly to the poor, it is even better for
your own selves; thereby will He remove from you many of
your ills. And Allah is aware of what you do. (Ch.2: Al-
Baqarah: 271-272)*

SOCIAL RESPONSIBILITIES

In Islam, it is considered highly essential that those in authority should be sensitive to the cause of the people to a degree that there is no need to form pressure groups.

According to the Holy Quran, the ruler is repeatedly held responsible and answerable to God for the state of affairs of those who are under him and placed under his trust. In one of the Traditions of the Holy Founder[sa] of Islam, we read:

$$\text{كُلُّكُم رَاعٍ وَكُلُّكُم مَسْئُولٌ عَنْ رَّعِيَّتِهِ}$$

Each of you is like a shepherd to whom the sheep do not belong. He is entrusted with the responsibility of tending the sheep. *You will be held answerable.*

This tradition mentions the various relationships in which one can be in charge of other human beings e.g. master over servant; the wife who is the lady of the house and the father as head of the family who are both responsible for the entire family; and the employer who is responsible for the employees under him, and so on and so forth, and each time the Holy Prophet[sa] repeated: *Remember you will be held responsible and answerable.*

AN EXAMPLE FROM EARLY ISLAM

Once Umar, the Second Caliph in Islam, was passing through a street in a suburb of Madinah at night. It was his custom to walk the streets incognito to see for himself at first hand what was happening to the people under his authority. He heard from a house the cries of children who seemed to be in some pain. His inquiry revealed that there were about three children sitting

157

around a fire on which a kettle or pot was boiling and their mother was sitting by them. He enquired what had happened. She said: *My children were hungry. I have nothing to feed them. It is only to cajole them that I have put some water and some stones in the kettle or pot to create the impression that food is being cooked. That is what you see.*

In deep pain and anguish, Umar immediately returned to his seat of government. He procured some flour, butter, meat and dates and put them in a bag. He asked a slave standing nearby for help in putting the bag on his back. The slave, in surprise asked Umar why he wanted to carry it himself and asked that he should be permitted to carry the bag instead. Umar replied: *No doubt you can carry this weight for me today, but who will carry my burden on the Day of Judgement?* He meant that on the Day of Judgement, the slave would not be in a position to answer on Umar's behalf as to how he discharged his responsibilities. He had to do it himself. It was also a sort of self-inflicted penance because Umar felt responsible for the misery of a helpless poor woman and her children whom he had just witnessed. He felt, in fact, that the entire township and its affairs were his ultimate responsibility - a trust he had to discharge himself.

It is impossible for the head of every government to physically emulate what Umar did, but in both spirit and attitude Umar remains an excellent model. This is the spirit which must be followed by modern societies everywhere. If the governments become sensitive to the cause and sufferings of the people, then, even before the people begin to give voice to their pain and sense of deprivation, those in authority would be compelled to take remedial measures, not because of demands from fear but from the impelling voice of their own conscience.

EXTENDED BOUNDARIES OF EXPENDITURE

The Holy Quran enlarges the boundaries of what should be spent in the cause of Allah to vast dimensions. An oft-repeated phrase in the Holy Quran, hard to come by elsewhere, is:

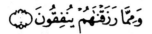

And the true believers *spend in Our cause of whatsoever we Ourselves have bestowed upon them. (Ch. 2: Al-Baqarah: 4)*

This covers all faculties, qualities and also, of course, every type of material possession, human relationship and ties. The phrase also covers such values as honour, peace, comfort, etc.

In short, nothing conceivable is beyond the domain of the Arabic expression WA MIMMA RAZAQNAAHUM.

Again, it is striking how the usage of the word MIN (lit. something of, of that) brings the advice within access of everyone. It does not mean that you should spend all or any fixed portion of that We have given you in Our cause. All that is required is that you should spend something of that which God has given you. The scope of *something* is so variable that even ordinary weak people who do not find the strength to make substantial sacrifices can at least participate to whatever degree they can afford. This is the atmosphere of social services which Islam endeavours to promote. It belongs partly to the social behaviour of man and partly concerns his economic activities.

In an economy where the entire society is possession oriented and is only concerned with what it can take, it is very hard and impractical to draw a line between what is foul and fair. Such a society is most likely to trespass into the doman of the rights of others than to remain within its own boundaries.

On the other hand, a society which is constantly reminded and trained to give to others more than their dues should be furthest from usurping the rights of others. It is hard to imagine how exploitation can flourish in such a climate.

SERVICE TO OTHERS

The principle of the Islamic concept of service is described in a single verse so beautifully and comprehensively. It states:

كُنتُمْ خَيْرَ أُمَّةٍ أُخْرِجَتْ لِلنَّاسِ تَأْمُرُونَ بِالْمَعْرُوفِ
وَتَنْهَوْنَ عَنِ الْمُنكَرِ وَتُؤْمِنُونَ بِاللَّهِ

O people of Islam! You are the best people ever raised for the good of mankind because you have been raised to serve others; you enjoin what is good and forbid evil and believe in Allah . . . (Ch.3: Al-Imran:111)

You will remain the best as long as you are service-minded. If you fail to serve others then you no longer have a right to boast of the superiority of Islam and the Muslim Ummah (community).

PROHIBITION OF DRINKING AND GAMBLING

When one talks of addiction, generally, drugs come to mind. There is another connotation of addiction in a wider sense which is seldom associated with the word addiction. I refer to society's regard for certain modes of pleasure, namely drinking and gambling, neither of which augurs well for the peace and good of society.

Gambling is institutionalised in almost all advanced countries of the world. But even in some Third World countries, where it is not institutionalised on such a large scale, gambling is found almost at every level as a small-time individual occupation. Drinking is the second addiction to which societies of the world have fallen prey.

The Holy Quran prohibits both gambling and drinking:

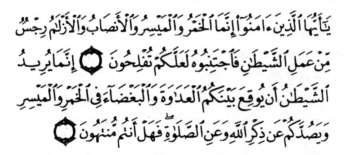

O ye who believe! Wine and the game of hazard and idols and divining arrows are only an abomination of Satan's handiwork. So shun each one of them that you may prosper. Satan desires only to create enmity and hatred among you by means of wine and the game of hazard, and to keep you back from the remembrance of Allah and from Prayer. But will you keep back? (Ch. 5: Al-Ma'idah: 91,92)

The Holy Prophet, may peace and blessings of Allah be upon him, declared drinking to be:

أُمُّ الـخَبَائِث

The Mother of All Evils

The two addictions are so widespread and universal in nature that it is hard to draw a dividing line. Politically, the East and West may never merge but, perhaps, in ever greater propensity towards gambling and drinking, East and West, and North and South, have already met.

Both drinking and gambling are socio-economic evils. The amount spent on drinking in one day in Great Britain is enough to feed the famine-stricken multitudes of Africa for many weeks. Yet, in the most poverty-striken countries of Africa and other continents, drinking is not considered a luxury that people cannot afford. Having failed to provide for the basic necessities of life and their children's education, there are millions of Africans who would still have access to the consumption of alcohol. In the poor south of India where factory-made wine is not available to all, home-made toddy serves as a substitute. However, poverty does deter the spread of the "mother of all evils" to a degree.

If the per capita income rises, so does the expenditure on drink. Until someone becomes an alcoholic, nobody seems to care much about it.

One may wonder why drinking and gambling should be treated as problems of the contemporary world while, in fact, they are as ancient as the records of human history go. Indeed, wine and gambling have been found in every age and part of the world; yet, by their very nature of being timeless, they can be considered as problems of all ages.

In economics, gambling is more objectionable than drinking. In gambling, money changes hands without pushing the wheel of economy just as money is exchanged for money without an underlying exchange of commodity in the money markets. In gambling, money changes hands without participating in the process of economic development and production of wealth. Though some economic purpose is served in the money markets, almost none is served in gambling. Under a free trade and industry environment, money does not change hands without serving the economy in material form. In trade and commerce, the exchange of value, more often than not, is beneficial for all concerned. It is inconceivable that the majority of traders should most often suffer losses. While in gambling, as a rule, a large majority of participants suffer losses most of the time. For instance, few casinos go bust. For the gain of a few, hundreds of thousands of people must suffer. The only value they get in exchange for the money they lose is the excitement and thrill of suspense until the realisation that they have lost their stake at last dawns upon them. After that they begin to wager again with a slim chance of recouping their losses until the tension and stresses grow far beyond the pleasure of excitement they receive in the bargain; the anguish and the heartache no longer remain a private matter for an individual but begin to tell on family relationships. In the poorer sections of society, the daily needs of family members have to be sacrificed at the altar of gambling. The Holy Quran, while prohibiting drinking and gambling, acknowledges that there is, of course, some partial benefit to be derived from them but most certainly their harm always outweighs their advantage:

يَسْتَلُونَكَ عَنِ الْخَمْرِ
وَالْمَيْسِرِ قُلْ فِيهِمَآ إِثْمٌ كَبِيرٌ وَمَنَـٰفِعُ لِلنَّاسِ وَإِثْمُهُمَآ
أَكْبَرُ مِن نَّفْعِهِمَا وَيَسْتَلُونَكَ مَاذَا يُنفِقُونَ قُلِ الْعَفْوَ
كَذَٰلِكَ يُبَيِّنُ اللَّهُ لَكُمُ الْأَيَـٰتِ لَعَلَّكُمْ تَتَفَكَّرُونَ ۝

They ask thee concerning liquor and gambling. Tell them: There is great harm in both and also some benefit for people, but their harm is greater than their benefit. And they also ask thee what shall they spend. Tell them: Whatever is spare. Thus does Allah make His commandments clear to you that you may reflect (Ch. 2: Al-Baqarah: 220)

It may be argued that to acquire pleasure from the money which one earns is nobody else's concern: let everyone enjoy himself as he pleases. Society has no right to interfere in individual freedom to the extent that one should be told where one may spend one's earnings.

But it should be remembered that most religious teachings are by way of admonitions and warnings. Coercive measures here on earth have no part to play in the teachings of any religion unless specific crimes are committed against others - crimes which are recognised as such even from a non-religious point of view. Murder, theft, fraud, corruption and usurpation of rights fall under this category. But there are other social crimes which, according to religions, are poisonous for society as a whole. Yet the penalty for such crimes is not meted out individually; society as a whole suffers. It is the broader social laws which pass the sentence.

Indulgence in liquor and gambling does not take very long to become over-indulgence for society as a whole. But that is no surprise.

Moreover, such societies always become progressively more expensive to maintain. A sizeable portion of the national wealth continues to be flushed down the drain. Frustration grows in this atmosphere. Crimes go hand in hand with both liquor and gambling. Miseries and tragedies of many homes where the peace of family life is shattered is the ever-increasing by-product of drinking and gambling. Many a broken home and ruined marriage are their direct outcome.

Alcoholism has serious economic and social consequences as indicated by the magazine *Scientific American.* Apart from domestic violence, there is child abuse, incest and rape due to the removal of inhibitions under the influence of alcohol and fetal alcohol syndrome.

Mortality statistics:

- 10 year decrease in life expectancy in alcoholics.

- Two times the usual death rate in men, three times the usual rate in women.

- Six times the usual suicide in alcoholics.

- Alcohol is a major factor in the four leading causes of death in men between the ages of 25 and 44: accidents (50 percent), homicide (60 percent), suicides, alcoholic cirrhosis.

Economic toll per year:

- Lost production:	$14.9*billion.*
- Health care costs:	$8.3*billion.*
- Accident losses:	$4.7*billion.*
- Fire losses:	$0.3*billion.*
- Cost of violent crimes:	$1.5*billion.*
- Cost of response by society to above:	$1.9 *billion.*
- Total cost of alcohol abuse:	$31.6*billion.*

Drinking, gambling, music, dancing and other modes of pleasure are largely considered innocent pursuits by most societies of the world. They are presented as essential parts of different cultures. Though the mode of expressions change from society to society the basic features remain the same. Barring sculpture, painting, etc., most of the pursuits mentioned earlier no longer remain as innocent features of culture but become hard task masters which sometimes overburden and break the backbone of society. Society is no longer the master of its trends. Drinking, gambling, music, dancing etc. invariably begin to attract increasing attention from society. The speed at which they capture the youth does not take very long to become a stampede.

Looking at such societies, one may be led to believe that the seeking of vain pleasures and total submission to the sensual desires is, in fact, the very purpose of man's creation.

Not so according to Islam.

إِنَّ فِى خَلْقِ ٱلسَّمَٰوَٰتِ وَٱلْأَرْضِ وَٱخْتِلَٰفِ ٱلَّيْلِ وَٱلنَّهَارِ لَأَيَٰتٍ لِّأُوْلِى ٱلْأَلْبَٰبِ ۝ ٱلَّذِينَ يَذْكُرُونَ ٱللَّهَ قِيَٰمًا وَقُعُودًا وَعَلَىٰ جُنُوبِهِمْ وَيَتَفَكَّرُونَ فِى خَلْقِ ٱلسَّمَٰوَٰتِ وَٱلْأَرْضِ رَبَّنَا مَا خَلَقْتَ هَٰذَا بَٰطِلًا سُبْحَٰنَكَ فَقِنَا عَذَابَ ٱلنَّارِ ۝

In the creation of the heavens and the earth and in the alternation of the night and day there are indeed signs for men of understanding. Those who remember Allah, standing, sitting and lying on their sides, and ponder over the creation of the heavens and the earth, say, 'Our Lord, Thou hast not created this in vain; Nay, Holy art Thou; save us then from the punishment of the fire'. (Ch. 3: Al-Imran: 191-191)

This is the declaration attributed by the Holy Quran to the wise servants of Allah who after pondering over the riddle of creation and life, spontaneously exclaim that whatever the purpose of creation be, it is not vanity.

These verses of the Holy Quran reminds one of the great expression of joy by Archimedes when he shouted *Eureka!*

Thus, there are two completely different climates. According to the Holy Quran, man has been created to achieve the noble goal of pursuing the path which leads to his Creator. In this wider meaning of worship, the Holy Quran declared:

$$\text{وَمَا خَلَقْتُ الْجِنَّ وَالْإِنسَ إِلَّا لِيَعْبُدُونِ} \bigcirc$$

I have not created Jinn and men but to worship Me. (Ch. 51: Al-Dhariyat: 57)

In examining each mode of seeking pleasure, one may not find much fault with any to justify their total ban. Particularly in the free societies of the world, it is very difficult for the people to understand why Islam is so puritan to the extent of dryness. Islam is not at all dry and boring, howsoever it may seem so from a distance. First of all, those who acquire a taste for goodness, also learn to draw sublime pleasure out of an act which may seem rather drab to the outsider. Secondly, the more fortunate among those who experience the true love of God, transcend to a state of sublimity from where worldly pleasures appear too lowly, base, meaningless and transient. Thirdly, in its much broader application, a society not given up to the pursuits of pleasure is not left empty-handed at the end of the day. In the final analysis, it turns not only to be an exchange of value - excitement, exhilaration, intense sensual experiences and explosive raptures are bartered for peace, tranquility, equilibrium, growing sense of security, nobility and contentment, which as a reward *per se* is the noblest of all rewards.

When the two social atmospheres and climates are compared as a whole, it is not difficult at all to understand that the tree of God's love and devotion to Him can seldom take root in the materialistic climate of a fun-loving society. Of course, there are exceptions but exceptions do not make the rule. The two climates are very different.

IV

ECONOMIC PEACE

1. Economic philosophies of Capitalism, Communism and Islam
2. Capitalism
3. Scientific Socialism
4. Islamic concept
5. Four characteristics of a capitalist society
6. Capitalism ultimately leads to destruction
7. The changing economic order
8. Islamic economic system
9. Zakat
10. Prohibition of interest
11. High interest rates in Britain
12. Other evils of interest
13. Interest as a threat to peace
14. Prohibition on hoarding of wealth
15. Simple lifestyle
16. Matrimonial expense
17. Accepting invitations from the poor
18. Moderation in eating habits
19. Borrowing money
20. Economic class differences
21. Islamic laws of inheritance
22. Prohibition of bribery
23. Commercial ethics
24. Basic needs
25. Worship as a means of economic unity
26. International obligations

Allah will abolish interest and will cause charity to increase. And Allah loves not anyone who is a confirmed disbeliever and an arch-sinner. (Ch. 2: Al-Baqarah: 277)

Nay, but you honour not the orphan, and you urge not one another to feed the poor, and you devour the heritage of the poor, and you love wealth with extreme love. (Ch. 89: Al-Fatir: 18-21)

ECONOMIC PHILOSOPHIES OF CAPITALISM, COMMUNISM AND ISLAM

The Islamic economic order neither belongs to capitalism nor to scientific socialism. The economic philosophy of Islam is scientific without being mechanical. It is disciplined without being over restrictive. It allows private possession and private enterprise but does not promote greed and the amassing of wealth in a few hands whereby a large section of society turns into destitutes, serfs and slaves to a cruel and relentless system of exploitation.

There are three fundamental differences in the economic philosophies of Capitalism, Communism and Islam.

CAPITALISM

In capitalism, capital is rewarded with interest. It is intrinsically accepted in principle that capital has a right to grow. Interest plays the central motive force for the amassing of capital which is then channelled as energy to set and keep the assembly line of production in motion. In short, interest acts as an incentive for keeping capital in circulation.

SCIENTIFIC SOCIALISM

In scientific socialism, although there is no incentive of interest to cycle and recycle capital into a productive mechanism, the state monopolises capital. So, there is no need for motivation.

In free private enterprise, whether one pays or does not have to pay interest, one's sense of personal ownership is sufficient to create an urge that one's capital should grow at the fastest possible rate. If one has to pay interest on borrowed money, the rate of interest acts as a benchmark. It works like a window through which one can monitor the comparative growth or diminution of capital. In the socialist economic system, however, there is neither this urge, because those who employ capital do not own it, nor is there any means of comparison whereby one can judge whether the rate of growth is economically sufficient or not.

In socialist scientific order, the forcible possession of the entire state's capital by the state itself renders the system of interest totally irrelevant and meaningless. The snag is that when you are not under any pressure to earn more than the interest you may have to pay, you lose all incentives and any sense of responsibility.

If the entire capital in circulation in a Communist state could, for instance, be valued from the point of view of how much interest it could earn had it been deposited in a bank, that would present us with one side of the picture. The second side of the picture could be conceived by assessing the economy on a profit and loss basis. Of course, it would present many complications such as assessing wages etc. But if financial experts put their heads to it, such hurdles may be overcome. A comparison of these two would present very interesting possibilities.

It is more than likely that the real culprits for the decline of standards of living could precisely be pinpointed in this way. Even without such a gigantic exercise, it is not difficult at all for one to determine the causes of such decline. I believe that because the state becomes the capitalist, it is deprived of a monitoring system to warn it of failures, wastage and blunders regarding the way it handles the state's capital because it has no financial obligations to fulfil and can employ capital without accountability. Such a situation is rife with inherent dangers. Lack of personal interest and a warning system on the profit or loss arising from the employment of capital, works havoc with the input-output ratio. The quantum of waste goes on increasing.

Again, there is no check placed on the policy of channelling capital. For instance, there is no mirror for the socialist governments to judge the real rate of economic growth in comparison to the free market economies of the outside world. An added problem is that communist states require much larger expenditure on defence, surveillance and law-enforcing agencies within the country. Other things being equal, this requires a disproportionate level of expenditure on defence and the maintenance of law and order. These and other similar factors take a heavy toll on the economy. The ultimate collapse of the economy can be delayed, of course, but cannot be averted altogether.

ISLAMIC CONCEPT

While communism provides no incentive for direct dedicated involvement in the production of wealth, despite banishing interest, Islam provides the incentive. Islam does away with the system of usury and interest without sharing the specific problems of the communist world, In the absence of interest dragging capital along non-productive channels, Islam checks idle capital. This check is a form of 'tax' known as *Zakat* which is levied not on income or profit but on the capital itself.

The contrast is very clear. In capitalist societies, capital is amassed in the hands of a few out of greed to increase capital through the accumulation of interest and is recycled into the economy with the set task of yielding a profit greater them the prevailing rate of interest. Failing this, the economy is bound to go into recession. In Islam, out of fear that any idle capital would be gradually eroded away through the imposition of

Zakat, anyone with surplus savings would have to employ it in earning profit to offset the effect of Zakat.

According to Islam, the answer to the economic problems of the world lies neither in scientific socialism nor capitalism. It is impossible to elaborate on this subject here but we must have a topical view of the economic imbalance created by capitalism to draw some lessons for the future.

FOUR CHARACTERISTICS OF A CAPITALIST SOCIETY

The signposts for determining that such an imbalance has arisen in a society are very clearly stated in the following verses of the Holy Quran:

Nay, but you honour not the orphan. And you urge not one another to feed the poor. And you devour the heritage of the other people wholly. And you love wealth with exceeding love. (Ch. 89: Al-Fajr: 18-21)

Briefly, these features are:
1. Dishonourable treatment of orphans.
2. Feeding of the poor is not promoted.
3. Usurpation of the heritage of others.
4. Endless amassing of wealth.

174

CAPITALISM ULTIMATELY LEADS TO DESTRUCTION

Without endorsing the philosophy of scientific socialism, Islam rejects some aspects of capitalism because:

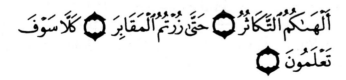

Mutual rivalry in seeking worldly increase diverts you from God. Till you reach the graves. Nay! you will soon come to know the truth. (Ch. 102: Al-Takathur: 2-4)

THE CHANGING ECONOMIC ORDER

Exploitation of poorer citizens by interest-based capitalism which gives birth to socialist rebellion seems to be relegated to history. But a deeper study would reveal that it is only a change of guise.

Already the world as a whole has been split into the haves and have-nots, thanks mainly to the exploitation by the advanced capitalist countries. Add to this situation the momentous return to capitalism by the repentant Eastern bloc. One shudders to visualise how much more blood would be sucked from the already enfeebled and anaemic nations of the Third World. But, it would seem that the vampires of capitalism must draw more blood.

It is clear that the age of confrontation between the two major opposing economic philosophies of capitalism and scientific socialism is over. The economic systems based on Marxism—

Lenninism have bowed out of the stage of human affairs. On the other hand, the so-called "free" economy of the West seems to be exultant over its apparent victory. Barring China, the Eastern bloc countries are still struggling to mitigate the miseries of the multitudes of have-nots in their respective countries in the wake of their new found freedom.

The economic gap between the East and West is not as big as that between the North and South. The First World countries of the North are divided on another plane from the Third World countries of Africa and South America. Though in terms of economic disparity, the gap between North and South America is certainly hurtful, it is nowhere near the gap between Europe and Africa. Africa, so close in proximity to Europe is, in terms of economic disparity, the farthest apart from Europe.

The sense of security that was once enjoyed by the weaker countries of the world because of the rivalries between the super-powers and any chance of the poorer nations benefitting from the thawing of the cold war will fast fade out. There is going to be much greater and more earnest competition between the USA, Russia and the rest of Europe to win, monopolise and secure the markets of the Third World countries.

Japan will no longer be the only serious rival to America. A new Europe emerging out of the rapid growth of the European Community and the prospective participation of Eastern Europe in a larger common market will pose a far more formidable competition to America than the rival states of Europe.

The teeming millions of East Europe and Russia are looking forward to and stand in dire need of raising their living standards. Merely the rehabilitation of a closed market would not be sufficient to meet this tall order which is likely to grow taller with the passage of time. The dire necessity of external markets to support the rising living standards in East Europe and Russia may be met by the EC, America and Japan. It offers little hope for the Third World countries — a bleak picture indeed for the Third World—much more so for the less fortunate people of Africa.

The politicians of the economically and politically advanced nations of the world are far more concerned by the capitalist economic revolution taking place in the Far East—Japan, South Korea, Formosa, Hong Kong and Singapore. It seems that the distance between the Far East and the West is being bridged over the heads of many less fortunate Asian countries Indonesia, Malaysia, Cambodia, Thailand, Burma, Bangladesh, India, Sri Lanka and Pakistan.

It is also possible that to meet the growing challenge from the gigantic economy of Japan and to put a check on its rapidly expanding economy, other Far Eastern countries would no longer remain beneficiaries of American know-how and capital. On the other hand, it is also possible that America may lean even more on its Far Eastern allies to meet new combined challenges from Japan and an economically much bigger and united Europe. This augurs ill for the future of mankind and may ultimately shatter the prospects for peace on a completely different plane than the ideological rivalries between capitalism and communism.

It is too early to predict how the changes in Eastern Europe and Russia may influence the economic balance of the world and whether their return to capitalism may be complete or partial or slow or rapid. Whatever happens, one thing is certain that these changes will further adversely influence the economies of the Third World.

Such a state of affairs cannot last indefinitely. Already, the world is heading towards a global catastrophe.

Islam has a word of advice for the presently exultant capitalist countries built on a hollow foundation of usury and interest. They are ultimately bound to tumble down and shatter to pieces. The so-called recent victory by capitalism over socialism will only provide transient peace. Capitalist philosophies by themselves will give birth to powerful demons which will rapidly grow to gigantic size in the absence of rivalries from socialism. The volcano of capitalism will finally erupt with such force that the whole world will shake, quake and convulse.

ISLAMIC ECONOMIC SYSTEM

As with the social system advocated by Islam, the Islamic economic system commences with the premise that all that is in the heaven and the earth has been created by God, Who has bestowed man various provisions on trust. As a trustee, man will be held accountable for the discharge of this trust. The possession or absence of wealth is a means of trial so that in both abundance and adversity, those who are mindful of their accountability may be distinguished from those who resort to callousness and scant attention to the sufferings of the rest of mankind.

The Holy Quran repeatedly reminds us:

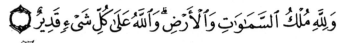

To Allah belongs the Kingdom of the heavens and the earth; and Allah has power over all things. (Ch. 3: Al-Imran: 190)

Then it teaches that if everything has been created by God for all, some of it should be shared amongst men.

$$\text{أَمْ لَهُمْ نَصِيبٌ مِّنَ ٱلْمُلْكِ فَإِذًا لَّا يُؤْتُونَ ٱلنَّاسَ نَقِيرًا ۝}$$

Have they a share in the Kingdom? Then would they not give men even so much as the little hollow in the back of a date stone? (Ch. 4: Al-Nisa:54)

$$\text{وَٱللَّهُ فَضَّلَ بَعْضَكُمْ عَلَىٰ بَعْضٍ فِى ٱلرِّزْقِ فَمَا ٱلَّذِينَ فُضِّلُوا۟ بِرَآدِّى رِزْقِهِمْ عَلَىٰ مَا مَلَكَتْ أَيْمَٰنُهُمْ فَهُمْ فِيهِ سَوَآءٌ أَفَبِنِعْمَةِ ٱللَّهِ يَجْحَدُونَ ۝}$$

Allah has favoured some of you above others in worldly gifts. But those more favoured will not restore any part of their worldly gifts to those under their control, so that they may be equal sharers in them. Will they then deny the favour of Allah? (Ch. 16: Al-Nahl: 72)

Man's responsibility is to discharge this trust honestly and equitably:

$$\text{إِنَّ ٱللَّهَ يَأْمُرُكُمْ أَن تُؤَدُّوا۟ ٱلْأَمَٰنَٰتِ إِلَىٰٓ أَهْلِهَا وَإِذَا حَكَمْتُم بَيْنَ ٱلنَّاسِ أَن تَحْكُمُوا۟ بِٱلْعَدْلِ إِنَّ ٱللَّهَ نِعِمَّا يَعِظُكُم بِهِ إِنَّ ٱللَّهَ كَانَ سَمِيعًۢا بَصِيرًا ۝}$$

Verily, Allah commands you to give over the trusts to those entitled to them, and that, when you judge between men, you judge with justice. Surely excellent is that with which Allah admonishes you! Allah is All-Hearing, All-Seeing. (Ch. 4: Al-Nisa 59)

The fact that material wealth is a source of trial is expressed in the Holy Quran as follows:

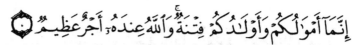

Verily, your wealth and your children are a trial; but with Allah is an immense reward. (Ch. 64: Al-Taghabun: 16)

An important concept of possession under Islam is that certain resources are taken out of individual ownership and placed in the hands of mankind as a whole. Thus, mineral resources and the produce of seas and oceans is not the exclusive property of any individual or group of people.

ZAKAT

Zakat is one of the five pillars of Islam—the others being the affirmation that there is no God but Allah and Muhammad is His Messenger; prayers; fasting during the month of Ramadhan; and pilgrimage to the House of Allah in Makkah. For instance, the Holy Quran commands:

Observe prayer and pay the Zakat and obey the Messenger that you may be shown mercy. (Ch. 24: Al-Nur: 57)

The Arabic word *Zakat* literally means to purify something and in the context of a mandatory levy would mean that the residual wealth after the deduction of Zakat had rendered it pure and lawful for the believers.

It is normally levied at 2.5% on disposable assets above specific thresholds which have remained in the hands of owners beyond one year. Although much has been said about the rate or percentage of this *tax*, we find no reference to any fixed percentage in the Holy Quran. In this respect, I beg to differ with

180

the dogmatic view of medieval scholars. I believe that the question of percentage remains flexible and should be determined according to the state of the economy in a particular country.

Zakat being a specific levy imposed upon capital beyond certain thresholds, it can only be utilised for certain categories of expenditure. These have been spelt out in the following verse of the Holy Quran:

$$\text{إِنَّمَا ٱلصَّدَقَٰتُ لِلْفُقَرَآءِ وَٱلْمَسَٰكِينِ وَٱلْعَٰمِلِينَ عَلَيْهَا وَٱلْمُؤَلَّفَةِ قُلُوبُهُمْ وَفِي ٱلرِّقَابِ وَٱلْغَٰرِمِينَ وَفِي سَبِيلِ ٱللَّهِ وَٱبْنِ ٱلسَّبِيلِ فَرِيضَةً مِّنَ ٱللَّهِ وَٱللَّهُ عَلِيمٌ حَكِيمٌ}$$

Alms are only for the poor and the needy, and for those employed in connection with their collection and distribution, and for those whose hearts are to be comforted, and for the freeing of slaves, and for those burdened with debt, and for those striving in the cause of Allah, and for the Wayfarers. This is an ordinance from Allah. Allah is All-Knowing, Wise. (Ch. 9: Al-Tauba: 60)

The Treasury is charged the administration of this ordinance. In the early history of Islam, Hadhrat Abu Bakr and Umar, the first two caliphs, were renowned for personally ensuring the speedy disbursement of alms in what became known as the first welfare state. This system had been at work with great success for centuries during the Abbaside period.

As has already been explained, the motive force of interest is replaced by the driving force of Zakat. When we examine this

181

system in operation, many differences between the Islamic economic order and other economic systems come to light. The features of a completely different economy begin to emerge.

No amount of idle money, irrespective of it being large or small, can survive for long without multiplying faster than the rate at which it is taxed. That is precisely how Zakat propels the economy in a truly Islamic state.

Imagine a situation where an individual with a small amount of capital is unable to directly participate in trade and there are no banks to credit him with interest on his deposit. Yet, if the deposit be sufficiently large to be taxable as Zakat, there are revenue collectors who knock at his door each year for a percentage of his capital, Zakat is not beyond a prescribed threshold. Such individuals have only two alternatives; either to personally employ their money profitably or to pool their resources to establish small or large enterprises.

This will promote joint-ventures, partnerships, the forming of small companies or public shareholding in larger companies on a strict profit and loss basis. Such companies will owe nothing to any financial institution to which they have to repay debts with interest. Hypothetically, when you compare the lot of such companies with that of their counterparts in capitalist economies, they will be found facing on completely different platforms during periods of trial and crisis. In the case of trade and industry facing a recession in a capitalist economy, the slow-down in production because of dwindling demand can push them to the brink of liquidation. The interest they have to pay to service their debts will go on mounting relentlessly until it will no longer be possible for such companies to remain afloat.

On the other hand, if an economy is run on Islamic principles, a slowdown in business and trade opportunities will only send trade and industry into a state of hibernation. That is how nature ensures survival of the fittest at the time of extreme stresses and adversities. When the input of energy decreases, output has to be lowered lest energy should drop below the critical level necessary for survival. As there is no relentless pressure of debt servicing in an Islamic financial system, it can withstand far greater pressure and challenges during a recession.

PROHIBITION OF INTEREST

The Islamic economic system runs on the total absence of the interest factor. Yet there is no historical nor current evidence to suggest that as a result of no interest, the demon of inflation went amok, and set the prices spiralling up beyond control. In the contemporary times, we have a very interesting opportunity to draw comparisons with regard to the influence of interest rates, or its absence, on inflation.

The government of China under Mao Tse Tsung's era made many experiments with the economy. Some faltered. Some produced excellent results. But during the entire reign of Mao Tse Tsung, interest was not allowed to play any part, either domestically or internationally. Yet, throughout this period, there was no prominent increase in inflation. In fact, when ultimately the overall production level increased, prices began to register a fall.

As compared to this, in the State of Israel, perhaps the world's most capitalist country, the rate of inflation has been amongst the highest recorded anywhere in the world, except, of course, in Latin American countries and the post-War exceptional phenomenon of inflation in Europe, particularly in Germany. But then those were not normal days. Other things being equal, the role of interest in any economy cannot be described as anything other than inflationary.

HIGH INTEREST RATES IN BRITAIN

The current hot debate in Great Britain regarding the pros and cons of high interest rates offers an interesting example for study. For a long time now, the Conservative government has kept interest rates precariously high with the sole declared purpose to curb private consumption and thus suppress inflation. The economy is already squeaking and groaning under the stresses this policy has caused.

Many a lesson can be drawn from this study. Among other things, this study presents a fit case of highly potent economic decisions being taken on the basis of a theory which in itself is debatable.

The notion that the higher the interest rate is raised the more will inflation be reduced seems to be the only reason to justify the maintenance of interest rates at an unnatural high level for so long.

In the case of our current study of what is happening in Great Britain, the rate of interest has never been the real culprit in the inflationary trend. There must have been mismanagement in many areas of the economy and an overall faulty economic policy which resulted in the relative high inflation rate of the present time. The raising of interest rates has only served to distract the attention from the root causes to an easy scapegoat. This strategy may show a measure of success in combating inflation to begin with but it has already set in motion powerful factors which would produce secondary effects. The country would be pushed to an unmanageable state of recession and unemployment would soar.

It is impossible to believe that advice from leading economists, experienced financial planners, central bankers and other experts is not available to the think-tank of the Conservative government. There has to be some reason for this prolonged wilful delay in lowering the high rate of interest on the hollow plea that it is essential for the survival of the national economy to push down the inflationary trend with the leverage of high interest rates. Could it be possible that the timing of lower interest rates is not politically suitable to the present government? Perhaps if it is delayed until close to the next general elections, the immediate relief felt by all sections of society from the cut in interest rates, could be turned to the political advantage of the Tories. If this is done too early on, the secondary effects to which I have already alluded may begin to manifest themselves and offset any gains from the temporary relief brought about by lower interest rates.

Some of the factors which may unleash this undesirable phenomenon are as follows:

(a) The high rate of interest has not only choked the buying power of the general public but has also squeezed the jugular vein of industry.

(b) It has certainly hurt a large section of the British public in its quest for the basic necessities of life. Those who borrowed large sums of money for a roof over their heads had calculated carefully before taking on a mortgage. They squeezed their ability to repay the mortgage and had squeezed their daily budget to meet repayments. Such people were already exercising restraint in unnecessary and imprudent expenditure. There was, in any case, little leeway to do so. This section of British society was certainly not responsible for inflationary trends. But, ironically, this is the section punished most severely by the so-called anti-inflationary measure of the government purportedly for the benefit of the general public. Meanwhile, the value of their houses has begun to nose-dive and they find themselves in an insoluble dilemma - unable to meet higher repayments and unable to find a buyer for their property.

(c) Inflation is a complex phenomenon. It is not the purpose of this address to devote unnecessarily longer time to this subject, but for reasons which will become apparent after a while, I have to beg the audience's indulgence.

Among other things, the ball of inflation can be set rolling when excessive money in the hands of the buyer artificially raises demand while the supply of goods remains low. Too much money for too few goods. There is more to buy and less to be bought. But, perhaps, in the case of the British economy, this situation did not prevail. The greater volume of money in circulation was supporting British industry to a large degree by increasing the consumption in the home market. Add to this the influence of tax cuts and moderate rates of exchange on the value of sterling in the international markets. This moderate exchange rate of sterling attracted overseas buyers to British manufactured goods to the advantage of British industry which was already being generally helped by the expanding home market.

The most logical outcome should have been a drop in the prices of manufactured goods. A rise in production should have absorbed fixed overheads leaving only marginal costs to be borne by ex-factory prices of such goods. Even a bigger profit margin should have left the manufacturers with sufficient cushion to reduce prices.

The prolonged high interest rates have reversed this natural growth of the British economy with dire consequences for the future. Meanwhile, foreign markets which slip out of their hands will be difficult to regain.

(d) The changes in Europe are transfusing more blood to the already robust economy of West Germany, or should one say Germany. The secondary negative effects enumerated earlier may augur ill for the British economy.

The present government may unsuccessfully manipulate the timing of the much needed drop in interest rates, but the next government, if it is Conservative, is going to inherit colossal problems from the erstwhile government of its own party.

The point which emerges from all this is a very important lesson for policy makers all over the world. Interest as a tool for controlling national economy meddles with the very concept of a free market economy. No economy run on the philosophy of interest-related capital can genuinely be declared to be free when its government has all the power to raise or lower interest rates.

The Islamic economic system provides no such measure of exploitation to the government.

OTHER EVILS OF INTEREST

Perhaps it will not be out of place to mention a few other aspects of interest. The inter-bank interest rate is only paid on wholesale deposits and not on savings account to the average depositor. Despite the compounding effect of interest, the return obtained on a small deposit is far below the true purchasing power of money. Although short term rates fluctuate, in the long run, interest earned on deposits is below the inflation rate. On the other hand, a similar principal sum invested in some business venture has potential for growth in real terms.

In an interest-motivated society, owners of capital are always ready to lend money without investigating the ability of the borrower to repay. On the borrower side, there are few who seriously consider their repayment ability. Little do they know that borrowing from the loan-sharks, the likes of Shylock and prestigious finance houses and banks, is tantamount to borrowing from their own future earnings. It encourages the habit of living beyond one's resources. It results in over-spending and an increasing inability to repay and honour one's pledges. Such societies give an unrealistic boost to production to meet consumer demand.

This evil aspect of interest run economies has to be further elaborated and illustrated.

In a society where *keeping up with the Joneses* becomes an obsession, the obsession is largely abetted by advertisements of the latest models of this and that. An introduction is provided to the general public of the luxurious lifestyle of the rich by displaying the latest design of sofas, luxurious chalets fitted with the most modern kitchen and bathroom appliances and gadgets.

People with less means available to buy all that they want are willy-nilly turned to false plastic money to fulfil their desires. Obviously, this means that they buy far more than their earnings. If this money was to be repaid even without interest, it would be tantamount to increasing one's buying capacity at present at the cost of lowering the same in the future.

If a man earns $1,000 per month and goes shopping for expensive articles with the help of borrowed money, say, to the tune of $40,000, his ability to repay will be determined by his net savings per month. Let us suppose that he can barely make the ends meet at $600. This will leave him with net savings of $400 per month. He will have to live within that tight budget for the next 100 months to repay the loan arising from his spending spree of $40,000 without interest. What he has, therefore, done is to borrow money from his future 100 months (i.e., 8 years and 4 months) to spend at the beginning of this period. The only advantage he has gained is to satiate his impatience and fulfil his desire instead of waiting for the next eight years or so.

But if he has also to pay interest on his $40,000 borrowing, his financial position will be far worse than the one discussed in the previous example. At an average rate of, say, 14 per cent, his total loan from his own future earnings would work out to be far greater than the actual money he borrowed. This will lower his ability to repay and lengthen the period of repayment to a considerable degree. Such a person will have to suffer patiently for some 20 years or so as a punishment for his impatience making monthly repayments of about $500 i.e. a total of about $120,000 to repay the loan with compound interest.

The loss is most certainly of the borrower and not of the lender. The lender is part of a very powerful system of exploitation which guarantees, after allowance for inflation and loan loss, that the lender ends up with more money in his pocket.

With inflation, the situation of the borrower in question will further worsen. His buying power will continue to decrease so that if it was difficult to live within $600, it will be impossible to cope with the same as time goes by. There are but a few who are fortunate enough to receive annual increments equal to the rate of inflation.

To further aggravate the situation, in a society where people become more pleasure-seeking, it is impossible for them to wait for a long period of sheer austerity imposed on them by themselves after a few moments of reckless spending. More money is borrowed with greater recklessness and the expenditure is increased far beyond the means of income. In fact, decades of one's future earnings with ever increasing debt-servicing and concomitant problems are pledged to the lending banks and financial institutions.

As a whole, such economies are inevitably heading for a major crisis. You cannot limitlessly pledge your future to the present before reaching the precipice of financial crisis arising from irresponsible spending which then raises the rate of inflation. To combat inflation by raising interest rates in the hope of making less money available for expenditure, is bound to trigger a chain of events culminating in economic recession.

It is bad enough at the national level but when the same factors create a recession in most countries of the world, a global recession looms large on mankind. Such global recessions pave the path for global wars and gigantic catastrophes.

Bankruptcies and liquidations begin to increase. Trade and commerce enters into the doldrums. The underlying unemployment rate begins to creep up. Real estate businesses start to collapse. The resultant overall frustration in every area aids and abets homelessness, deprivation, fraud and crime. If this happens, it should not surprise anyone, least of all the stout champions of capitalism.

In the capitalist economy the situation is not limited to private individuals being financed beyond their means to repay. In fact, the future of the entire industry is jeopardised at the cost of temporary gains. To begin with, of course, the industry of the country benefits to a great degree. This helps in lowering the price of homemade goods. The transfer of money to an individual not only boosts his buying power but also has an impact on the productivity of the national industry. An increase in demand is followed by more production and with rising production, lower costs are achieved. It gives the national industry a competitive edge in international markets. All seems silvery and rosy. Then comes the hangover.

When, because of impatience and excessive spending beyond its means, the society as a whole is deeply indebted to the banks, the buying power of the entire society gradually comes to the end of its tether. Such industry has no alternative but to seek larger foreign markets to remain afloat and competitive. The smaller the country's economic base the sooner it reaches the end of the blind alley. The larger the economic base, the longer will be the period of ultimate realisation of the impending crisis.

Let us turn to the USA to see how things may work there. Without doubt, it is a country with the largest home-market to support its industry, so much so that some economists believe that even if America is cut off from the international community, the broad base of the home-market would guarantee the survival of its industry. But such economists do not take account of other related factors. If you apply, for instance, the case discussed earlier to the America scenario, you will certainly begin to see that there can be no logical conclusion other than the one drawn earlier. It is only a question of time. With a huge budget deficit and trillions of dollars in outstanding debts, the USA as a whole has already overspent and the American public is under very heavy debt to its own future. The buying power of the nation as a whole is bound to slow down or lending houses will have to go bankrupt. It is only a question of size. But the inevitable laws of nature must operate and apply equally to all similar situations.

In a hot summer, pools and ponds warm up quickly to the ambient situation but it takes a bit longer for the lakes. Likewise, smaller seas get warmed up sooner than the larger ones. Yet, they all follow the same inevitable fate. It takes the Pacific Ocean so long to warm up that by the time it reaches that stage, winter is already set in most of the countries bordering on this gigantic mass of water. That is why the climate is more temperate than that of land bordering smaller oceans.

Such also is the case of the oceans of the economy. The very philosophy of spending from borrowed money is basically so crooked that to expect straight-forward honest results would be madness.

Another important factor should also be brought to the focus of one's attention. When industry and the national economy reach choking point, poorer and less developed countries face ever-increasing danger of suffering from the fallout of the explosive situation of the developed and advanced countries.

It begins with greater urgency by political leaders of the industrialised countries to sell more goods in the markets to save industry from slowing down and to maintain the standard of living of its people. The problem they face are twofold:

(a) the people are accustomed to modern comforts; and,

(b) for the sake of its own survival, industry continues to excite them with new inventions and devices which bring comfort and pleasure to their homes.

No political government can survive the pressure of a public which continues to demand higher living standards. The economy must be kept afloat at whatever cost possible.

Obviously the Third World countries have to be bled more than before for the maintenance of artificially high standards of life in the advanced countries. What about the new challenge of the reshaping economies of the USSR and Eastern Europe and what about the growing need for foreign markets by the newly emerging capitalist states of the erstwhile communist world? Again, what about the havoc which the western media is already playing with the desires and ambitions of the poor and almost destitute common people of socialist and Third World countries? All these factors put together will certainly not change the face of the earth for the better.

INTEREST AS A THREAT TO PEACE

This is the import of the warning so powerfully delivered to mankind 1400 years ago by the Holy Quran with regard to the holocaust to which the interest based economies would ultimately lead mankind.

ٱلَّذِينَ يَأْكُلُونَ ٱلرِّبَوٰا۟ لَا يَقُومُونَ إِلَّا كَمَا يَقُومُ ٱلَّذِى يَتَخَبَّطُهُ ٱلشَّيْطَٰنُ مِنَ ٱلْمَسِّ ذَٰلِكَ بِأَنَّهُمْ قَالُوٓا۟ إِنَّمَا ٱلْبَيْعُ مِثْلُ ٱلرِّبَوٰا۟ وَأَحَلَّ ٱللَّهُ ٱلْبَيْعَ وَحَرَّمَ ٱلرِّبَوٰا۟ فَمَن جَآءَهُۥ مَوْعِظَةٌ مِّن رَّبِّهِۦ فَٱنتَهَىٰ فَلَهُۥ مَا سَلَفَ وَأَمْرُهُۥٓ إِلَى ٱللَّهِ وَمَنْ عَادَ فَأُو۟لَٰٓئِكَ أَصْحَٰبُ ٱلنَّارِ هُمْ فِيهَا خَٰلِدُونَ ۝ يَمْحَقُ ٱللَّهُ ٱلرِّبَوٰا۟ وَيُرْبِى ٱلصَّدَقَٰتِ وَٱللَّهُ لَا يُحِبُّ كُلَّ كَفَّارٍ أَثِيمٍ ۝ إِنَّ ٱلَّذِينَ ءَامَنُوا۟ وَعَمِلُوا۟ ٱلصَّٰلِحَٰتِ وَأَقَامُوا۟ ٱلصَّلَوٰةَ وَءَاتَوُا۟ ٱلزَّكَوٰةَ لَهُمْ أَجْرُهُمْ عِندَ رَبِّهِمْ وَلَا خَوْفٌ عَلَيْهِمْ وَلَا هُمْ يَحْزَنُونَ ۝ يَٰٓأَيُّهَا ٱلَّذِينَ ءَامَنُوا۟ ٱتَّقُوا۟ ٱللَّهَ وَذَرُوا۟ مَا بَقِىَ مِنَ ٱلرِّبَوٰٓا۟ إِن كُنتُم مُّؤْمِنِينَ ۝ فَإِن لَّمْ تَفْعَلُوا۟ فَأْذَنُوا۟ بِحَرْبٍ مِّنَ ٱللَّهِ وَرَسُولِهِۦ وَإِن تُبْتُمْ فَلَكُمْ رُءُوسُ

أَمْوَالِكُمْ لَا تَظْلِمُونَ وَلَا تُظْلَمُونَ ۞ وَإِن كَانَ
ذُو عُسْرَةٍ فَنَظِرَةٌ إِلَىٰ مَيْسَرَةٍ ۚ وَأَن تَصَدَّقُوا خَيْرٌ لَّكُمْ
إِن كُنتُمْ تَعْلَمُونَ ۞

*Those who devour interest stand like one whom Satan has
smitten with insanity. That is so because they keep saying: The
business of buying and selling is also like lending money on
interest: whereas Allah has made buying and selling lawful and
has made the taking of interest unlawful. Remember, therefore,
that he who desists because of the admonition that has come to
him from the Lord, may retain what he has received in the past;
and his affair is committed to Allah. But those who revert to the
practice, they are the inmates of the Fire, therein shall they
abide. Allah will wipe out interest and foster charity. And Allah
loves not confirmed disbelievers and arch-sinners. Surely,
those who believe and act righteously and observe Prayer and
pay the Zakat, shall have their reward with their Lord. No fear
shall come on them nor shall they grieve. O ye who believe!
fear Allah and relinquish what remains of interest, if you are
believers. But if you do not do it, then beware of war from
Allah and His Messenger; and if you repent, then you shall
have your original sums; thus you shall not wrong, nor shall
you be wronged. And if any debtor be in straitened
circumstances, then grant him respite till a time of ease. And
that you remit charity shall be better for you, if only you knew.
(Ch. 2: Al-Baqarah: 276-281)*

The warning about a war from God in the verses just cited
means that the laws of nature governed by God would begin to
punish the capitalist society when the factors which have been
discussed earlier ultimately lead man to economic imbalance
and warfare. Disorders, disturbances and wars always follow
exploitation and usurpation of the rights of the poor. *We warn*

you about a war with God and His Messenger means that the state which thrives on interest would inevitably end up in a situation where the nations will rise in arms against each other.

Time does not permit me to elaborate this aspect of interest. In the Holy Quran, verses prohibiting interest always follow verses on warfare. This indicates the inter-relation of interest and war. Those who are familiar with the history of the First and Second World Wars would remember that capitalism played a disastrous role in not only causing but also prolonging those wars.

PROHIBITION ON HOARDING OF WEALTH

Islam rejects every form of exploitation and unfair means like the hoarding of wealth, capital, commodities and supplies which set in motion spiralling prices and end in general inflation. The Holy Quran states:

يَٰٓأَيُّهَا ٱلَّذِينَ ءَامَنُوٓاْ إِنَّ كَثِيرًا مِّنَ ٱلۡأَحۡبَارِ وَٱلرُّهۡبَانِ لَيَأۡكُلُونَ أَمۡوَٰلَ ٱلنَّاسِ بِٱلۡبَٰطِلِ وَيَصُدُّونَ عَن سَبِيلِ ٱللَّهِ وَٱلَّذِينَ يَكۡنِزُونَ ٱلذَّهَبَ وَٱلۡفِضَّةَ وَلَا يُنفِقُونَهَا فِي سَبِيلِ ٱللَّهِ فَبَشِّرۡهُم بِعَذَابٍ أَلِيمٖ ۝ يَوۡمَ يُحۡمَىٰ عَلَيۡهَا فِي نَارِ جَهَنَّمَ فَتُكۡوَىٰ بِهَا جِبَاهُهُمۡ وَجُنُوبُهُمۡ وَظُهُورُهُمۡ هَٰذَا مَا كَنَزۡتُمۡ لِأَنفُسِكُمۡ فَذُوقُواْ مَا كُنتُمۡ تَكۡنِزُونَ ۝

O ye who believe! Surely, many of the priests and monks devour the wealth of men by false means and turn men away from the way of Allah. And those who hoard up gold and silver and spend it not in the way of Allah—give to them the tidings of a painful punishment. On the day when it shall be made hot in the fire of Hell, and their foreheads and their sides and their backs shall be branded therewith and it shall be said to them: 'This is what you treasured up for yourselves; so now taste what you used to treasure up.' (Ch. 9: Al-Tauba: 34-35)

Yet Islam grants freedom to individuals to earn money by any lawful means within the Islamic code of economic behaviour. Thus there is the freedom and right for individuals to possess property and enter into private enterprise.

In shaping the economies of their countries, the focus of attention of most governments is on how a member of society earns his livelihood. Taxation is imposed on sales turnover, profit from trade and commerce and earnings from employment. Having done that, there is little further interference in the financial affairs of the individual. Broadly speaking, national interest is limited to the income side but what or how an individual spends his earned or hoarded income is no concern of most states. If he so pleases, an individual may flush his income or wealth down the drain. He may acquire a lavish and extravagant lifestyle or, despite his wealth, he may live in hardship if he chooses. It is no business of the state to interfere with how he intends to spend or employ his money.

Nevertheless, this is an area where religions do step in and, by way of admonishment or counsel, not only tell an individual how he should earn his daily bread but also guide him as to how he should or should not spend what he has earned. Most injunctions relating to expenditure are primarily moral and spiritual guidelines. For instance, when Islam prohibits expenditure on drinking and gambling and over-indulgence in various pursuits of pleasure, though such injunctions may not directly aim at shaping the expenditure budget, they are a by-product of the moral and spiritual teachings of a religion. In capitalist economies, such injunctions are considered as an invasion of privacy and an interference with the right of an individual to spend as he or she pleases. But this attitude is not new to man.

According to the Holy Quran, earlier people and civilizations displayed exactly the same attitude towards religions which sometimes resulted in a debate as to the justification of religions to interfere with people's personal affairs. When Shuaib[as], an ancient Prophet, attempted to educate the people of Midian on how best they should spend their wealth and what they should refrain from, he was rebuked by his people:

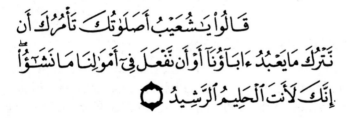

They replied, 'O Shu'aib, does thy Prayer bid that we should leave what our fathers worshipped, or that we cease to do whatever we may please with our wealth? Thou art indeed very intelligent and right-minded'. (Ch. 11; Hud:88)

SIMPLE LIFESTYLE

Islam advocates a simple life style. It prohibits extravagance and encourages expenditure:

وَلَا تَجْعَلْ يَدَكَ مَغْلُولَةً إِلَىٰ عُنُقِكَ وَلَا تَبْسُطْهَا كُلَّ ٱلْبَسْطِ
فَتَقْعُدَ مَلُومًا مَّحْسُورًا ۝

*Keep not thy hand chained to thy neck, nor stretch it out an
entire stretching, lest thou sit down blamed or exhausted. (Ch.
17: Bani-Israel:30)*

وَءَاتِ ذَا ٱلْقُرْبَىٰ حَقَّهُ
وَٱلْمِسْكِينَ وَٱبْنَ ٱلسَّبِيلِ وَلَا تُبَذِّرْ تَبْذِيرًا ۝ إِنَّ ٱلْمُبَذِّرِينَ
كَانُوٓا۟ إِخْوَٰنَ ٱلشَّيَٰطِينِ وَكَانَ ٱلشَّيْطَٰنُ لِرَبِّهِۦ كَفُورًا ۝

*Give thou to the kinsman his due, and to the poor and the
wayfarer, and squander not thy wealth extravagantly. Verily,
the extravagant are brothers of Satan, and Satan is ungrateful
to his Lord. (Ch. 17: Bani-Israel: 27-28)*

MATRIMONIAL EXPENSE

The style of marriage ceremonies between the rich and poor
families can be a sensitive area which may cause terrible anguish
and heartache to the poor parents with daughters of marriageable
age.

Lavish wedding receptions with a grand display of pomp,
opulence and pageantry are roundly condemned in Islam. In fact,
we observe from the early history of Islam that wedding
ceremonies were so simple as to appear colourless events in the
sight of many. Although influenced by the customs and tradition
of the surrounding societies, many innovations and malpractices
have crept into Muslim marriage styles of the rich, and basic
formal ceremony remains exactly the same – plain, simple and
inexpensive for the rich and poor alike.

The announcement of marriage i.e. NIKAH is pronounced mostly in mosques in the presence of all and sundry and where the rich and poor are gathered alike. The mosque is a house of worship and is no place for pompous display.

As far as the reception feasts and other related expressions of joy are concerned, the rich are very firmly warned that any feast to which the poor have not been invited is cursed in the sight of God. Thus, amongst the most well dressed richest members of society, you will find the most poorly dressed poor people mixing freely with the rich – a grand eye opener for the rich and a special opportunity for the poor to taste some of the delicacies, fruits and dishes of the wealthy people.

ACCEPTING INVITATIONS FROM THE POOR

The rich and the more highly placed people in the social order are strongly advised to accept the invitation of the poorest should such a person invite them to his humble home. Of course, it is not a must for the rich who may have their own prior commitments and difficulties, but it was a constant practice of the Holy Founder of Islam to accept the invitation from even the very poorest. All those who love him as their holy Master are very proudly influenced by this admonition. Although in contemporary society, to always accept all such invitations would place the rich with no other preoccupation, but to eat with the poor, the spirit of this injunction can still be kept alive by occasionally accepting such invitations.

We have already stated that wine and gambling is prohibited. Lavish expenditure on revelry is therefore obviated. This general admonition condemning lavish expenditure and a high flying lifestyle applies not only to marriages, but all spheres of human activity. The beauty of this teaching is that it is not enforced by compulsion but is prompted by words of advice and love.

MODERATION IN EATING HABITS

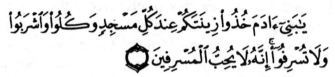

O children of Adam! look to your adornment at every time and place of worship, and eat and drink but exceed not the bounds; surely, He does not love those who exceed the bounds. (Ch. 7: Al-A'raf: 32)

Time does not permit me to dwell on the need to wage a war against hunger to which end the prevention of food wastage is an important stepping stone. Nonetheless, I shall briefly refer to this subject later.

BORROWING MONEY

As far as borrowing money for the basic necessities of life is concerned, Islam strongly and repeatedly propounds that loans for exigencies and emergencies be without interest. Those with means should help those who need financial assistance. It is also clearly laid down that if the debtor is unable to return the loan in due time because of his straitened circumstances, he must be granted a greater period of grace. Close relatives may assist a debtor. Debts can be recovered from a deceased person's estate. Zakat can also be used to alleviate the financial obligations of one burdened with debt. If the rich can write the loan off, it would be better still in the sight of God. Nevertheless, a debtor who can afford to return the loan must fulfil his promise in repaying the loan within its appointed term and should add an ex-gratia amount thereon. This is not, however, obligatory nor predetermined since it would then fall under the broad definition of interest. The Holy Quran teaches:

يَٰٓأَيُّهَا ٱلَّذِينَ ءَامَنُوٓاْ إِذَا تَدَايَنتُم بِدَيْنٍ إِلَىٰٓ أَجَلٍ مُّسَمًّى
فَٱكْتُبُوهُ وَلْيَكْتُب بَّيْنَكُمْ كَاتِبٌۢ بِٱلْعَدْلِ وَلَا يَأْبَ
كَاتِبٌ أَن يَكْتُبَ كَمَا عَلَّمَهُ ٱللَّهُ فَلْيَكْتُبْ وَلْيُمْلِلِ
ٱلَّذِي عَلَيْهِ ٱلْحَقُّ وَلْيَتَّقِ ٱللَّهَ رَبَّهُۥ وَلَا يَبْخَسْ مِنْهُ شَيْـًٔا
فَإِن كَانَ ٱلَّذِي عَلَيْهِ ٱلْحَقُّ سَفِيهًا أَوْ ضَعِيفًا أَوْ لَا يَسْتَطِيعُ
أَن يُمِلَّ هُوَ فَلْيُمْلِلْ وَلِيُّهُۥ بِٱلْعَدْلِ وَٱسْتَشْهِدُواْ شَهِيدَيْنِ
مِن رِّجَالِكُمْ فَإِن لَّمْ يَكُونَا رَجُلَيْنِ فَرَجُلٌ وَٱمْرَأَتَانِ
مِمَّن تَرْضَوْنَ مِنَ ٱلشُّهَدَآءِ أَن تَضِلَّ إِحْدَىٰهُمَا فَتُذَكِّرَ
إِحْدَىٰهُمَا ٱلْأُخْرَىٰ وَلَا يَأْبَ ٱلشُّهَدَآءُ إِذَا مَا دُعُواْ وَلَا تَسْـَٔمُوٓاْ
أَن تَكْتُبُوهُ صَغِيرًا أَوْ كَبِيرًا إِلَىٰٓ أَجَلِهِۦ ذَٰلِكُمْ أَقْسَطُ
عِندَ ٱللَّهِ وَأَقْوَمُ لِلشَّهَٰدَةِ وَأَدْنَىٰٓ أَلَّا تَرْتَابُوٓاْ إِلَّآ أَن تَكُونَ
تِجَٰرَةً حَاضِرَةً تُدِيرُونَهَا بَيْنَكُمْ فَلَيْسَ عَلَيْكُمْ جُنَاحٌ
أَلَّا تَكْتُبُوهَا وَأَشْهِدُوٓاْ إِذَا تَبَايَعْتُمْ وَلَا يُضَآرَّ كَاتِبٌ
وَلَا شَهِيدٌ وَإِن تَفْعَلُواْ فَإِنَّهُۥ فُسُوقٌۢ بِكُمْ وَٱتَّقُواْ
ٱللَّهَ وَيُعَلِّمُكُمُ ٱللَّهُ وَٱللَّهُ بِكُلِّ شَيْءٍ عَلِيمٌ ۝

201

وَإِن كُنتُمْ عَلَىٰ سَفَرٍ وَلَمْ تَجِدُواْ كَاتِبًا فَرِهَٰنٌ مَّقْبُوضَةٌ

فَإِنْ أَمِنَ بَعْضُكُم بَعْضًا فَلْيُؤَدِّ ٱلَّذِى ٱؤْتُمِنَ أَمَٰنَتَهُۥ وَلْيَتَّقِ

ٱللَّهَ رَبَّهُۥ وَلَا تَكْتُمُواْ ٱلشَّهَٰدَةَ وَمَن يَكْتُمْهَا فَإِنَّهُۥٓ

ءَاثِمٌ قَلْبُهُۥ وَٱللَّهُ بِمَا تَعْمَلُونَ عَلِيمٌ

O ye who believe, when you take a loan, one from another, for a
term, reduce the transaction *to writing; and let a scribe record*
it in your presence faithfully. And no scribe should refuse to set
it down in *writing, because Allah has taught him, so he should*
write. And let him who undertakes the liability dictate; and he
should fear Allah, his Lord, and not diminish anything
therefrom. But if the person incurring the liability should be of
defective intelligence, or a minor, or unable to dictate then let
his guardian dictate faithfully. And procure two witnesses from
among your men; and if two men be not available, then one
man and two women, of such as you like as witnesses, so that if
either of the two women should be in danger of forgetting, the
other may refresh her memory. And the witnesses should not
refuse to testify when they are called upon to do so. Whether
the transaction be large of small, do not be disinclined to write
it down, together with the appointed time of payment. This is
more equitable in the sight of Allah, makes testimony surer and
is more likely to exclude doubts. In case of ready transactions
when goods and money pass from hand to hand, it shall be no
sin for you to reduce them to writing. And have witnesses when
you buy or sell. And let no harm befall a scribe or a witness
and if you do such a thing it shall certainly be disobedience on
your part. And be ever mindful of your duty to Allah. And Allah
grants you knowledge and Allah knows all things well. And
should you be on a journey and not find a scribe, the
alternative is a pledge with possession. And when one of you

202

entrusts something to another, then let him who is entrusted render back his trust when he is called upon to do so, and let him be mindful of his duty to Allah, his Lord. And conceal not testimony; and whoever conceals it is one whose heart is certainly sinful. Remember Allah knows well all that you do. (Ch. 2: Al-Baqarah: 283-284)

It is very important to remember that these verses have been completely misapplied and used entirely out of context by those medieval minded scholars who insist that according to Islam a single woman's testimony is not sufficient. They say that for each legal requirement, two women's testimony is essential in comparison to one man's wherever one man's testimony is sufficient. Having totally misconstrued the meaning of these verses, they have falsely envisaged the role of male and female witnesses in Islamic jurisprudence. They think that when the Holy Quran requires one man as a witness, the testimony of two women will be substituted in lieu thereof; where two men's testimony is required, four women's testimony will be required; and where four male persons are required as witnesses, eight women will be required to testify the same.

This concept is so unrealistic and alien to Quranic teachings that one is exasperated to see such medievalist stance on this important judicial issue.

The following points should be noted regarding these verses:

1. The verses do not at all require both women to testify.

2. The role of the second women is clearly specified and confined to be that of an assistant.

3. If the second woman who is not testifying finds any part of the statement of the witness as indicative of the witness not having fully understood the spirit of the bargain, she may remind her and assist the witness in revising her understanding or refreshing her memory.

4. It is entirely up to that woman who is testifying to agree or disagree with her assistant. Her testimony remains as a single independent testimony and in case she does not agree with her partner, her's would be the last word.

After this brief digression, let us return to the subject proper.

Reducing loan agreements to writing with the debtor dictating the terms in the presence of witnesses for the sale of goods; being absolutely honest and mindful of God in fulfilling one's undertakings; and trustees discharging the trust honestly form the essential features of contractual obligations in Islam.

It should be noted that in an economy where lending tends to be interest free, the lender will not unnecessarily flush the economy with loans and credit. Therefore, the buying power of society will remain within realistic limits and related to the present. The tendency to borrow from the future will automatically be averted. An industry founded on this platform is bound to remain solid and able to survive the vicissitudes of economic hazards.

Public wealth should not circulate in the higher plane of the wealthy but should flow in the direction of the lower plane of the poor.

Islam cultivates a life style which is simple and, though strictly speaking not austere, is in no way glamorous and profligate to the extent that it begins to offend the poorer sections, causes heartache and widens the distance between the two sections of society.

ECONOMIC CLASS DIFFERENCES

It should be well understood here that classes are created not merely by the accumulation of wealth in fewer hands but by the division of capital among owners and the labourer or by landlords and those who cultivate the land.

There is much more to the creation of a class society. It is impossible to mention all the factors and how they jointly and severally contribute towards the creation of classes.

A study of traditional Indian society should provide an excellent example of the existence of a class structure evolved over thousands of years. The entire course of this evolution was influenced not by the distribution of wealth but by racial, social, religious and political factors. A long history of invasions, internal strife, struggle for survival and domination is preserved in the caste system of India which has carved so many classes.

Marx took serious note of this situation. In a series of letters to New York's *Herald Tribune*, he considered the state of society in India as being at variance with the philosophy of scientific socialism. He concluded that the existence of this caste system rendered India the least likely country to turn to communism.

From the Islamic point of view, the creation of classes in a society begins to hurt only when there is no code of ethics governing the way money should be spent. Imagine a society where people live a simple life, with no lavish expenditure on their clothing, food or accommodation and where the contrasts in the style of life are not so distinctly marked. No matter how much wealth may have accumulated in a few hands, it is the expenditure which hurts rather than the accumulation of wealth in a few hands. It only begins to hurt when it is unevenly or imprudently spent or wasted. It is the luxurious life style of the rich and all its concomitant flair, display, pomp and pageantry, which, when observed from the lowly vantage point of the miserable and suffering poor struggling for survival, the uneven distribution of wealth begins to create unbridgeable chasms between the two.

Therefore, Islam does not unduly interfere with the freedom of an individual to earn and to keep. On the contrary, it promotes and encourages the private sector more than the public sector. It lays down a well-defined code concerning the style of life which when followed to the letter and spirit, would make life as a whole refreshingly simple for all.

As this aspect of Islamic economic philosophy has been discussed earlier, we need not dwell upon it further.

ISLAMIC LAW OF INHERITANCE

The Islamic law of inheritance also plays an important role in the distribution of wealth from the deceased to his dependents. Prescribed shares must be distributed amongst parents, spouses, children, relatives and kith and kin. One cannot deprive them of their rights of inheritance granted to them by God unless there be a good reason, the validity of which will be determined by the courts in an Islamic state and not the individual. At best, a person can bequeath a maximum of one third of his disposable possessions to other people or societies of his choice. (*Al-Nisa:* 8-13). These measures effectively prevent the accumulation of wealth in fewer hands.

Under the Islamic law of inheritance, the rule of primogeniture or those which involve the impartiality of estates or the unrestricted power of bequest at the whimsical pleasure of the testator are prevented. Both movable and immovable property continues to be divided and sub-divided in each generation and within three or four generations, even large estates are parcelled out into small holdings so that no permanent division is created among the people by a monopoly of the ownership of the land.

PROHIBITION OF BRIBERY

وَلَا تَأْكُلُوٓاْ أَمْوَٰلَكُم بَيْنَكُم
بِٱلْبَٰطِلِ وَتُدْلُواْ بِهَآ إِلَى ٱلْحُكَّامِ لِتَأْكُلُواْ فَرِيقًا مِّنْ
أَمْوَٰلِ ٱلنَّاسِ بِٱلْإِثْمِ وَأَنتُمْ تَعْلَمُونَ ۝

Do not devour your wealth among yourselves through falsehood, and offer it not as a bribe to the authorities that you may knowingly devour a part of the wealth of other people with injustice. (Ch. 2: Al-Baqarah: 189)

Again I have to omit this aspect which is particularly noticeable in the form of corruption and bribery in the Third World countries but shall refer to it under individual peace.

COMMERCIAL ETHICS

Islam neither disagrees with capitalism nor totally rejects scientific socialism but retains their good points and attitudes.

Following are some examples where 1400 years ago, Islam advised a code of sound commercial ethics which modern man has ultimately discovered the hard way:

(1) Islamic commercial relations are based upon absolute trust and honesty. *(Al-Baqarah: 283-284)*

(2) Islam forbids the use of false weights and the giving of short measure. *(Al-Tatfif: 2-4)*

(3) Traders are forbidden from selling defective articles or

goods which are rotten or rendered useless. A trader must not try to conceal any defects of an article which he offers for sale. *(Muslim)* If such an article is sold without the buyer's prior knowledge, he has a right to return it when he discovers the fault or defect and obtain a refund. *(Hadith)*

(4) A trader is prohibited from charging different rates to different customers though he has discretion to offer concessional discounts to any customer(s). He is free to fix any rate he considers reasonable. *(Bukhari and Muslim)*

(5) Islam forbids false competition or cartels which create false competition. It also forbids the inflating of prices at an auction by false bids or procuring bogus offers to deceive a prospective buyer. *(Bukhari and Muslim)*

(6) Likewise, Islam recommends that the purchase and sale of goods take place in the open preferably in the presence of witnesses and that the buyer be put on alert on what he purchases. *(Al-Baqarah: 283-284; Muslim)*

To cut a long story short, Islam adopts the strategy of decreasing the gap between the rich and poor by:

(a) imposing certain inhibitions as have already been mentioned before e.g. drinking, gambling, etc.

(b) prohibiting the hoarding of wealth and its accumulation by interest.

(c) encouraging private enterprise

(d) promoting the rapid circulation of wealth

(e) the use of repeated admonition, persuasion and instruction appealing to the nobility in man to voluntarily adopt a humble, meek and simple lifestyle which is not too far removed from the reach of a poor man.

The object of this exercise is to make man more sensitive to the feeling of others and to choke and kill in him the bestial and sadistic impulses. A Holy War in the real sense of the words is waged against vanity, hypocrisy, superficiality, snobbishness, pride and arrogance. All that is refined and noble in man is brought out and he is made so sensitive to the sufferings of others that he sometimes feels it to be a crime to live in luxury and comfort while others suffer and eke out an existence of misery and wretchedness.

Of course, such highly cultured people who form the vanguard of sublime human values are always in a small minority but the overall consciousness in society for the well-being of others is raised to such a respectable level that it becomes impossible for them to remain concerned only with their own necessities and comforts, oblivious of the miserable state of the less fortunate section of society. Their concern in life no longer remains introvert. They learn to live with a wider consciousness of life around them. They feel uneasy unless they materially participate in ameliorating the sufferings and raising the standards of life of others.

The characteristics of such society of believers is described in one of the earliest verses in the Holy Quran and cited previously in this address:

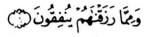

And spend out of what We have provided for them.
(Ch. 2: Al-Baqarah:4)

BASIC NEEDS

In the previous section on socio-economic peace, we have seen how Islam has revolutionised the concept of alms for the poor and needy. As far as the rights of individuals in the national cake are concerned, the Holy Quran gives us the criteria whereby we can determine how much wealth, which should have flowed to the common man, has been transferred into the hands of a few capitalists:

Those in whose wealth there is a recognised right for one who asks for help *and for one who does not. (Ch. 70: Al-Ma'arij: 25-26)*

These verses address the rich and remind them that part of their wealth comprises that which by right belongs to the beggar and the destitute.

How can we judge that an imbalance has arisen in society by the transfer of rights due to the poor into the hands of a few rich people? The yardstick for this criteria is certain guaranteed rights.

According to Islam, there are four basic needs of man which must be fulfilled. The Holy Quran states:

It is provided *for thee that thou wilt not hunger therein, nor wilt thou be naked. And that thou wilt not thirst therein, nor wilt thou be exposed to the sun. (Ch. 20: Ta-ha: 119-120)*

Thus, Islam establishes minimum rights in the form of a four point charter by defining the basic needs which a state should procure:

1. Food
2. Clothing
3. Water
4. Shelter

Even in England and the United States of America, there are hundreds of thousands of people without shelter and those who have to dip into dustbins to find some scrap of food to satiate their hunger.

Such ugly scenes expose the inherent weakness of the capitalist society and bring to the surface the symptoms of a deep underlying malaise. Materialism in its ultimate form breeds selfishness and callousness and dulls human sensibilities to the sufferings of others.

Of course there are even uglier scenes of misery caused by extreme poverty in most Third World countries, but then society as a whole is poor and the countries themselves are run on the same capitalist principles. Hence, it is not a question of whether the majority population of such countries is Christian, Jewish, Hindu, Muslim or pagan – the system essentially remains capitalist in nature.

Crime flourishes and vice prospers in the ghettos which are a blemish on the face of humanity itself in the so-called developed nations of the world.

There are regions in Africa and in other countries where even portable water is not available to large sections of society. If you even get one square meal a day, you consider yourself lucky. Water becomes an every day problem. There are countries in the world which have all the potential and resources to change their lot within a matter of a few years without feeling the pinch themselves. Yet such countries do not care to commit their resources to ameliorate the sufferings of the hundreds of millions of people in poorer countries.

From the Islamic point of view, this question is very important. According to Islam, it is not just the sufferings of one man for which the society of that country is responsible but it is the sufferings of any human being in any society, that is to say, humanity which has neither geographical boundaries, nor colour, creed or political demarcations. Humanity at large is responsible and human beings as such are answerable to God. Whenever famine, malnutrition or sufferings from any other natural disaster strikes any community, it must be treated as a human problem. All societies and states of the world must participate to help mitigate the sufferings.

It is a shame that despite all the advancement in science and technology, the elimination of thirst and hunger has not received the attention it needs. There must be a system whereby the sum total of human wealth can be quickly and efficiently channelled to those areas where hunger strikes or famine plays havoc with humanity or wherever people have been rendered destitute and homeless.

Governments have both national and international responsibilities. These responsibilities on the national level are to fulfil the basic needs of each member of society by ensuring that all are fed adequately, clothed, and provided with water and shelter. The international duty, to which further reference will be made later, is to fully participate in pooling resources to meet the challenges of widescale natural disasters or man-made calamities and to help such countries as are by themselves incapable of appropriately handling the crisis.

As such, it is the duty of the state to set the matters aright by transferring back to the beggars and poor people what truly belongs to them. So the four fundamental requirements of food, clothing, water, and shelter, will have preference over all other considerations.

In other words, in a truly Islamic state there can neither be a beggar nor a destitute without food, clothing, water and shelter.

These overall requirements being guaranteed, the minimum responsibility of the state is discharged. But the society as a whole is supposed to do much more than this.

Man cannot live by bread alone is a profound maxim. Add to this the requirement of healthy water, appropriate clothing and a roof over his head. Yet, all these requirements put together cannot make life complete. Man will always be in search of something more than the bare necessities of life. So there has to be something else to be done by the society to remove the drabness, add some colour to the life of the poor and to make them share some of the pleasures of the wealthy.

Again, it is not enough that the more fortunate members of society should share their wealth with the less fortunate members of society. But it is also necessary that they share the miseries that go with poverty which afflicts a very large number of human beings. There has to be some system of the intermixing of the rich and the poor whereby, of their own volition, the upper layers of society mix with the people at lower levels to personally witness what it really means to live in poverty. Islam proposes many measures which make it impossible for the various classes to be compartmentalised and insulated in their own spheres. We have briefly mentioned some of these measures earlier.

WORSHIP AS A MEANS OF ECONOMIC UNITY

1) Commencing with the affirmation of there being no god other than the One God, establishes the unity of God and His creation thereby uniting mankind under the Almighty Creator.

2) The five daily Prayers which are to be said in congregation is perhaps one of the most effective of all the measures in this regard. The rich and the poor and the small and the big, are required, without exception, to say their Prayers in mosques, if accessible. If not all, at least a large section of Muslim society is responsible for abiding by this injunction. The percentage of those who regularly pray five times a day may be lower in some countries and higher in others, but it is a common experience shared to a greater or lesser degree by a majority of Muslims.

The system of Prayer in itself is a grand message of the equality of man. The one who reaches the mosque first occupies the place of his choice and none, howsoever highly placed in society he may be, can ever think of displacing him. At the time of Prayer, all stand together – shoulder to shoulder – with no gap in between. The most impeccably dressed may have standing adjacent to him someone clad in tattered rags. The weak and pale and the healthy and robust all meet together daily on an equal platform where the message invariably repeated is: *God is the Greatest*

To see eye to eye the misery in which some members of a locality are living and to meet them daily, leaves a very powerful effect on the heart of a man living in comparative comfort. The message is loud and clear that you must do something to ameliorate their sufferings and lift their standards or be degraded yourself in the estimation of God as well as your own estimations.

The area of this contact is broadened further on each Friday where Muslims gather at a central mosque so that people from richer neighbourhoods meet those from poorer areas. It is extended still further on each of the bi-annual festivals which are preceded by *fitrana*, a fund raised by voluntary contributions for the relief of the poor.

3) The Muslim month of fasting also sets on an equal plane the rich and poor. The rich endure thirst and hunger to remind themselves of the lot of the poor for whom thirst and hunger is but a way of life.

4) Zakat transfers the due right of the poor from the capital of the wealthy.

5) Then, finally, the fifth pillar of Islam is pilgrimage, often described as the greatest spectacle of human unity. The female pilgrims are permitted to wear simple sewn clothes. The male pilgrims are clad in two unsewn sheets – a uniform for both the rich and the poor.

But that is not all. Apart from the above acts of worship, there are many other measures introduced and implemented in a Muslim society which continuously bridge the gap between various sections of society and provide the much needed ventilation and convection for a healthy environment in which the rich are allowed to remain reasonably rich but are also required to care for the poor.

A similar principle was expounded by Jesus, on whom be peace, when he said, *the meek shall inherit the earth*. It is a great pity that despite this moral injunction, capitalism has singularly failed to care for the poor and the meek members of society.

INTERNATIONAL OBLIGATIONS

Discussing the alternative course of action to be adopted during periods of any natural disaster or great calamity afflicting any society, (see basic needs mentioned earlier) the Holy Quran describes the right choice in the following sequence:

It is the feeding of a slave; or feeding on a day of hunger an orphan, near of kin; or a poor man lying in the dust. (Ch. 90: Al-Balad: 14-17)

In other words, the right choices are:

1. The genuine and true service of mankind which is acceptable to God has been described here. The foremost of those that need any help is that man should help those who are under any bondage or ties. Any service contrary to this concept is regarded by God as worthless. In the light of this, the modern system of providing financial aid to less developed countries with preconditions and strings attached to the aid is totally rejected.

2. The next choice is the feeding of an orphan even if he or she has a guardian to support him or her.

3. The final choice is the feeding of a destitute who is so helpless as though he had beaten the dust.

Although addressed in the singular, this verse (15) is evidently describing a widescale crisis. The connotation of the word *Yaum* (lit. day) and the general style of expression is so obvious.

Upon reflection, the implications of this verse paint a very clear picture of how big, wealthy and powerful nations treat the poorer ones who stand in dire need at times of extreme helplessness. They are provided with aid but with strings attached. Thus the very purpose and spirit of helping others is destroyed. They are liberated apparently from one misery only to be led into the snare of another.

The entire contemporary system of international aid with strings attached is crisply described here in such few words. The believers are told not to take undue advantage of helpless people by relieving the sufferings of poor individuals or nations and at the same time depriving them of their liberty.

The word *orphan* is used in a wider sense as it applies to dependent individuals as well as nations. Such nations, who like orphans with wealthy relations have been abandoned by their kith and kin, should not be left unaided because they might be helped by others who are primarily responsible for them.

The case of the oil rich states is a fit example. If only a few states of the Gulf had joined hands to relieve immense sufferings of humanity at large, they could have resolved the problem of hunger and drought in African without feeling a pinch. The mountains of money they have in bank deposits and foreign assets in western countries generates interest and income which alone is sufficient to allay the misery and suffering to Africa. In any case, Islam forbids them from spending such interest for their own use.

The case of a multitudinous sea of hunger, misery and want from the numerous calamities in Bangladesh is another deserving case to be studied in this context. They have been abandoned by the rest of the worled to their own lot. The aid, if any, which trickles down to them is virtually ineffective for relieving their misery.

Such nations must be considered *orphan* nations according to the wider definition of the term. When such orphan nations are abandoned by their own kith and kin, this constitutes a serious crime in the sight of God.

People have a very naive and even crooked attitude towards God and nature for the sufferings of the poorer nations whilst, most certainly, it is man himself who is to be blamed for his utter callousness and disregard. If we fill the hearts of human beings with that special quality and are able to suffer for the sake of others, the world can still be turned into a paradise.

In the world outside Islam, the same selfish attitude prevails. if Ethiopia, for instance, happens to have close ties with the Soviet Union, aid should not be withheld on the pretext that it is for the Soviet Union to discharge its responsibility as a patron. If millions of Muslims in Sudan are dying of hunger, their plight should not be ignored on the plea that wealthy nations like Saudi Arabia and other oil-rich Muslims states, being virtually their kith and kin, have the ultimate responsibility to feed them. This is the true import of the Arabic expression *Yateeman Za Maqrabate* (lit. an orphan, near of kin).

Again, it is pointed out in this verse that individuals or nations who suffer through individual or national economic crises, must be helped to make them stand on their own feet. This scenario applies to many Third World countries whose economy is rapidly crumbling because timely, widescale help is not provided.

The third choice is *Au Miskeenan Za Martabate* which applies to such economies as are reduced to dust and the entire economic system of the nation has collapsed. According to the Holy Quran, feeding the people in such countries is not enough. It is the responsibility of man to adopt measures to restore and rehabilitate their economies.

Unfortunately, trade relations in this contemporary age represent the exact opposite. The flow of wealth is always in the direction of the richer and more advanced countries while the economies of poorer countries sink deeper in the red.

I am not an economist, but understand this much at least that it is impossible for the Third World countries to retain bilateral trade relations with the advanced countries and yet prevent the flow of wealth from their countries to those of the rich by ensuring that export revenues equal the import bill.

Another important factor to bear in mind is that in all economically advanced nations, there is a constant urge for an improvement in living standards. The poorer nations are encouraged to borrow money to match the rising living standards of the developed world. Push button technology leads to an easier and more comfortable life, even if such addictions to modern amenities, ultimately, may adversely influence the human character of hardiness. But if the people in advanced countries want to restore blood to their own cheeks and restore their own physical health, how can the wealthier nations be expected to relieve the poorer nations from a state of pernicious, terminal anaemia when their own thirst for more blood knows no bound and when their standard of living must continue to rise, and all that money can buy must constantly be transferred into their own economies?

This mad race for rising living standards without discrimination is not only robbing the poorer nations of their chance of survival but is also robbing the advanced nations themselves of their peace of mind and contentment of heart. The whole society is tantalised in the pursuit of artificially created needs so that everyone lives in a constant state of wanting something to keep up with the Joneses. This again is a state of affairs which can potentially lead to war.

This tendency is strongly discouraged in Islam. Islam presents to you a picture of a society in which people live within their means and there is some saving for a rainy day, not only at an individual and family level, but also on a national basis.

For poorer countries, such a situation is potent with dangers because when the advanced countries suffer from the new challenges of competition from emerging economies, and their own economies begin to stagnate, they would become more callous in their relationship with the Third World or poorer countries. This is inevitable because, somehow or the other, the governments of richer countries must maintain a reasonable standard of life for the people who have become addicted to them.

Ultimately these situations aggravate and culminate in factors which create wars. It is such wars that Islam seeks to prevent.

V

POLITICAL PEACE

1. No outright condemnation of any political system
2. Monarchy
3. Defining democracy
4. Islamic definition of democracy
5. Two pillars of Islamic concept of democracy
6. Mutual consultation preferred
7. The confusion as to the true nature of Islamic government
8. Divine Authority
9. Mullahism
10. Divided loyalties between the state and religion
11. Should religion have exclusive legislative authority?
12. Islamic statecraft
13. International relations: the principle of absolute justice equally applicable to all.
14. The role of the United Nations Organisation

Verily, Allah commands you to give over the trusts to those entitled to them, and that when you judge between men, you judge with justice. And surely excellent is what Allah admonishes you with! Allah is All-Hearing, All-Seeing. (Ch.4: Al-Nisa: 59)

POLITICAL PEACE

Political peace has to be carefully examined at the national and international level.

As far as national politics is concerned, the foremost issue is which political system is good or bad for man. Again, we need to discover whether it is the failure of political systems and their inherent defects which are responsible for the miseries and dissatisfaction of a people or is it something else. Is the system to be blamed or those who run it? Can immoral selfish, greedy, or corrupt political leadership which rises to power by democratic means be really good and beneficial for society as against benign dictatorship, for instance?

In order to establish and guarantee international peace, Islam has a word of advice for the contemporary politicians.

Islam lays extraordinary stress on introducing absolute morality to all spheres of human activity- politics being no exception.

NO OUTRIGHT CONDEMNATION OF ANY POLITICAL SYSTEM

We begin with the observation that no political system is mentioned in Islam as the only valid system against all others.

There is no doubt the Holy Quran speaks of a democratic system where the rulers can be elected by the people, but it is not the only system recommended by Islam. Nor can it be the fundamental prerogative of a universal religion to choose a single system of government without due regard to the fact that it is not practically possible for a single system to be applicable to all regions and societies of the world.

Democracy has not developed enough even in the most advanced nations of the world to reach the stage of polity which is the ultimate political vision of democracy. With the rise of capitalism and the building of extremely powerful machinery in capitalist countries, truly democratic elections cannot be held anywhere.

Add to this the growing problem of corruption, and the coming into being of the Mafia and other pressure groups. One can safely conclude that democracy is not in safe hands even in the most democratic countries of the world. Then, how can it be suitable in the Third World?

So, to say that western democracy can prevail in African, Asian or South American countries or the so-called Islamic countries of the world would be tantamount to making a hollow and unrealistic claim.

As far as I am concerned, Islamic teachings do not reject any political system of the world, but Islam leaves it to the choice of the people and historically established traditions prevailing in any country. What Islam emphasises is not the form of government but how the government should discharge itself.

Provided a system of rule conforms to the Islamic ideal in the discharge of the trust owed to the subjects, different systems of government, such as feudal lordship, monarchy, democracy, etc., can be accommodated under Islam.

MONARCHY

Monarchy is mentioned repeatedly in the Holy Quran without being condemned as an institution.

A prophet of Israel reminds the Israelites of Talut:

وَقَالَ لَهُمْ نَبِيُّهُمْ إِنَّ اللَّهَ قَدْ بَعَثَ لَكُمْ طَالُوتَ مَلِكًا
قَالُوٓاْ أَنَّىٰ يَكُونُ لَهُ ٱلْمُلْكُ عَلَيْنَا وَنَحْنُ أَحَقُّ بِٱلْمُلْكِ
مِنْهُ وَلَمْ يُؤْتَ سَعَةً مِّنَ ٱلْمَالِۚ قَالَ إِنَّ ٱللَّهَ ٱصْطَفَىٰهُ
عَلَيْكُمْ وَزَادَهُ بَسْطَةً فِى ٱلْعِلْمِ وَٱلْجِسْمِۖ وَٱللَّهُ
يُؤْتِى مُلْكَهُۥ مَن يَشَآءُۚ وَٱللَّهُ وَٰسِعٌ عَلِيمٌ ۝

Their Prophet said to them: Allah has appointed for you Talut
as a King. They demurred said, saying: How can he have
sovereignty over us while we are better entitled to sovereignty
than he, and he has not even been granted abundance of
wealth? He answered; Surely Allah has granted him superiority
over you and has given him a large portion of knowledge and
strength. And Allah bestows sovereignty upon whom He
pleases. Allah is Lord of vast bounty, All-Knowing. (Ch.2 Al-
Baqarah:248)

Monarchy is also mentioned in the broader sense of the people
being the monarch themselves:

وَإِذْ قَالَ مُوسَىٰ لِقَوْمِهِۦ يَٰقَوْمِ ٱذْكُرُواْ
نِعْمَةَ ٱللَّهِ عَلَيْكُمْ إِذْ جَعَلَ فِيكُمْ أَنۢبِيَآءَ وَجَعَلَكُم مُّلُوكًا
وَءَاتَىٰكُم مَّا لَمْ يُؤْتِ أَحَدًا مِّنَ ٱلْعَٰلَمِينَ ۝

Call to mind when Moses said to his people: O my
people, recall the favour that Allah bestowed upon you when
He appointed Prophets among you and made you Kings, and
gave you that which He had not given to any other of the
peoples. (Ch.5 Al-Ma'idah:21)

Again, sovereignties created or expanded by conquest in general do not enjoy a good reputation as we find in the verse about the Queen of Sheba advising her counsel.

The Queen of Sheba's decision is set out as follows:

$$\text{قَالَتْ إِنَّ ٱلْمُلُوكَ إِذَا دَخَلُوا قَرْيَةً}$$

$$\text{أَفْسَدُوهَا وَجَعَلُوٓا أَعِزَّةَ أَهْلِهَآ أَذِلَّةً وَكَذَٰلِكَ يَفْعَلُونَ ۝}$$

She said; Surely when mighty kings invade a country, they despoil it and humiliate its leading people. And that has been their way. (Ch.27 Al-Naml:35)

Kings can be good or bad, of course, just as democratically elected prime ministers and presidents can also be good or bad.

But the Holy Quran mentions a category of kings who were appointed by God. They are of the type, such as King Solomon[as], who was not only a king as understood by the Jews and Christians, but also a Prophet of God according to the Holy Quran.

This demonstrates that sometimes the offices of prophethood and sovereignty combine in one person and they are sovereigns directly commissioned by God.

Another type of sovereignty through the authority of a Prophet is mentioned in the Holy Quran. The following verse illustrates this fact:

$$\text{يَٰٓأَيُّهَا ٱلَّذِينَ ءَامَنُوٓا أَطِيعُوا ٱللَّهَ وَأَطِيعُوا ٱلرَّسُولَ وَأُولِي}$$

$$\text{ٱلْأَمْرِ مِنكُمْ فَإِن تَنَٰزَعْتُمْ فِى شَىْءٍ فَرُدُّوهُ إِلَى ٱللَّهِ وَٱلرَّسُولِ إِن كُنتُمْ}$$

$$\text{تُؤْمِنُونَ بِٱللَّهِ وَٱلْيَوْمِ ٱلْءَاخِرِ ذَٰلِكَ خَيْرٌ وَأَحْسَنُ تَأْوِيلًا ۝}$$

O ye who believe, obey Allah and obey His Messenger and those who are in authority among you. Then if you differ in anything among yourselves, refer it to Allah and His Messenger if you are believers in Allah and His Messenger and the Last Day. That is the best and most commendable in the end. (Ch.4 Al-Nisa:60)

We have this verse not only to enumerate the categories of sovereignty but to emphasise that according to the Holy Quran, sometimes democratic choices are not necessarily always the right ones. It is quite likely that the overwhelming majority of people fail to recognise the essential qualities of great leadership in a person and protest against his election if he is imposed upon them. By all political criteria, his appointment would be decried as dictatorial. The choice may be against popular will but is certainly not against public interest.

The inherent weakness in the democratic form of elections is that the masses make their choice on superficial impressions and latest assessment and are incapable of judging for themselves the sound qualities of leadership which are best suited for their ultimate benefit.

It seems that in the history of God's favoured people, there have been times when their political survival required divine intervention. At such times, God takes the choice of a king, sovereign or leader into His own hands. It should not be inferred from this that all monarchs of leaders are divinely chosen by God or sanctified as such. This misconcept which has been common in the medieval Christian system is not shared by the Holy Quran. For instance, King Richard laments:

Not all the waters of rough rude seas can wash the balm of an anointed King (Shakespeare).

DEFINING DEMOCRACY

The concept of democracy, despite its Greek origins, is based on Abraham Lincoln's brief definition of *government of the people, by the people, for the people.* It is a very interesting cliche indeed but seldom applied in totality anywhere in the world.

The third part of this definition *for the people* is very vague and rife with dangers. What can be declared to be *for the people* with full confidence? In a system of majority rule, it can very often happen that what is considered to be *for the people* is merely for the majority and not for the remaining minority.

In a democratic system, it is also possible for vital decisions to be taken solely on the basis of absolute majority. Yet, when you further dissect and analyse the facts and figures, you discover that it was in reality a minority decision, democratically passed, and imposed on the majority. One of the numerous possibilities is that the ruling party is voted into power on a first past the post basis having obtained a minor majority in most constituencies. Again, if the turnout on polling day is rather low, it becomes dubious if the ruling party does in fact enjoy the support of the majority. Even if the party emerges with an overall majority of the electorate, many things may happen during the term of its tenure. Public opinion may change drastically so that the sitting government is no longer a true representative of the majority. After all, a gradual process of change of heart by the electorate manifests itself at each change of government.

Even if the government remains popular with its voters, it is not unlikely that when certain key decisions are made, a considerable number of the ruling party's members do not agree at heart with the majority but may have voted out of party loyalty. If the difference is in the strength of the ruling party over the opposition party or parties, then, more often than not, the so-called majority decision would in reality be a minority decision imposed on the people.

It is also noteworthy that the concept of what is seen as good *for the people* changes from time to time. If decisions are not taken on absolute principles but what one considers to be good *for the people*, or at least what the party considers to be good, it may lead to a constant shift in policy from time to time. What appears good today may be bad tomorrow and good the day after.

For the man in the street, this can be a tricky situation. The experimentation of communism on such a large scale for over half a century was after all based on the same slogan of *for the people*. Not all socialist states were dictatorial.

It should also be noted that the line separating the socialist states from the democratic ones, as far as *government by the people* is concerned, is very thin and sometimes non-existent. How can one condemn all world governments elected in socialist countries as having been brought to power not *by the people?* Of course, in a totalitarian state, it is possible to dictate the choice of candidates to the electorate in such a manner as leaves them little room to elect any alternates. Yet similar and other high-handed tactics can also be employed, save for a few exceptions in the Western world, in countries with a democratic system of government.

In fact, democracy in most parts of the world is not given a free hand and the elections are seldom *by the people*. With election-rigging, horse trading, rule of fear through police tactics and other similar corrupt measures, the spirit and substance of democracy in the world are attenuated with adulteration so that there is little of democracy left in the end.

ISLAMIC DEFINITION OF DEMOCRACY

According to the Holy Quran, people have a free choice to adopt any system of rule which suits them. Democracy, sovereignty, tribal or feudal systems are valid provided they are accepted by the people as the traditional heritage of their society.

However, it seems that democracy is preferred and highly commended in the Holy Quran. The Muslims are advised to have a democratic system though not exactly on the pattern of western style democracy.

Islam does not present a hollow definition of democracy anywhere in the Holy Quran. It only deals with principles of vital significance and leaves the rest to the people. Follow and benefit, or stray and be destroyed.

TWO PILLARS OF ISLAMIC CONCEPT OF DEMOCRACY

There are only two pillars to the Islamic concept of democracy. These are:

1. Democratic process of elections must be based on trust and integrity.

Islam teaches that whenever you exercise your vote, do it with the consciousness that God is watching over you and will hold you responsible for your decision. Vote for those who are most capable of discharging their national trust and are in themselves trustworthy. Implicit in this teaching is the requirement that the ones entitled to vote, must exercise their voting right unless there are circumstances beyond their control or impediments exist in the exercise of that right.

2. Governments must function on the principle of absolute justice.

The second pillar of Islamic democracy is that whenever you make decisions, make them on the principle of absolute justice. Be the matter political, religious, social or economic, justice may never be compromised. After the formation of government, voting within the party should also always remain oriented towards justice. Hence no partisan interest or political consideration should be permitted to influence the process of decision-making. In the long run, every decision taken in this spirit is bound to be truly *of the people, by the people and for the people.*

MUTUAL CONSULTATION PREFERRED

The substance of democracy is very clearly discussed in the Holy Quran and as far as the advice to Muslims is concerned, though monarchy has never been ruled out as an irreligious and ungodly institution, democracy is most certainly preferred to all other forms of government.

Describing the ideal Muslim society, the Holy Quran declares:

فَمَآ أُوتِيتُم مِّن شَىۡءٍ فَمَتَٰعُ

ٱلۡحَيَوٰةِ ٱلدُّنۡيَا وَمَا عِندَ ٱللَّهِ خَيۡرٌ وَأَبۡقَىٰ لِلَّذِينَ ءَامَنُواْ وَعَلَىٰ رَبِّهِمۡ

يَتَوَكَّلُونَ ۞ وَٱلَّذِينَ يَجۡتَنِبُونَ كَبَٰٓئِرَ ٱلۡإِثۡمِ وَٱلۡفَوَٰحِشَ وَإِذَا مَا

غَضِبُواْ هُمۡ يَغۡفِرُونَ ۞ وَٱلَّذِينَ ٱسۡتَجَابُواْ لِرَبِّهِمۡ وَأَقَامُواْ ٱلصَّلَوٰةَ

وَأَمۡرُهُمۡ شُورَىٰ بَيۡنَهُمۡ وَمِمَّا رَزَقۡنَٰهُمۡ يُنفِقُونَ ۞ وَٱلَّذِينَ إِذَآ أَصَابَهُمُ

ٱلۡبَغۡىُ هُمۡ يَنتَصِرُونَ ۞

Whatever you have been given is only a temporary provision of
this life, but that which is with Allah is better and more lasting

for those who believe and put their trust in their Lord; and those who eschew the graver sin and indecencies, and when they are wroth they forgive; and those who hearken to their Lord, and observe Prayer and whose affairs are administered by mutual consultation, and who spend out of whatever We have provided for them; and those who, when a wrong is done them, defend themselves. (Ch.42 Al-Shura:37–40)

The Arabic words AMRO HUM SHOORA BAINAHUM *(whose affairs are administered by mutual consultation)* relate to the political life of the Muslim society, clearly indicating that in matters of government, its decisions are made through mutual consultation, which, of course, reminds one of the first part of the definition of democracy i.e. *government of the people.* The common will of the people becomes the ruling will of the people through mutual consultation.

The second part of the definition of democracy relates to *by the people.* This is clearly referred to in the following part of the verse:

إِنَّ اللَّهَ يَأْمُرُكُمْ أَن تُؤَدُّوا الْأَمَٰنَٰتِ إِلَىٰٓ أَهْلِهَا

Allah commands you to make over the trusts to those best fitted to discharge them. (Ch.4 Al-Nisa:59)

This means that whenever you express your will to choose your rulers, always place the trust where it rightfully belongs.

The right of the people to choose their rulers is of course mentioned but incidentally. The real emphasis is on how one should exercise this right. The Muslims are reminded that it is not just a question of their personal will which they can exercise in any way that they please, but far more than that, it is a question of national trust. In matters of trust, you are not left with many choices. You must discharge the trust with all honesty, integrity and a spirit of selflessness. The trust must repose where it truly belongs.

Many Muslim scholars quote this verse simply to indicate that Islam propounds the system and theory of democracy as understood in the Western political philosophy, but it is only partly true.

The system of consultation mentioned in the Holy Quran has no room for the party politics of the contemporary western democracies nor does it give licence to the style and spirit of political debates in democratically elected parliaments and houses of representatives. As we have discussed this aspect in detail, no more is necessary here.

It should also be noted with regards to the second part of the definition of democracy that according to this concept of mutual consultation, the right to vote belongs to the voters almost absolutely without any provisos or conditions infringing this right.

According to the established norms of democracy, the voter can cast his vote in favour of a puppet, or spoil or toss his ballot paper in a dustbin instead of the ballot box. He will remain irreproachable, nor can he be censured for violating any principles of democracy.

According to the Quranic definition, however, a voter is not the absolute master of his vote, but a trustee. As a trustee, he must discharge his trust fairly and squarely and place it where he feels it truly belongs. He must be vigilant and aware that he will be held responsible for his act in the sight of God.

In view of this Islamic concept, if a political party has nominated a candidate who an individual party member considers will fail to discharge his national trust, that member should quit the party rather than vote for someone who does not merit the trust. Loyalty to a party is not allowed to interfere in his choice.

Again, a trust must be discharged in good faith. Therefore, every voter must participate fully in exercising his vote during the elections unless he is unable to do so. Otherwise, he will have failed in the discharge of his own trust. The concept of abstention or refraining from exercising the vote, as happens in the USA where reportedly almost half the electorate actually bothers to vote, has no room in the Islamic concept of democracy.

THE CONFUSION AS TO THE TRUE NATURE OF ISLAMIC GOVERNMENT

It is becoming popular among Muslim political thinkers of the contemporary age to claim that Islam stands for democracy. According to their political philosophy, God being the ultimate authority, sovereignty belongs to Him.

DIVINE AUTHORITY

Absolute sovereignty belongs to God. The Holy Quran sums up His domain in the following verse:

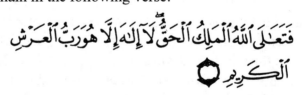

Then exalted be Allah, the True King. There is no god but He, the Lord of the Glorious Throne. (Ch.23 Al-Mu'minun:117)

The fundamental principle, that ultimately all rights to govern belong to God and He is the Lord of Sovereignty, is mentioned

234

in different ways in the Holy Qur'an of which the above verse is but one example.

In the running of political affairs, God's sovereignty is expressed in two ways:

a) The Law *(Shariah)* as derived from the Holy Quran, the conduct of the Holy Prophet[sa] of Islam and also from the established traditions attributed to him by early Muslims are supreme. They bear essential guidelines for legislation and no democratically elected government can interfere with the express Will of God.

b) No legislative process would be valid in contradiction of the aforesaid principle.

Unfortunately, however, there is no unanimity among the scholars of various sects of Islam as to what are the clear cut Laws *(Shariah)*. On this, all the scholars are agreed that legislation is the prerogative of God and that He has expressed His Will through the Quranic revelation to the Holy Founder[sa] of Islam.

Regarding the manner in which Muslim governments should be run, the popular idea is that in the day to day administrative matters, affairs and measures, the government, as representatives of the people, becomes instrumental in the expression of God's Will. As sovereignty belongs to the people by way of delegated power, therefore, such a system is democratic.

MULLAHISM

This is the rigid view of the so-called orthodoxy who would come to an understanding with the modern democratic tendencies of the Muslim populace only on the condition that the *Mullah* (nearest translation Muslim "clergy") be granted the ultimate right to judge the validity of democratic decisions on the basis of *Shariah.*

If accepted, this demand would be tantamount to placing ultimate legislative authority not in the hands of God but in the hands of the orthodox or some other school of clergy. When you consider the awesome power placed in their hands in the background of fundamental differences prevailing among the Muslim clergy itself regarding their understanding of what is and what is not *Shariah,* the consequences appear horrendous. There are so many schools of jurisprudence among the orthodoxy. Even within each school of jurisprudence, the clergy is not always unanimous on every edict. Again, their position regarding what the actual Will of God as expressed in Islamic *Shariah* is has been changing in different periods of history.

This presents a complex problem to the contemporary world of Islam which still seems to be in search of its true identity. It is gradually becoming more apparent to Muslim intellectuals that the only meeting point amongst the clergy is their uncompromising demand for the enforcement of Shariah.

The Iranian revolution has further whetted the appetite of the *Mullah* in countries where Sunni Muslims are a majority. According to them, if Khomeini can succeed, why must they fail? Beyond this lies their fantasia — the land of their dreams.

The masses are confused. Would you prefer the Word of God and that of the Holy Prophet[sa] of Islam or would you rather have men under a godless and fearless society to guide and shape your political manifestos? This question is extremely difficult for a common person, who finds himself in a state of bewilderment and confusion. The masses in many Muslim countries adore Islam and would readily die for the Will of God and the honour of the Holy Prophet of Islam, may peace and blessings of Allah be upon him. Yet there is something within the whole scenario which leaves them confused, disturbed and very uneasy. Despite their love of God and that of the Holy Prophet[sa], it invokes many a bloody memory of governments in the past which were either under the influence of *Mullahs* or exploited *Mullahism* to their political advantage.

As for the Muslim politicians, they seem to be divided and indecisive. Some cannot resist exploiting this situation by siding with the *Mullah* and patronising them. They cherish the secret hope, however, that at the time of elections, it will not be the *Mullah* but they who will be elected as stalwart champions of *Shariah*. The masses would prefer to trust them more as guardians of *Shariah* than the *Mullah*. Life would be easier and more down to earth in their hands than under the stiff and uncompromising control of the "custodians of heaven". Most scrupulous amongst the politicians are the foresighted ones who consider this to be a dangerous game. Alas! They are fast turning into a minority. Politics and hypocrisy and truth and scruples, or for that matter any noble virtue, do not seem to go hand in hand. By and large, the intellectuals are inclined ever more towards democracy. They love Islam but are afraid of theocratic rule. They view democracy not as an alternative to Islam, but genuinely believe that as a political philosophy, it is the Holy Quran itself which propounds democracy:

Those who hearken to their Lord, and observe Prayer, and whose affairs are decided by mutual consultation, and who spend out of what we have provided for them. (Ch.42 Al-Shura:39)

وَشَاوِرْهُمْ فِى ٱلْأَمْرِ فَإِذَا عَزَمْتَ فَتَوَكَّلْ عَلَى ٱللَّهِ إِنَّ ٱللَّهَ
يُحِبُّ ٱلْمُتَوَكِّلِينَ ۞

And consult them in matters of administration; and
when thou art determined, then put thy trust wholly in Allah.
Surely, Allah loves those who put their trust in Him. (Ch:3: Al-
Imran:160)

As a net result of this tug of war between various factions, young Muslim countries, like Pakistan, find themselves in a rigmarole of confusion and contradiction. The electorate is temperamentally averse to the return of the Mullah to the constituent assemblies in any sizeable number. Even at the height of Shariah fever, hardly five to ten percent of the Mullahs succeed in winning elections. Yet, having committed themselves to the Law of God in return for additional support from the Mullah, the politicians find themselves in a very unenviable position. Deep within, they are fully convinced that the acceptance of Shariah is in reality paradoxical to the principle of legislature through a democratically elected house of representatives.

If the authority for legislation lies with God, which a Muslim cannot deny, then, as a logical consequence, it is the divines and the Mullahs who possess the prerogative of understanding and defining the law of Shariah. In this scenario, the whole exercise of electing legislative bodies would become futile and meaningless. After all, members of Parliament are not required to sign only on the dotted lines where the Mullah so indicates.

It is rather tragic that neither the politician nor the intellectual has ever genuinely attempted to understand the form or forms of government which the Holy Quran really propounds or recognises.

DIVIDED LOYALTIES BETWEEN THE STATE AND RELIGION

There is no contradiction between the Word of God and Act of God. There is no clash between loyalty to one's state and religion in Islam. But this question does not relate to Islam alone.

There are many episodes in human history where many an established state was confronted with this question.

The Roman Empire, particularly, during the first three centuries of the Christian period, blamed Christianity for split loyalties between the Empire and Christianity. This allegation from the state resulted in extremely barbaric and inhumane persecution of early Christians in their homes for the alleged crime of treason and disloyalty to the Emperor.

Such struggle between the Church and the state has always been an important factor in shaping European history. Napoleon Bonaparte, for instance, blamed Roman Catholicism for divided loyalties and asserted that the first loyalty would be to the French people and the government of France and no Vatican Pope would be permitted to govern the affairs of Roman Catholics in France nor would Roman Catholicism be permitted to interfere in the affairs of the state.

In recent history, my own community, the Ahmadi Muslims, in Pakistan faced serious problems on similar grounds. As the influence of medievalist clergy began to rise under the patronage of General Muhammad Zia-ul-Haq, the longest ruling military dictator of Pakistan, Ahmadis became increasingly popular victims of this age-old accusation of divided loyalties. The Government of Pakistan under General Zia even proceeded to issue a sort of White Paper against Ahmadis proclaiming that Ahmadis were neither loyal to Islam nor to the state of Pakistan.

It was the same spirit of madness possessing new subjects. The wine remains the same though the goblets have changed.

More recently, during the notorious Salman Rushdie affair, Muslims in Britain and many parts of Europe, faced a similar problem of being accused of possessing divided loyalties. Although its intensity did not reach a fever pitch, yet the potent damage it poses to inter-community relations should not be under-estimated.

SHOULD RELIGION HAVE EXCLUSIVE LEGISLATIVE AUTHORITY ?

It is a universal phenomenon, therefore, which has never been seriously investigated. Neither politicians nor religious leaders have ever resolved the thin blue dividing line between religion and the state.

As far as the Christians are concerned, this issue should have stood resolved once for all when Jesus, on whom be peace, gave his historic reply to the Pharisees:

> Then he said to them: Pay back, therefore, Caesar's things to Caesar, but God's things to God. (Matthew 22:21)

These few words are profoundly rich with wisdom; all that need be said has been.

Religion and statecraft are two of the many wheels of the wagon of society. It is, in reality, irrelevant whether there are two, four and eight wheels as long as they keep their orientation correct and revolve within their orbits. There can be no question of mutual conflict or confrontation.

In total agreement with its earlier divine teachings, the Holy Quran elaborates this theme by clearly demarcating the sphere of activities of each component of society. It will be oversimplifying the matter if one conceives that there is no meeting point or common ground which religion and the state share with each other. They do indeed overlap, but only in a spirit of cooperation with each other. There is no intent to monopolise.

For instance, a large part of moral education in each religion becomes an integral part of legislation in every state of the world. In some states, it may constitute a small part; in others a relatively larger part of the law. The penalties prescribed may be mild or harsh but religious disapprovals against many crimes which are penalised are always traceable without reference to religion. Though they may be in disagreement with many secular laws, yet, as far as people belonging to different religions are concerned, they seldom choose to come in confrontation with the established government on such issues.

This applies not only to Muslims or Christians but to all religions of the world equally as well. Of course, the pure Hindu laws of MANUSMARTI are at complete variance with the secular rule of political governments in India. Yet, somehow, people seem to live in a state of compromise.

If religious law were invoked seriously against the prevailing political systems in different countries, the world would most certainly turn into a blood bath. But fortunately for man, this is not so.

As far as Islam is concerned, there should be no such problem because the ultimate and unyielding principle propounded by Islam in this regard is the principle of absolute justice. This principle remains central and fundamental to all forms of governments which claim to be Islamic in spirit.

Alas! This most pivotal point in understanding the Islamic concept of statecraft is little, if at all, understood by the political thinkers in Islam. They fail to make a distinction between the application of the common law relating to crimes which are universal in nature and without any religious bearing and such crimes as are specific to certain injunctions of that religion. Therefore, only adherents of such religions are liable for prosecution.

These two categories are not clearly defined. There is a fair size of grey area where common crimes can have religious or moral bearing as well as rank as offences against accepted human norms. For instance, the act of stealing is a crime varying in degrees of condemnation and prescribed punishment. Similarly, there is the question of murder, drinking and public disorder which are partially or wholly forbidden by many religions. Some religions have prescribed specific punishments for these offences.

The question then arises as to how a state should dispense with such crimes. This question raises further the question of whether Islam at all gives a clear-cut and well defined formula for a Muslim government and for a non-Muslim government to adopt. If a Muslim government has been defined as such in Islam, then other very important questions will be raised e.g. the validity of any state considering itself under some specific religious instruction and imposing that religion's teachings upon all its citizens irrespective of whether or not they belong to that religion.

Religions have a duty to draw the attention of the legislature to moral issues. It is not necessary that all legislation be placed under the jurisdiction of religions.

With so many different sects and shades of varying beliefs between one sect and another and one religion and another, nothing short of total confusion and anarchy would be the result. Take for instance the punishment for alcohol. Although it is forbidden in the Holy Quran, there is no punishment specified by the Quran itself. Reliance is placed on some traditions which are challenged by various schools of jurisprudence. In one locality or country, the punishment would be one thing and completely another elsewhere. Ignorance of the law would be rampant. What holds true for Islam is also true for other faiths. The Talmudic law would be totally impractical. The same can be said about Christianity.

A believer of any religion can practise his beliefs even under a secular law. He can abide by truth without any state law interfering with his ability to speak the truth. He can observe his Prayers and perform his acts of worship without the need of a specific law being passed by the state to permit him to do so.

This question can also be examined from another interesting angle. If Islam agrees with the question of a Muslim government in countries where Muslims are in the majority, then by the same token of absolute justice, Islam must concede the right to other governments to govern the countries according to the dictates of the religion of the majority. Therefore, in the next door neighbour, India, Pakistan will have to concede Hindu law for all Indian citizens. That being so, it will indeed be a very tragic day for more than one hundred million Indian Muslims who would lose all their rights to honourable survival in India. Again, if India is to be ruled by *Manusmarti*, why should the state of Israel be denied the right to rule the Jews as well as the gentiles by the law of Talmud? If this happens, life would become extremely miserable not only for the people of Israel but also a large number of Jews themselves.

But this concept of different religious states in different countries can only have a valid place in Islam if it propounds that in countries with a Muslim majority, Islamic Shariah (law) must prevail by force of law. This will again create a universally paradoxic situation because on the one hand, in the name of absolute justice, all states will be provided with the right to impose upon its people the law of the majority religion. On the other hand, each act of the religious minority in the countries of the world, would be brought under the severe rule of a religion in which they do not believe. This will be an affront to the very concept of absolute justice.

This dilemma has neither been addressed nor attempted to be resolved by the proponents of Islamic law in the so-called Muslim states. According to my understanding of Islamic teachings, all states should be run on the same principle of absolute justice and as such every state becomes a Muslim state.

In view of these arguments and the over-riding concept of there being no compulsion in matters of faith, religion does not need to be the predominant legislative authority in the political affairs of a state.

ISLAMIC STATECRAFT

My study has unambiguously revealed to me that the Holy Quran deals with the subject of government without making any distinction whatsoever between a Muslim and a non-Muslim state.

The instructions on how a state should be run are common to humanity though it is the believers who are primarily addressed in the Holy Quran. The Holy Quran speaks of statecraft equally applicable to Hindus, Sikhs, Buddhists, Confucianist, Christians, Jews and Muslims etc.

The essence of this instruction is contained in the verse quoted earlier and other similar verses which we quote now.

$$\text{فَلَا وَرَبِّكَ لَا يُؤْمِنُونَ حَتَّىٰ يُحَكِّمُوكَ فِيمَا شَجَرَ}$$
$$\text{بَيْنَهُمْ ثُمَّ لَا يَجِدُوا۟ فِىٓ أَنفُسِهِمْ حَرَجًا مِّمَّا قَضَيْتَ}$$
$$\text{وَيُسَلِّمُوا۟ تَسْلِيمًا ۝}$$

But no, by thy Lord, they will not truly believe until they make thee judge in all that is in dispute between them and they find not in their hearts any demur concerning that which thou decidest and submit with full submission. (Ch.4: Al-Nisa:66)

$$\text{يَـٰٓأَيُّهَا ٱلَّذِينَ ءَامَنُوا۟ كُونُوا۟ قَوَّٰمِينَ بِٱلْقِسْطِ شُهَدَآءَ لِلَّهِ}$$
$$\text{وَلَوْ عَلَىٰٓ أَنفُسِكُمْ أَوِ ٱلْوَٰلِدَيْنِ وَٱلْأَقْرَبِينَ إِن يَكُنْ غَنِيًّا}$$
$$\text{أَوْ فَقِيرًا فَٱللَّهُ أَوْلَىٰ بِهِمَا فَلَا تَتَّبِعُوا۟ ٱلْهَوَىٰٓ أَن تَعْدِلُوا۟ وَإِن}$$
$$\text{تَلْوُۥٓا۟ أَوْ تُعْرِضُوا۟ فَإِنَّ ٱللَّهَ كَانَ بِمَا تَعْمَلُونَ خَبِيرًا ۝}$$

O ye who believe, be strict in observing justice and bear witness only for the sake of Allah, even if it be against your ownselves or against parents on kindred. Whether the person be rich or poor. In either case, Allah is more regardful of him than you could be. Therefore, follow not vain desires so that you may act equitably. And if you conceal the truth or evade it, then remember that Allah is well aware of that which you do. (Ch. 4; Al-Nisa:136)

The Traditions of the Holy Prophet[sa] of Islam are very clear on this subject. He holds every ruler and anyone in authority over another, in the way he treats his subjects or those under his authority, as being directly answerable to God. But since these discussions have already been exhausted earlier, we need not discuss them further.

The substance of this study is that Islam propounds a completely neutral central government in which the matters of statecraft are common and equally applicable to all subjects of the state and religious differences are allowed to play no part therein.

Islam most certainly admonishes Muslims to follow the rule of the law in all worldly matters.

يَٰٓأَيُّهَا ٱلَّذِينَ ءَامَنُوٓاْ أَطِيعُواْ ٱللَّهَ وَأَطِيعُواْ ٱلرَّسُولَ وَأُوْلِى ٱلْأَمْرِ مِنكُمْ فَإِن تَنَٰزَعْتُمْ فِى شَىْءٍ فَرُدُّوهُ إِلَى ٱللَّهِ وَٱلرَّسُولِ إِن كُنتُمْ تُؤْمِنُونَ بِٱللَّهِ وَٱلْيَوْمِ ٱلْءَاخِرِ ذَٰلِكَ خَيْرٌ وَأَحْسَنُ تَأْوِيلًا ۝

O ye who believe, obey Allah and obey His Messenger and those who are in authority among you. Then if you differ in anything refer it to Allah and His Messenger if you are believers in Allah and the Last Day. That is the best and most commendable in the end. (Ch.4 Al-Nisa:60)

But as far as relations between man and God are concerned, it is an area exclusive to religion and the state has no right to interfere. There is total freedom of mind and heart in the affairs of belief and profession of faith. It is a fundamental right of man not only to believe in anything which he so pleases, but also to worship God or idols as dictated by his religion or pagan belief.

According to Islam, therefore, religion has no right to interfere in areas exclusive to the state nor has the state any right to interfere in areas commonly shared by them. Rights and responsibilities are so clearly defined in Islam that any question of a clash is obviated. Many verses relating to this subject have already been quoted in the section dealing with religious peace.

Unfortunately, there is a tendency among many secular states to sometimes extend the domain of secularisation beyond its natural borders. The same is true of theocratic states or states unduly influenced by a religious hierarchy.

Though one may not sympathise with them, one can understand to a degree the lopsided views of states governed by religious fanatics. But when one observes such an immature attitude in the so-called advanced and broad-minded people of secular countries, it is hard to believe. This is not the only thing difficult to understand in the political behaviour of man.

As long as politics remains rigidly wedded to national interest and contributes to its philosophy, there can be no such thing as absolute morality. As long as political attitudes are governed by national prejudices and truth, honesty, justice and fair play are discarded whenever they clash with the perceived national interest, and as long as this remains the definition of loyalty to one's state, the political behaviour of man will remain dubious, controversial and ever paradoxical.

The Holy Quran mentions the responsibilities of government and people. Some of these responsibilities have been mentioned in the earlier sections of this lecture - the provision of food, clothing, shelter and the basic needs of its citizens; the principles of international aid; answerability to both the government and the people; their interplay; absolute justice; and sensibility to the problems of the people so that they do not have to raise their voice in demand of their rights.

In a true Islamic system of government, it is the responsibility of the government to be watchful so that people do not have to resort to strikes, industrial strife, demonstration, sabotage or cause of complaint, to get their rights. Let us turn briefly to some other responsibilities.

The Holy Quran states:

وَإِمَّا تَخَافَنَّ مِن قَوْمٍ خِيَانَةً فَأَنۢبِذْ إِلَيْهِمْ عَلَىٰ سَوَآءٍ إِنَّ ٱللَّهَ لَا يُحِبُّ ٱلْخَآئِنِينَ ۝

If thou apprehend treachery from the people who have made a pact with thee, terminate the pact and their covenant with equity in a manner that should occasion no prejudice. Surely, Allah loves not the treacherous. (Ch. 8: Al-Anfal:59)

Those who govern may not govern in a manner so as to promote disorder, chaos, suffering and pain but should work diligently and effectively so as to establish peace in every sphere of society.

أَمَّن يُجِيبُ ٱلْمُضْطَرَّ إِذَا دَعَاهُ وَيَكْشِفُ ٱلسُّوٓءَ وَيَجْعَلُكُمْ خُلَفَآءَ ٱلْأَرْضِ أَءِلَٰهٌ مَّعَ ٱللَّهِ قَلِيلًا مَّا تَذَكَّرُونَ ۝

Or, Who responds to the afflicted person when he calls upon Him, and removes the affliction, and will make you inheritors of the earth? Then, is there a god beside Allah? Little is it that you heed. (Ch.27 Al-Naml:63)

INTERNATIONAL RELATIONS; THE PRINCIPLE OF ABSOLUTE JUSTICE EQUALLY APPLICABLE TO ALL

Even the politicians and the statesmen of today stand in need of Islamic teachings. It is a faith whose cornerstone in international affairs is absolute justice.

يَٰٓأَيُّهَا ٱلَّذِينَ ءَامَنُوا۟ كُونُوا۟ قَوَّٰمِينَ لِلَّهِ شُهَدَآءَ بِٱلْقِسْطِ وَلَا يَجْرِمَنَّكُمْ شَنَـَٔانُ قَوْمٍ عَلَىٰٓ

أَلَّا تَعْدِلُوا اَعْدِلُوا هُوَ اَقْرَبُ لِلتَّقْوَى وَاتَّقُوا اللَّهَ إِنَّ
اللَّهَ خَبِيرٌ بِمَا تَعْمَلُونَ ۝

*O ye who believe! be steadfast in the cause of Allah,
bearing witness in equity; and let not a people's enmity incite
you to act otherwise than with justice. Be always just, that is
nearer to righteousness. And fear Allah. Surely, Allah is aware
of what you do. (Ch.5 Al-Maidah:9)*

I cannot claim to have read everything about all major religions
of the world but neither am I entirely ignorant of their teachings.
During my studies, however, I have failed to find a similar
injunction as the verse under discussion in their scriptures. Even
the mention of international relations is rare. If a similar
teaching is also found in another religion, then let me assure you
that Islam is in full agreement with that teaching for therein lies
the key to world peace.

The world at large is worried today at the future prospects of
world peace. The momentous and epoch-making changes in the
socialist world and the improving relationship of the
superpowers offer a glimmer of hope. The world is in an
exultant mood. The general consensus of opinion amongst
leading politicians seems to be extremely optimistic, even
euphoric, at the likely outcome of the momentous revolutionary
changes we are witnessing today.

The West, in particular, seems to be over confident and jubilant.
It is becoming increasingly difficult for the Americans to
suppress their jubilation at what they consider to be a grandslam
victory over the communist hemisphere, a victory viewed by
some as good over evil and of right over wrong.

It will be out of place to analyse in detail the current geo-political situation and its outcome. Perhaps I will be able to devote a few hours to this subject at the UK Ahmadiyya Muslim Community's Annual conference at the end of July this year (1990).

THE ROLE OF THE UNITED NATIONS ORGANISATION

Of the many debates raging around the future prospects of world peace as a result of the recent events, one in particular needs special mention. It relates to the role that the United Nations Organisation is going to play in being able to secure and maintain (i.e. make and keep) world peace far more effectively than ever before.

With the cold war between the two super-giants coming to an end, it is said that there is a fair chance of closing the gap between their hitherto divergent outlooks: less veto in the Security Council's sessions, it seems, and more united decisions on how global problems should be resolved. This may present a completely new look to the Security Council of the future.

The only snag so far is the danger of China playing the odd-man out, but in view of China's immensely complicated economic and political problems, it should not be impossible to convince China of the advantages of agreement.

Whether this dream comes true or not is beside the point. Given that the Security Council as well as the United Nations emerged as the most powerful political instrument to influence the events of the globe and coerce smaller nations to submit to the supreme will of the nations of the world, such a scenario was inconceivable prior to the tumbling of the Berlin Wall. But the question remains, nay, it looms larger on the political horizon than ever before, whether or not the United Nations in its new role of combined judicial and executive powers of such enormous proportion, will be actually able to achieve global peace?

I beg to be excused if I may sound over-pessimistic, but my answer to this question is a very apologetic, 'No'. The issue of war and peace in the world does not only hang by the thread of superpower relationships. It is a deep and complex question with its roots embedded in the political philosophies and moral attitudes of the nations of the world.

Moreover, economic disparity and the widening gap between the haves and have-nots of the world are bound to play an important role in the future events of the world. Some effects have already been discussed in the previous section of this address. Unless the principle of absolute justice in the economic relationship between countries is accepted and strictly adhered to and unfair market practices which exploit the resources of the poor are removed by and for all members of the United Nations, no peace can ever be guaranteed or even visualised for the nations of the world. As long as the relationship of the United Nations Organisation with its individual member states is not more clearly defined than at present, the prospects of world peace will remain bleak.

There is a need to devise some measure to prevent governments from being cruel to their own subjects. Some instrument has to be made available to the United Nations to justly fight injustice wherever it prevails. Till then, one cannot dream of peace for the world.

How far the United Nations can interfere with the so-called internal affairs of a country is a very sensitive question and yet vital to the attainment of world peace. But if, in the final analysis, the policy of the United Nations is not governed by the principle of absolute justice, and different standards are applied to individual nations, then providing greater leverage to the United Nations Organisations to interfere in the internal affairs of a state may create more problems than it can resolve. Therefore, this issue requires a thorough, cool and detached study.

What has happened so far is simply that the Soviet Union and Eastern bloc countries have been compelled to confess the failure of scientific socialist philosophies in improving the quality of life in the Soviet Union and her neighbouring East European countries. This has created great confusion.

The fog is yet to clear before we can see the shape of things to be. Will it be a total defeat for scientific socialism followed by a mad rush back to capitalism in its entirety or will there be new experimentation with mixed economies? Will there be a complete breakdown of strict central control by totalitarian governments or will the totalitarian control itself break down into pieces resulting in a near state of anarchy? Or, will there be a gradual transition into totalitarian state control to a new compromised system of give and take between the state and individual so that, with the passage of time, civil liberties are progressively introduced and fundamental human rights restored?

It is important to wait for the outcome of a new struggle between Mr. Gorbachev's ideas of *perestroika* and *glasnost* on the one hand and the attitude of the strict orthodox in the communist hierarchy. To the best of my knowledge, most of the benefits in the USSR's classless society are mutually shared by the party hierarchy, civil service and the defence forces. The vital question is what role are they going to play at this critical nascent stage of the bloodless counter-revolution which is now taking shape?

This and similar questions have to be answered before one can reasonably visualise the impact of these changes on the prospects of world peace.

Merely a detente between the two superpowers in itself does not bring any hope of peace. On the contrary it invokes many phantoms of lurking dangers for the Third World countries in particular. It was the mistrust prevailing between the two superpowers and their jealousies which, in fact, provided a sort of canopy for weaker nations. Also, it was the ability of the weaker nations to change sides and allegiances from the West to East or vice-a-versa which gave them a small measure of manoeuvrability and bargaining power. But this is no longer so. What hope can these weaker nations entertain now to survive respectably as independent nations in the future?

The thought at this stage shifts to the UNO—a bastion of peace and the only torch of hope for the establishment of a new world order. At least, one wishes it was so. However, upon a closer critical examination, a completely bleak, oppressive and even threatening picture emerges.

In the newly emerging balance of power, will not the United Nations be practically governed by only one superpower? This presents the smaller and weaker nations no chance to escape the inevitable fate of hunted animals.

The present United Nations has proved again and again to be a powerful organisation working not for justice but for the political ends of whichever nation has the greatest lobbying power. The concept of right and wrong has never played a part in the decision-making process of the United Nations in our recent memory nor in the present set up can it play a meaningful role in the future. Politics and diplomacy are too deeply and inextricably rooted in the soil of modern politics to leave any room for absolute justice to take root and be given a fair chance of survival. It is a hard and bitter fact, which no man with respect for truth can deny, that this great and awesome institution has been reduced to an arena of intricate diplomatic activities, lobbying, secret paramours and power struggles, all carried out in the name of world peace.

According to the Holy Quran, therefore, what the world needs is an institution which sets itself the task of establishing justice. Without absolute justice, no peace is conceivable. One can wage wars in protestation in the name of peace, stifle conscience and still dissent for the purported aim of establishing peace, but all that one can achieve is death but not peace.

Alas! Few among the great politicians of the world understand the difference between death and peace.

Death is born out of inequity, tyranny and persecution by the mighty. Peace is the child of justice.

The Holy Quran often speaks of peace but always in relation to justice. Peace is oft-mentioned as conditional to the dispensation of justice.

In a situation erupting into belligerence and active hostility between two Muslim individuals or nations, the Holy Quran has this to propose:

وَإِن طَآئِفَتَانِ مِنَ ٱلْمُؤْمِنِينَ ٱقْتَتَلُوا۟ فَأَصْلِحُوا۟ بَيْنَهُمَا فَإِن بَغَتْ إِحْدَىٰهُمَا عَلَى ٱلْأُخْرَىٰ فَقَٰتِلُوا۟ ٱلَّتِى تَبْغِى حَتَّىٰ تَفِىٓءَ إِلَىٰٓ أَمْرِ ٱللَّهِ فَإِن فَآءَتْ فَأَصْلِحُوا۟ بَيْنَهُمَا بِٱلْعَدْلِ وَأَقْسِطُوٓا۟ إِنَّ ٱللَّهَ

يُحِبُّ ٱلۡمُقۡسِطِينَ ۝ إِنَّمَا ٱلۡمُؤۡمِنُونَ إِخۡوَةٌ فَأَصۡلِحُوا بَيۡنَ
أَخَوَيۡكُمۡ وَٱتَّقُوا ٱللَّهَ لَعَلَّكُمۡ تُرۡحَمُونَ ۝

In case two parties among the believers, be they individuals or nations, *fight each other, bring about reconciliation between them. If,* however, *one of them* persists in belligerence and *transgresses against the other, bring* your collective *might to bear upon the one that transgresses to force him until he agrees* that his dispute be resolved *in accordance with the word of Allah. Then if both parties* having so submitted, *effect reconciliation between them* and make them resolve their dispute *with equity and* We advise that you must exercise absolute justice, *act justly. Remember, Allah loves the just. All believers are brothers, so make peace between your brothers and be mindful of* your duty to *Allah that you may be shown mercy. (Ch.49 Al-Hujurat:10–11)*

In the above verse, non-Muslims are not mentioned for the obvious reason that they cannot be expected to submit to the teachings of the Quran. Yet, the verse serves as an excellent model for the whole world to follow.

While the eyes of the world are turning to the United Nations and the Security Council in the hope that it will acquire a more active, wider and meaningful role in resolving international disputes and thus transforming the world into a more secure, safe and peaceful abode, there is very little in the past record of the performance of the United Nations to give credence to this wishful thinking. A world arena of lobbying, intrigue, intense diplomatic activity aimed at formation of pressure groups and attempts to gain an upper hand over one's opponents by any means available, where scruples have no part to play and human conscience is barred entry, may of course be called a House of

255

Nations even though in conflict and disarray. But it would be an irony to call such a house a house of United Nations. If that be the concept of unity, I for one would much rather risk survival in a community of Nations which are disunited but united in truth and justice.

The will to muster power to crush adversaries and still the voice of dissent is a most vital question which every nation must address and resolve. One wonders with a deep sense of sorrow as to how long the member nations of this august House would continue to shut their eyes and refuse to open their minds to the dangers inherent in the style in which the affairs of nations are run.

World peace hangs precariously on the string of a feeble hope that justice will prevail and justice will be done.

VI
INDIVIDUAL PEACE

1. To be at peace with oneself
2. Vying with one another in good deeds
3. Love between kith and kin
4. Serving others
5. Seeking the pleasure of God
6. A constant awareness of other human beings
7. A wider sphere of loving care
8. The object of man's creation
9. Without God, there can be no peace

Those who believe and whose hearts find comfort in the remembrance of Allah. Aye! It is in the remembrance of Allah that hearts can find comfort. (Ch. 13: Al-R'ad:29)

TO BE AT PEACE WITH ONESELF

In the end, though last but not the least, let me emphasise that the quality and attitude of individual members of society play a most significant role in the creation of a peaceful or disorderly society.

We have discussed so far the architecture and design of the religious, social, economic and political edifices that Islam plans to erect. As to the nature of bricks required to be used as building material, Islam lays great emphasis on the character and qualities of the individual.

This is a wide subject spread over the length and breadth of the Holy Quran. Following are the essential features which I understand Islam attempts to inculcate in every member of society.

VYING WITH ONE ANOTHER IN GOOD DEEDS

According to Islam, both desires and ambitions are activated and curtailed under divine guidance so that a perfect balance is achieved. Without such a balance, it is impossible to achieve social peace. Islam promotes such desires and ambitions as are largely independent of one's financial state of affairs and are available to individuals at all levels at no or nominal cost.

The ambition to rise above the common run of people, and to attain distinction is but natural. However, this natural desire to excel and rise above others, if left undisciplined and uncurtailed can become unwholesome. Jealousy and foul play, for instance, can poison the spirit of free competition to a degree that the entire society begins to suffer rather than benefit from the advantages of a competitive spirit.

The tendency to use drugs in sports is but a small example; but competition in industry, trade and commerce in the national and international spheres, provides us with extremely ugly examples of the absence of level playing fields.

The type of foul play differs in the Third World countries from that in the more advanced nations. In the Third World, corruption, adulteration, breach of trust, fraud and deceit are but a few instruments freely employed to achieve a quick economic gain. That is why in all spheres of human activity, religious and moral education is required to be employed. The lack of such education can lead to dire consequences.

Islam provides us with detailed instructions covering the entire field of competitive conduct. Alas! In the Muslim countries, themselves, where one hears so much of Islamisation and Islamic fundamentalism, seldom does one come across a serious attempt to Islamise industry, trade, commerce and economic relations - a tragedy of the first order, indeed.

The following verse of the Holy Quran presents the essence of Islamic teaching in this field:

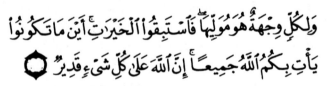

Everyone had an ultimate goal to pursue which dominates him. We fix that goal for you, do you, then vie with one another in goodness. Wherever you be, Allah will bring you all together. Surely, Allah has the power to do all that He wills. (Ch.2 Al-Baqarah:149)

In this brief statement, boundless wisdom is miraculously compressed and preserved. It serves as a guiding principle covering competition of all types and in all fields. Goodness must stand supreme. It must remain the ultimate goal. It must itself become the object of all competition. All foul play and meanness is completely banished at a single stroke.

If time could permit, we could go into greater length and provide ample illustrations from Islamic teachings as to how competition should be kept healthy, pure and correct. Seldom do people realise that real peace of mind and heart lies in the realisation of one's being good and not in some fabulous feat achieved by employing bad and foul means.

Such individuals are never at peace with either society or themselves. To casual observers, they present a facade of great attainment and consequential satisfaction but it is more a hollow victory rather than a real triumph.

A close friend of a late multi-millionaire from Pakistan once told me a surprising tale of utter despondency. Once he complimented his friend on his great achievement and success. Instead of being pleased, the multi-millionaire's spontaneous reaction was most surprising. He opened up the front buttons of his shirt and moved his hand as if he was about to rend his chest apart using his nails like the claws of an animal. He exclaimed: Woe to this success. If one could tear open my chest and see within, one would find nothing but a raging fire.

Some confess to this hard reality; some do not. None can defeat human nature. One can succeed in amassing colossal wealth and have access to all amenities and luxuries of life. But there is no begrudging the fact that there are few, if any, rich people who are truly happy and content. Their condition is described in the Holy Quran as follows:

261

Woe to every backbiter, slanderer, who amasses wealth and keeps counting it. He thinks that his wealth will make him immortal. Nay, he shall surely be cast into the crushing torment. And what should make thee know what the crushing torment is? It is Allah's kindled fire which rises over the hearts. It will be closed in on them, in widely extended columns. (Ch. 104; Al-Humazah:2–10)

Yet truly sincere satisfaction will continue to evade one unless one satisfies the ingrained urge in human nature to do good, be good and lead a noble life.

LOVE BETWEEN KITH AND KIN

The promotion of love between kith and kin to build a strongly bonded family system has already been discussed under social peace. Here it is being mentioned to highlight the need to improve the quality of the individual who performs a role in the society similar to that of a brick. Without improving the quality of the brick, the quality of the building cannot be improved.

SERVING OTHERS

The emphasis in Islam is on being able to draw pleasure from being of service to others rather than vice-a-versa. The following part of a verse of the Holy Quran delivers this message:

كُنتُمْ خَيْرَ أُمَّةٍ أُخْرِجَتْ لِلنَّاسِ تَأْمُرُونَ بِالْمَعْرُوفِ
وَتَنْهَوْنَ عَنِ الْمُنكَرِ وَتُؤْمِنُونَ بِاللَّهِ

You are the best of the people by virtue of being of service to and raised for the benefit of mankind; you enjoin good, and forbid evil and believe in Allah. (CH.3: Al-Imran:111)

This indicates that a Muslim is not given precedence over others arbitrarily. Just to be a Muslim would not automatically imply that he or she is better than others. One has to earn this title by being of service to others so that the flow of favours is from that one to the others.

Defining the meaning of KHAIR, which means both better and best, the Holy Prophet once said:

The upper hand is better than the lower hand: the upper hands gives and spends, the lower hand begs and receives. (Narrated by Ibn Umar Bukhari and Muslim)

In the Holy Quran and the Traditions of the Holy Prophet[sa], this aspect is so highly emphasised that some Companions of the Holy Prophet[sa], set new and lofty standards in this area of human excellence. Not only did they endeavour to be of service to others but were hesitant to receive and beg favours from others.

Auf ibn Malik Ashj'ai relates: *Seven, eight or nine of us were with the Holy Prophet[sa], on one occasion when he said: Will you not make a covenant with the Messenger of Allah? We had only shortly before made our covenant. So we said: We have made our covenant with you, Messenger of Allah. The Holy Prophet[sa] repeated his question and we made the same response adding: What covenant shall we now make with you? He said: That you will worship Allah and will not associate aught with Him, that you will observe the five obligatory Prayers, will obey Allah, and will*

263

not ask anyone for anything. Thereafter, I have noticed that if a riding whip fell from the hand of one of them, he would not ask anyone to restore it for him. (Muslim)

The emphasis on service is not just a dry and austere approach, but an attempt to refine human attitudes and to inculcate in man a taste for more sophisticated values. Once more refined tastes are developed, human beings can be trained to enjoy being of service to others far more than merely being recipient of favours and service provided by others.

One half of faith is service to God's creation.

The motto in Islam seems to be that an act of goodness is a reward in itself. It is beyond the realm of argument; it can only be experienced.

SEEKING THE PLEASURE OF GOD

In cultivating higher values in human behaviour, Islam does not stop short at that. Islam creates amongst its followers a consciousness that appreciation by God of all one's goodness is all that matters and should matter. This emphasis obviates the urge for showing-off one's good deeds to merit applause from human observers. It is more than sufficient for a true believer that all his deeds, whether good or bad, are in the knowledge of the All-Seeing God. Speaking of this, the Holy Quran observes:

يَـرَهُ ۞ وَمَن يَعْـمَلْ مِثْقَالَ ذَرَّةٍ شَرًّا يَـرَهُ ۞

*On that day the earth will narrate its account, for thy Lord has
so directed it. On that day people will come forth in diverse
groups that they may be shown* the consequences of *their
actions. Then whose will have done a good deed* even as small
and *insignificant as a minute particle will see it* had been
noticed by God *and whose will have done an evil* deed as small
and *insignificant as a minute particle will* also *see it* had been
noticed by God. *(Ch.99: Al-Zilzal:5–9)*

It should be noted that this is an important step in the direction
of reforming human society. It is the only effective cure for the
vanity of man and his urge to display and exult.

In a wider definition of charity, the Holy Prophet, included the
following acts which merit a reward from God:

Charity is due from every limb of a person on every day on
which the sun rises. Doing justice between two persons is
charity, to help a person ride his mount or to place his baggage
on it is charity, removing from a path that occasions
inconvenience is charity. (Narrated by Abu Hurairah: *Bukhari
and Muslim*)

If a Muslim plants a tree, then whatever is eaten from it is
charity on his part and whatever is stolen from it is charity and
whatever is subtracted from it is charity. (Narrated by Jabir:
Muslim)

Shield yourselves against the Fire, even if it be by giving away
half a date in charity, and if that should be lacking, by saying a
good word. (Narrated by Adiyy ibn Hatim: *Bukhari*)

If a person should have nothing, he should work with his hands
to his own benefit and also give away alms. If he is unable to
work, he should help a needy helpless one. If he cannot even do

that, he should urge others to goodness. If he lacks that also, he should restrain himself from doing evil. That too is charity. (Narrated by Abu Musa Ashari: *Bukhari and Muslim*)

Even a morsel of food fed in your wife's mouth earns the love of God.

A CONSTANT AWARENESS OF OTHER HUMAN BEINGS

Islam develops sensibility and sensitivity to the pains and sufferings of others. We have already discussed this aspect under the section dealing with socio-economic and political peace. No further comments are needed here.

A WIDER SPHERE OF LOVING CARE

Islam widens one's sphere and the ability to love not only one's fellow human beings but also the entire creation of God.

As Islam claims to be the last revealed religion addressed not only to a people but the whole of mankind, one normally expects that the Prophet of Islam[sa] should accordingly be described as a source of light and blessing for all mankind. But one is surprised to read, instead, that the Holy Prophet, is described in the Holy Quran as

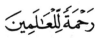

A blessing for the entire universe. (Ch.21 Al-Anbiya:108)

The word `ALAM' in Arabic means a world or the whole world. The word used here, however, is `AL-ALAMEEN' which is the plural of *Alam* (the whole world). As such, we have translated it here as the entire universe.

A sceptic may not be convinced of the validity of such a tall title. But a deeper understanding of the relationship of the office of universal prophethood, which the Holy Prophet[sa], undoubtedly possessed, can reveal the wisdom of the title *a blessing for the entire universe.*

THE OBJECT OF MAN'S CREATION

According to the Quranic concept of creation, the philosophy of the creation of just the inanimate universe would have served little purpose other than being, God forbid, a futile act on the part of the Creator. Who would know and who would share the knowledge with the Creator of the existence of things? It would have been tantamount to the creation of nothing less.

The purpose of creation was to create a consciousness and ultimately to improve, widen and enhance the quality of that consciousness to the purpose of creation.

This is not a simple objective and needs a separate full discussion which would be beyond the scope of today's address. The relevant part, to put it simply, is that the ultimate purpose of creation was to create a conscious being of the highest order who would not only voluntarily submit to the most consummate beauty of God as reflected in His creation directly, but would also lead fellow creation of the highest order (i.e. mankind) to this ultimate goal of creation, or at least, make it possible for those among them who desire to follow Him.

Hypothetically, remove the ultimate object of creation for a while, and suddenly the entire *raison d'etre* for the creation and maintenance of this universe would collapse.

In its simplified example, the reason for the planting of a seedling and nurturing, irrigating, pruning and maintenance of a fruit tree is the fruit itself. If there was to be no fruit, there would be no tree. All the effort in planting, nursing and maintaining the fruit tree without the concept of a fruit as the end product would be totally vain and meaningless. As such, the entire fruit tree, inclusive of its roots, stalk, stem, twigs, leaves and buds virtually remain obliged to the fruit. Though preceding in time, all parts of the tree remain obliged to their ultimate purpose. It is the beneficence of the purpose which creates the instrument of creation itself.

In light of this relationship between the supreme object of creation and the rest of the universe, when one studies the teachings of Islam, one would be surprised to realise that Islam encompasses not only the relationship between man and God and God and man, but also man's relationship with the animal kingdom and the inanimate world around him.

All that exists becomes sacred not because of its superiority to man but because it is created specifically by the Lord of creation for man, directly or indirectly. Nothing in the universe remains meaningless any longer or remote and disconnected. Even the remotest stars acquire a meaning and a place in the scheme of human creation. This is what is repeatedly discussed in the Holy Quran from different angles of which the following are a few examples:

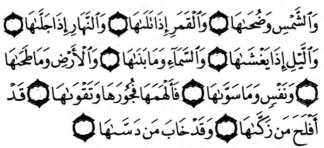

268

We call to witness the sun and its growing brightness, and the moon when it *follows it, and the day* when it *reveals its glory, and the night* when it *draws a veil over it, and the heaven and* the purpose of *its making, and the earth* and the purpose of *its spreading out, and the soul and its perfect* proportioning *and He revealed to it the right and wrong* of everything, *he indeed prospers who purifies it, and he is ruined who corrupts it.* (Ch.91 Al-Shams:2–11)

وَسَخَّرَ لَكُم مَّا فِى السَّمَوَتِ وَمَا فِى الْأَرْضِ جَمِيعًا مِّنْهُ إِنَّ فِى ذَلِكَ لَآيَتٍ لِّقَوْمٍ يَتَفَكَّرُونَ ۝

He has subjected to you whatsoever is in the heavens and whatsoever is in the earth, all of it is from Him. In that surely are Signs for a people who reflect. (Ch.45 Al-Jathiyah:14)

وَسَخَّرَ لَكُمُ الَّيْلَ وَالنَّهَارَ وَالشَّمْسَ وَالْقَمَرَ وَالنُّجُومُ مُسَخَّرَتٌ بِأَمْرِهِ إِنَّ فِى ذَلِكَ لَآيَتٍ لِّقَوْمٍ يَعْقِلُونَ ۝

He has constrained to your service the night and the day and the sun and the moon and the stars too have been constrained to your service by His command. Surely in all this there are signs for a people who make use of their understanding. (Ch.16 Al-Nahl:13)

أَلَمْ تَرَوْا أَنَّ اللَّهَ سَخَّرَ لَكُم مَّا فِى السَّمَوَتِ وَمَا فِى الْأَرْضِ وَأَسْبَغَ عَلَيْكُمْ نِعَمَهُ ظَهِرَةً وَبَاطِنَةً وَمِنَ النَّاسِ مَن يُجَدِلُ فِى اللَّهِ بِغَيْرِ عِلْمٍ وَلَا هُدًى وَلَا كِتَبٍ مُّنِيرٍ ۝

Have you not seen that Allah has constrained to your service whatever is in the heavens and whatever is in the earth, and poured out His favours to you, visible and hidden? Yet there are some among men who dispute concerning Allah, without knowledge or guidance, or the authority of *an illuminating Book. (Ch.31 Luqman:21)*

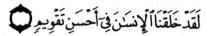

Surely, We have created man in the best mould. (Ch.95 Al-Tin:5)

Many other verses and even small chapters of the Holy Quran are devoted entirely to this subject explaining that man is a micro-universe which has received influence from all forms of creation. Even the remotest star has contributed to this micro-universe of man.

But this relationship is not that of a servant to his master but that of the master to his servant. The masters do not bow and prostrate before those who serve them. Man, therefore, emerges as the master of the whole universe and the servant of only the One Who is the Lord and Creator of the universe.

How different is this philosophy from that of many other religions which teach not only idol worship but also nature worship in so many forms. In their philosophies, the moon, star(s), the sun, oceans, trees, rain, lightning, thunderstorms or even animals such as cows, snakes, or birds, all appear in a way superior to man. Man is taught to worship them as gods by virtue of their superiority of some sort over man. In short, man is placed at the lowest order of things and is made subservient to everything which was only created to serve him.

In the Islamic understanding of the scheme of things, man is the master, in a manner of speaking, of all creation. Man, therefore, stands under the greatest obligation to the Creator because it is he who has benefitted most from the creation of God ,Who has constrained everything to the service of man.

In other words, man is emancipated from all bondage by accepting just one bondage - that of his Creator. Man is the personification and symbol of the conscience and the consciousness of the entire universe. When he bows and prostrates before his Creator, in him bows and prostrates the whole cosmos. When he returns to the Creator, the entire universe returns, in a manner of speaking, to the Creator.

This ultimate realisation and the shaping of one's life to this goal is, according to Islam, the ultimate peace.

A phrase in the Holy Quran, oft repeated by Muslims, encompasses this philosophy in a few words:

إِنَّا لِلَّهِ وَإِنَّا إِلَيْهِ رَاجِعُونَ

We belong to Allah and to Him must we ultimately return. (Ch.2 Al-Baqarah:157)

Few understand that here the meaning of 'return' is not physical but spiritual. It is not just a statement of fact but a reminder of the purpose of man's creation. Just as a salmon cannot find peace until it returns to the place of its origin-its spawning ground, the human heart cannot find peace without spiritually returning to its source of creation. This is the meaning of the verse:

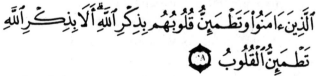

Those who believe and whose hearts find peace in the remembrance of Allah because it is only in the remembrance of Allah that hearts can find peace. . . . . (Ch.13: Al-R'ad:29)

WITHOUT GOD, THERE CAN BE NO PEACE

Man cannot live at peace with himself nor can peace be vouchsafed for society without this formula; no other formula can work. It is only the love of God which can bring about true respect for His creation. The higher the order of creation, the nearer it becomes to the Creator and the stronger the bond between the created and the Creator grows.

Man begins to respect other men with a higher and nobler object; i.e. out of his respect and the obligation owed to his Creator, man begins to respect mankind. One can, therefore, say that in essence, it is the love of God which is transformed into the love for His creation. Hypothetically, remove God from the scenario for a while, and suddenly human relationships acquire a completely different perspective.

The vacuum created by the non-existence of God is suddenly filled by man's ego. It is a very naive and extremely ignorant philosophy that man can live without God. What atheism ultimately achieves is not just the death of one God but it suddenly brings to life a myriad of gods. Every conscious being that exists, suddenly acquires the role of a god unto himself or itself. Ego, selfishness and the total commitment to serve one's own ends grows stronger and all-powerful.

Societies which are built with the bricks of such individuals, always remain egoistic, and self-oriented. There is no logic left in being beneficial to others without an ulterior motive. There is no external reference point left in the form of a beneficent God, Who is the only binding and meeting point of all forms of creation.

This is the ultimate Islamic philosophy. Without returning to God, one cannot attain peace, and without that peace, peace in society cannot be built. All human efforts to create peace from selfish ulterior motives are bound to fail and come to nothing.

If there is no God, there is no peace. That is the ultimate wisdom.

Thank you

APPENDIX

QURANIC VERSES QUOTED IN THIS BOOK

INDEX

278

279

280